LIFE IS STILL GOOD

Life is Still Good

Rob Szymaszek:

*One Man's Coaching Philosophy
Applied to the
Toughest Challenge of His Life*

Bryant Carpenter

*To Bob:
Go for it, especially
on Fourth Down!
All The Best,*

PLAIDSWEDE PUBLISHING
Concord, New Hampshire

ISBN 978-0-9790784-4-6
Library of Congress Control Number: 2007937287

Designed and composed in Adobe Garamond Pro
at Hobblebush Books, Brookline, New Hampshire
(www.hobblebush.com)

Cover photo by Bill Lischeid

Printed in the United States of America

Published by:

PLAIDSWEDE PUBLISHING
P. O. Box 269 · Concord, New Hampshire 03302-0269
www.plaidswede.com

For Diane and for Laura

Contents

Rob Szymaszek 2000

Jennifer, Diane and Rob Szymaszek at 2002
Connecticut–Rhode Island All–Star Game

PREGAME: SZYMASZEK

LIFE HAD ALWAYS been good to me. I had the good fortune to be born into a loving, nurturing family, anchored by my World War II veteran father and my loving mother. Being the middle child of three, I learned early to receive recognition between my older, beautiful sister and my extremely intelligent younger sister. I would participate in sports. This gave me a positive identity at home and made Dad proud.

Fortunately, the combination of my family's loving support and the lessons learned on the gridiron both as a player and coach helped prepare me to take on the biggest challenge of my life. Throughout this entire ordeal of fighting brain cancer, despite the many obstacles and constant ups and downs of the insidious disease, this foundation has been my unwavering strength.

I have been known by many of my friends to be an eternal optimist. There is no doubt that core attitude has helped me in my struggle. Throughout the story you are about to read, please bear in mind this book is not meant as an embellishment of my personal football career. It is meant as a book of inspiration and encouragement. In spite of all the events that follow, *life is still good.*

PRE-GAME: CARPENTER

I WASN'T SUPPOSED to be starting quarterback on this book. In the preseason of his ambition, when Rob Szymaszek looked around and saw precious little reading material on the shelf for brain tumor patients, he sought the aid of an older and wiser sportswriter whom he'd known far longer than he'd known me.

What he didn't know was that I'd been in training all my life for the exact game plan he envisioned. He didn't know the single event that had shaped me most was my sister's battle with childhood cancer.

Laura: She was only 7. I don't need the photographs to remind me of how hollowed out, how skeletal she looked in those months of 1977 and 1978, years that retain the length of decades in my memory. So much is seared there.

She wasn't supposed to make it. So many other children on that fifth floor of the UConn Health Center did not. So I know first-hand the cruelty of the disease.

I know the miracles, too. My sister, the little girl with the 5-percent chance, is now a grown woman, married, with two children. She's a nurse, and her first job was at the very hospital, on the very floor, where she was once a patient.

That's my favorite story of all time. The one that follows of Rob Szymaszek ranks way up there, too.

Bryant Carpenter and his sister Laura, 1994

PART I

CHAPTER 1

September 1, 2001

THE FIRST SUNLIGHT spilled through the windows and that was enough to get Rob Szymaszek springing out of bed.

Not that Rob could sleep in anyway, even on a Saturday, because this was it, the start of another football season, his 25th as head coach at Maloney High School in Meriden, Connecticut. Twenty-five years and the mind still raced and the adrenaline still pumped as August turned to September and preseason made the pivot from conditioning and drills to helmets and scrimmages. Opening night looms and suddenly offseason's eight-month window has winnowed to two weeks—a compression of urgency and anxiety, even for a veteran coach and eternal optimist like Rob.

Are we ready? *Are we ready?*

The Maloney Spartans had their first scrimmage that morning. The Tomahawks were coming in from Glastonbury High. Kickoff was hours away and still Rob couldn't get there fast enough. He showered and shaved in the slanting morning light spilling over the trap-rock ridge to the east. Meriden, a small city of about 60,000 where Rob was born and raised (and where his wife Diane was born and raised, and where they in turn raised their daughter Jennifer) is bracketed on the east and west by these ridges. The cliffs reach to nearly 1,000 feet. They stand sheer above the tree lines and glimmer when the light arrives low at dawn and departs at sunset.

Meriden lies in the bowl in between, its socio-economic strata descending with the slopes. Fine homes on the heights give way to rings of suburban-style neighborhoods of ranches, capes and split-levels, which give way to multi-family rentals once home to the blue-collar work force (much of it Polish) that fueled the city's factories (much of it silver). Like many New England industrial towns, Meriden's factories shut down or relocated to cheaper labor markets. The city's downtown, once thriving, was further sapped by a shopping mall out on the West Side. For all the talk and sweat of downtown renewal, railroad tracks still ran past empty buildings and tenement housing. The tracks split the city in two. A symbolic touch: Since the late 1950s, when Meriden High closed and Maloney High was built on the East Side and Platt High went up on the West, the city often divided into camps whose rivalries extended far beyond athletic fields. Several times a day Amtrak trains rumble through, and traffic in the heart of Meriden comes to a standstill.

Rob's well-kept Colonial sits on a hill at the end of a comfortable cul-de-sac on the East Side. It faces east. East all the way: Rob went to Maloney; Diane went to Maloney. They worked there—Rob as a guidance counselor, Diane as an art teacher. Rob had played football for Maloney. Now he coached for Maloney. The team motto, "Spartan Pride," wasn't just a slogan, the green Maloney block "M" not just a fashion statement. For the scrimmage, Rob donned one of his Maloney shirts: white with green trim and the green M, short-sleeved and collared, tucked into white shorts. Always presentable, even when casual: No ragged sweats for this coach.

The sun rose higher and Rob zipped out the door. It was still early, plenty of time to stop and pick up coffee for the assistant coaches. It's only three miles from Rob's house to the school, a straight shot down the commercial strip of East Main, then a right onto Gravel Street. He popped in a James Taylor cassette tape and hit the road.

In my mind I'm going to Carolina; I'm going to Carolina in my mind.

Under a cloudless, absolutely blue late-summer sky even the gas stations, strip plazas and highway interchange hotels of East Main seemed fresh. The recent heat and humidity of late August had been shooed away by cool high-pressure out of Canada, bringing with it the sort of crispness that reminds a coach that leaves will soon be turning and falling with a twilight that will come sooner and steal time from afternoon practice.

Fall and football: Rob could smell it.

Photo by Bill Lischeid

Coach Szymaszek warming up with his team

Arriving at school, he wheeled around the building to the empty back parking lot and hopped out of his Acura Legend, green Maloney duffel bag slung over a shoulder. Down below, at the bottom of a steep hill, lay the practice field. How much of his life had been spent on that field? Thirty years: three as a player, two as a volunteer assistant just out of college and then 25 as head man. He'd been only 26 when he was put in charge. Now, at age 51, still putting in a hundred push-ups and sit-ups a day, he looked and felt almost as good as when he started.

He had high aspirations for 2001. Nothing unusual there. Even when Maloney didn't have much, the glass was half-full and rising, and those teams typically responded to Rob's dogged belief and overachieved. Being a medium-sized school, Maloney rarely had big numbers as far as the roster went, but the Spartans were always game and they worked like hell. That was the essence of "Spartan Pride," an underdog pluck scoffed at by some. But it enabled Maloney to compete year after year in a conference dominated by larger schools. In 2001, the Spartans were poised to more than hold their own. Offseason weightlifting had been dedicated, spring practice spirited. The team went to summer camp at Syracuse University and George DeLeone, the Orangemen's associate head coach at the time, said Maloney had the best offensive line in camp. Maloney went to another camp at Rob's alma mater, Southern Connecticut State, and the coaches there raved about the Spartans, too. The summer passing league team had won games by four or five touchdowns.

Preseason began with a solid week of conditioning. The team made it through triple sessions that ran from seven in the morning to seven at night. No footballs, just workouts in the August heat, with the finishing gauntlet of "Burma Roads," a drill in which the players lined up at midfield and crawled across the field in 5-yard increments down to the goal line. Across the 50, down the sideline to the 45, back across the field, down to the 40 and so on and so on. "This program isn't for the faint of heart," as Rob once told me. If one player keeled over and couldn't make it, the whole team started over back at the 50. So the goal wasn't merely finishing, but fostering a sense of team. The Spartans were a mix of white, black and Hispanic players. The Spartans were all in this together, a shared trial to be overcome. So players pulled for each other. Players who had completed the circuit would go back and help the big linemen huffing down the stretch or the guys who hadn't kept in shape during the offseason. It was no time to point fingers. If one went down, they all went down.

Coach Szymaszek and the Spartans huddle up
after their September 1, 2001 scrimmage.

Triple-session conditioning gave way to triple-session practices. The humidity persisted; there were no days off. The players were on the field at 7:30 a.m. Offensive and defensive sessions were run before the full heat of the day bore down. Then the team would break for two hours, eat a catered lunch, rest, digest and get back on the field for special teams work. That was always the lightest and shortest session. By four o'clock the kids hit the showers and Rob and his assistant coaches reconvened to brainstorm.

"We need a tight end, coach."

"Maybe we can move so-and-so from here."

"Will so-and-so buy into the move?"

"So long as we stress 'we're thinking about the team, not about me' he will."

Get the team into shape, go over team rules, go over plays, issue equipment, re-order missing equipment, get players into the right positions, get players onto the same page, boost egos, massage egos, make sure everyone had breakfast, lunch and a way to get home at night: It all ran together and it was a lot of ground to cover as preseason hurtled forward.

This cool first Saturday of September was a reward for that work. A scrimmage was a chance to smack somebody wearing a different uniform, a chance to gauge where you really stood as a team. As it turned out, Maloney didn't play well against Glastonbury. This was surprising. Given all that would follow that day, it was also a harbinger.

Rob put the kids through Maloney's "Green Bay" running regimen after the game—ten 100-yard sprints, eight 80s, six 60s, four 40s, two 20s—and then they hit the showers. Jetting water echoed around the tiles. Not much shouting today. A stream of players coursed through the small coaching office to use the telephone or double-check the practice schedule or the playbook, or ask for a form they'd forgotten to fill out or a gold chain that was suddenly missing.

"What time you want us here again tomorrow, coach?"

"Coach, do I drive block or pull on Z-right-19?"

"Is it OK if my grandmother signs this, coach?"

"Never mind, coach, I found it!"

The noise rose, crested, ebbed away. As usual, one shower was left running. As usual, Rob and Mike Falis, his assistant coach of 17 years, were the last to leave.

"See ya Monday."

"Yeah, have a great weekend."

Rob slid back into his car, far less peppy than he'd been that morning. He was uptight. There was tension in his neck, where it always gathered during the season and lingered for a month even after it was over. The team's play had been so disappointing, so un-Spartan-like. It wasn't so much the lack of execution that bothered Rob, but the lack of intensity, of enthusiasm. If a football team lacks those elements, it's beaten at square one. Then Rob caught himself. This had been just one preseason Saturday in early September. The Spartans had the ingredients to compete for a league title, maybe even reach the state playoffs, which they hadn't seen since 1998.

And it was such a beautiful day, so absolutely blue. The sun shone. The cliffs were free of shadow.

The day would be salvaged. Rob had an afternoon appointment down in Westport with Staples High head coach Marce Petroccio. Since meeting at a football clinic in the early 80s they'd made it a preseason ritual to get together, watch game film and exchange ideas. This year's trip would help shake off a bad scrimmage, Rob figured. He'd spend a few hours in Westport, then return home and take Jennifer out for her annual back-to-school dinner. It was the last one. Jen was 21. The next day she was off to New York for her senior year at Sarah Lawrence.

Rob swung by the house to get changed. Only Mr. Diffley, the family's golden retriever, was home. He roused himself from his blanket behind the kitchen table when Rob came through the door from the garage.

"Hey, Diff, hey old buddy, how's my buddy!"

Rob gave Mr. Diffley the two-handed, under-the-jaws rub that he loved. Mr. Diffley smacked his chops and licked Rob's face. Diff could chase a bad mood, but Rob was still tense. A slight headache was forming. Though not prone to drinking in the middle of the day or before he drove, Rob popped a beer, hoping to relax. He waited a while, and then hopped on the Wilbur Cross Parkway. A straight shot from Meriden to upscale Fairfield County.

As he drove, Rob replayed the day's scrimmage in his mind—the missed tackles, the missed assignments. Well, what was broken would be fixed. The big preseason jamboree was coming up on Friday at Ceppa Field, Meriden's downtown sports facility. The Spartans would be under the lights, in a real Friday night game situation, with the arch-rival Platt Panthers on the other sidelines. Platt and Maloney wouldn't play each other until Thanksgiving. On Friday they'd take turns scrimmaging the two out-of-town teams that rounded out the jamboree. But the Spartans would be watching the Panthers and the Panthers would be watching the Spartans, a cool opening salvo in an annual cold war that exploded every Thanksgiving. In the meantime, Maloney needed work. Punt coverage, kickoff returns, swarming to the ball on defense: The Spartans had failed on all counts against Glastonbury.

Rob drove, mentally mapping out practice schedules as he navigated the curves of the parkway through Hamden. He passed the exit to Southern Connecticut State where he'd played defensive back in the late 60s and his position coach, Ron Carbone, referred to him as the All-American boy. *I should give Ron a call.* He drove through the tunnel under New Haven's West Rock, the radio signal fading out, then back in. Rob hardly noticed. *We played so poorly. But we have the makings. The playoffs: Why not? We can get there. It starts now for the Maloney Spartans.*

The parkway cut its southwesterly sweep toward the coastal towns of Milford and Stratford. Rob noticed bumper-to-bumper traffic creeping up the northbound lanes and made a mental note. *Take I-95 and 91 back home; we have those dinner reservations.* Rob went on . . . sort of. He was oddly detached from his surroundings. *These are weird perceptions. Am I really driving in this car? Am I sleeping?*

He went on, assuming it was fatigue, assuming it would pass. It didn't.

What was it? Rob felt dizzy, faint, a little nauseous. *It couldn't have been that one beer.* It was unlike anything he'd ever experienced, and it was getting stronger. Something wasn't right.

At the exit connecting the parkway with I-95, Rob decided to head for home. He followed the signs, the curves of the road, focusing through the faintness, hands tight on the wheel, telling himself, "you're OK; you're driving fine."

Or was he dreaming he was driving?

Yes, this is a dream. I'll wake up it and I'll be home and Diane and I will get ready to go out to dinner with Jen and—THUMP

What the . . . Did I just hit that guard rail? No. No, this is just a dream. I'll wake up and —

THUMP

*Did I just hit that car? No. No, I'm not doing that. I am not possibly doing that. This is some kind of an illusion—*THUMP-THUMP

What's with the steering wheel? What is that noise? Do I have a flat?

There was a thumping and it was constant and it snapped Rob out of what he later described as a trance-like state. *Get off the road,* he told himself. He glanced in the rearview mirror. That's when he saw the swirling red lights. This was no dream.

Rob jockeyed over to the shoulder ahead of the cruiser. A state police officer strode up.

"Do you know you have two flat tires?" the cop asked above the droning, zipping whine of passing cars.

"No sir," Rob replied, "but I know something is wrong."

"Do you know we just got a report that you were bouncing off the median and that you also bounced off a car?"

"No sir, but . . . yes sir. I had this perception it was happening, but I don't remember it."

"Did you have anything to drink?"

He barked that. Rob told him about the scrimmage and the Maloney High School football team he coached, and he told him about the beer.

"Sir, I can handle one beer."

"Empty your pockets."

Boy, he's a blunt son of a gun. Rob emptied his pockets. His Land's End shirt was new. It still had the extra buttons in a little plastic bag in one of the pockets. The cop saw the bag and accused Rob of doing cocaine.

"Cocaine? Sir, in all honesty, I wouldn't know what it looks like. I know it's supposed to be white, but I've never seen cocaine, sir."

Rob was trying to be polite—his dad had been a policeman for 30 years—but was he slurring his speech?

The cop was saying something about having to press charges. He asked for license and registration. Rob handed them over, and as the cop started back to his car, Rob got out of his. He had those flats to change. He was still queasy and his legs were buffeted by the wind of the passing cars. The cop turned and shouted above it.

September 1, 2001

"Hey, where are you going?"

"I've got to get these tires changed, officer. I'm taking my daughter out. Right before she goes back to college we go out to a great restaurant. She's going back to school tomorrow morning –"

"Get back in the car."

"This is the end of the summer vacation –"

"Get back in the car."

"Officer, just let me get the tires and I'll get things set up."

Rob headed for the trunk. The cop came charging back.

"Did you hear me? I said get back in the car!"

"Sir, all I want to do is change my tires."

"I TOLD YOU TO GET BACK IN THE FUCKING CAR!"

The cop was howling as he threw Rob to the pavement, pulled his arms back and slapped on handcuffs.

"Officer, what's going on?"

Rob had never been handcuffed or manhandled. He'd never been in trouble. He came from a law-abiding family. His dad had been a police sergeant for 30 years.

"Officer!"

"We just had an officer get beat up with a crowbar someone pulled out of their trunk," the policeman seethed. "You're lucky I didn't freakin' shoot you! How did I know you weren't going back there for a gun?"

He tightened the cuffs.

"Sir, is this necessary?"

"You bet your freaking life it's necessary."

The cuffs were tight. Rob's wrists began to bleed. He could feel his hands going numb.

"Sir, can you loosen these up?"

No response.

It was painful. The cuts would scar.

13

"You're in big trouble now."

"What did I do, sir?"

Rob kept repeating it: What did I do, what did I do? Looking back, he gives the state trooper the benefit of the doubt. He must have been incoherent; another officer had recently been assaulted. But at the time Rob was growing more queasy and confused. Cars flew by on the highway, heads turning and then turning back away, leaving a windy concussion in their wake, heading somewhere safe and fun and normal on a beautiful late-summer Saturday. And here was Rob Szymaszek, coach of Maloney football, son of Sgt. Bob Szymaszek, the All-American boy, handcuffed, disoriented and ducking his head to get in the back of a police car that had its lights flashing.

He was taken to nearby barracks in Bridgeport, fingerprinted and made to give a blood sample. That was for the drug test. It was negative, but Rob's blood sugar was extremely low, so the cops gave him something that looked and tasted like cake frosting. He ate it. He felt they knew what they were doing. He had to. He was tired, disoriented.

You get one phone call, and Rob called home. Diane and Jennifer would be getting in from walking Mr. Diffley, getting ready to go out for dinner. Would they hear the phone ringing over the running water, the bathroom fan, the hair dryers? Were they wondering where he was? What time was it anyway?

Jen answered the phone and Rob tried to explain. She could make out only "jail" and "accident" and "police suspecting" through the stuttering and the slurring.

"Dad, what's wrong with you?"

"Nothing, honey. I, uh, had an accident. I'm, uh, down at the state police in . . . um . . ."

"Are you OK, Dad?"

"Yeah, I'm OK."

"Dad, you sound—something's wrong. Dad, what's wrong?"

Jen handed the phone to Diane. She heard it, too.

"Rob, what's wrong with you?"

"Hon, I don't know what's wrong with me."

"You're slurring your words."

He was awfully tired. Too tired to talk, explain.

"Hon, you just need to come down here."

Diane asked to speak to the police officer. He was cordial, gave her directions. He'd thawed toward Rob, too, assured he was no crowbar-toting, drugged-out psycho. The handcuffs were off, but Rob was still confused and worried. He'd never been in a police barracks before except to visit his dad at work. When he was small his dad would take him in the back to see the cells and the guys they had in lockup. "Dad, what's he in jail for?" Rob would whisper because he didn't want the bad guys to hear. Now here he was in his own holding cell, charged with evading responsibility in an incident being classified as a hit and run.

It was an hour drive for Diane and Jen. Rob felt instant security when they arrived. They instantly saw something was wrong. They'd known it just from hearing his voice on the phone, and they'd talked on the ride down.

"Maybe he got a concussion from the accident," Jen said. "Maybe it was a stroke like Pa."

That wasn't too farfetched. Rob's dad—"Pa" to Jen—had suffered a severe stroke 10 years earlier at age 68 that left him aphasic, unable to speak beyond a few words.

Diane tried to keep her hands firm on the steering wheel.

"Maybe he had some kind of nervous breakdown."

She said it even though she knew it made no sense. There

was nothing extraordinarily stressful going on in her husband's life. It was just her gut reaction. Instinctively, Diane feared the unimaginable.

She and Jen just knew. Seeing Rob confirmed it. He's typically upbeat and vibrant, with a warm smile to match a robust voice. Now he was slow, subdued and lethargic.

Diane took one anxious look and told the policeman, "That's not my husband. Something's wrong. Whatever happened as far as the accident, there's some reason for it. There is something wrong."

"No. The doctor here says he's OK."

"No. No, he's not. I've got to take him to a hospital."

Rob was released on his own recognizance. Pulling away from the police barracks, with Diane driving and Jen in the back, he tried telling them what happened, about the weird perceptions and the flat tires and the handcuffs, but he was out of it. He couldn't think straight. He couldn't talk straight. He couldn't sit up straight. In the rearview mirror, Diane and Jennifer exchanged glances of bewilderment and worry.

"Oh God, something is not right," Diane said. "You have got to get to a hospital."

"No, I'm fine."

"Rob!"

"Why do we have to go to the hospital?"

But he knew. He could hear the spacey disconnection in his voice. *Is that actually me talking?* Rob suggested MidState Medical Center. That's the Meriden hospital. If he went there, he'd be closer to the football team. "I wasn't thinking big," Rob would later admit. "I was thinking really, really small."

Diane was not. She got off I-95 in downtown New Haven and followed the blue "H" signs to the emergency room of Yale-New Haven Hospital.

* * *

Doctors later theorized Rob had suffered a simple-partial seizure while driving. It would account for the "fuzzy brain" sensations he experienced.

There's no doubt about the seizure he suffered in the emergency room: a grand mal, the severest of seizures. If Rob had suffered it while driving, he'd most likely be dead. When you have a small seizure like a simple-partial, it's a matter of a neuron or two misfiring in the brain. With a grand mal, it's a massive malfunction.

Right away the doctors in the ER suspected Rob's brain was the issue, but they were thinking encephalitis or some other infectious disease. They had Rob lying in a room that was curtained off. Jen and Diane were sitting outside—Jen frustrated because she couldn't get answers, Diane upset that the ER staff had left Rob alone.

The curtain kept Diane from seeing the grand mal seizure come over Rob, but she heard it. Bolting to her feet, she darted around the curtain. "He's having a seizure!" Rob has no recollection of any of it. He didn't hear Diane screaming. He didn't see the ER personnel come sprinting.

"He's having a seizure! He's having a seizure!"

Diane saw Rob's whole body tighten. He's a muscular guy, tight to begin with, but Diane could see his legs were unnaturally rigid. She was afraid he would bite off his tongue.

"He's having a seizure!"

It diminished, passed. Rob remembers none of it.

There was no back-to-school dinner for Jen that night. No football practice the next day. The grand mal cemented the inevitable. Rob was admitted to Yale-New Haven and placed in intensive care. A gorgeous, blue-sky day that started on the sidelines of a familiar football field ended eons later in a strange bed.

Rob's world, his wife's, his daughter's, was turned upside down between a sunrise and sunset, in a single pass of the sun over Meriden from eastern ridge to western. Light to shadow on the trap-rock faces. That day the Szymaszeks learned how quickly life can drop off a cliff. How steep the fall they would come to know.

CHAPTER 2

World Turned Upside Down

THE PHONE AT Mike Falis's house rang shortly before 7:30 . Sunday morning. It was Diane, her voice steady but subdued.

"Mike, is there practice today with the kids?"

"No, they're off. They don't come in till Monday. Rob knows that."

"Rob's in the hospital."

"The hospital?"

Mike had been with Rob only the day before, on the field, coaching their butts off, putting the players through the Green Bays, re-assessing the roster—the last, as usual, to leave.

"See ya Monday."

"Yeah, have a great weekend."

"Diane, I don't understand."

Mike got down to Yale-New Haven around two in the afternoon. By then word had filtered out and some of the Maloney players were already there. Rob was hooked up to an IV and a little out of sorts, but to Mike and the guys he looked OK and sounded OK. They talked football. Rob had already gone over the game tape from Saturday's scrimmage. With no good place to sleep at Yale-New Haven, Diane had gone home about 1 a.m. the night before, agitated but exhausted. She slept a few hours and returned to the hospital first thing Sunday morning. Before she left home, Rob called. "Hey Di, can you bring the VCR and the game tape?" And so, for perhaps the first time, Yale-New Haven became a satellite coaching office and football film was broken down by an in-patient.

After the players left, Rob and Mike went over plans for Monday's Labor Day scrimmage with Lyman Hall High School. Not that Rob and Mike really needed to. They were so often on the same page. Mike had been Rob's top assistant for 17 seasons. They had been Spartans together as kids.

"Don't forget punt coverage and, Mike, remind them about effort. We did not have all-out effort on every play yesterday."

Was that game really played only yesterday?

As Mike was leaving Rob mentioned the wedding of a former player they had attended only a few weeks before. The reception had been held at a banquet hall down on the Connecticut shore. Rob and Mike and their wives drank cocktails at sunset and watched the boats come in off Long Island Sound.

"I wonder if all those margaritas I had set this thing off," Rob joked.

If only the explanation was so simple, so light-hearted, so harmless. The grand mal seizure Rob had suffered in the emergency room was a strong indication something was seriously wrong. Exactly what it was would take more than a week to determine.

In the meantime, Rob wasn't going anywhere. After a while he was in constant mini-seizures. He felt unfocused, as if he were at the eye doctor's office trying on pair after pair of eyeglasses and none were quite the right prescription. He was nauseous, too, as if he'd had too many beers and the room was spinning.

Except that it didn't stop. And it went on for days.

Diane was at the hospital almost constantly. Maloney principal Gladys Labbas was accommodating. Gladys and Rob had often butted heads in the past. They didn't exactly assign equal importance to the sport of football and the coaching of it. Yet during that long first week of September 2001, Gladys let Diane leave school early or take entire days off to get down to Yale-New Haven, and Rob wouldn't forget it.

Jennifer was making trips back and forth from the Sarah Lawrence campus in Bronxville, N.Y. She had been away from school the previous year, having spent her junior semesters in El Salvador and Mexico. Now here it was her senior year, the homestretch. She had wanted to hit the ground running. That wasn't going to happen.

"My entire being is here with you," she told her father.

Her teachers and advisors understood. She was dealing with a hard new subject. Jen took both a student's and daughter's approach to Rob's condition. She asked questions. She made sure all possibilities were explored. She scoured the Internet for information. She craved answers.

And she couldn't help but wonder: Is this the last week I have with my dad?

For a while, there were no answers. The doctors at Yale-New Haven ran all sorts of tests: CAT scans, MRIs, spinal taps. Rob's brain signals were constantly monitored. Swelling was found in the right temporal lobe. What was causing it? The mosquito-borne West Nile virus was a leading suspect. The virus had first appeared in North America only two years before. Symptoms in severe cases include disorientation, convulsions and enceph-alitis—swelling of the brain. Doctors specializing in infectious diseases were brought in. They were on Rob like mosquitoes. Eventually, West Nile was ruled out.

So what was it?

Early in the week, Rob was still thinking the problem was minor. He'd find out what it was, deal with it and be on his way back to the field in time for Friday night's jamboree at Ceppa

Field. The team played very well in its Labor Day scrimmage. Immediately after the game Mike called Rob to fill him in. Before hanging up Mike held up his cell phone in the team huddle. The players shouted out and wished Coach well. Rob was touched by the call, but it drove him crazy as well. It was September; it was football time. He had to get back. He belonged on the field talking directly to those players, not in a hospital bed listening to their shouts over a cell phone. He should be linked up to a sideline headset, not a bedside IV.

Mike Falis holds up his cell phone so the Spartans can wish Coach Szymaszek well.

Rob wasn't exactly out of the loop while in the hospital. After 25 years, he was a well-known and well-respected member of the state coaching fraternity. Colleagues from other schools, though busy with their own hectic preseason preparations, paid visits. Jack Siedlecki and his Yale football staff stopped by. In walked Ron Carbone, Rob's old position coach at Southern Connecticut and the man Rob looked up to as mentor.

So many visitors, but Rob was in and out of lucidity. Some people would later ask, "Rob, don't you remember me calling or seeing you in the hospital?" and, sadly, Rob could not.

He does recall Ray Carleglio, a buddy from North Haven, stopping in. He and Rob's neighborhood buddy Donny Maleto liked to play the horses from time to time at Sports Haven in New Haven, so Ray thought to drop off that day's Racing Form.

"Bobby, I just want you to know, any time you want the Racing Form brought up to this room, just give me a call."

Betting on horse races is not one of Rob's hobbies that Diane particularly cares for. "*Who* offered to do that?" she wanted to know.

As the week went on and testing continued, it was harder to laugh and harder to think about football. *Never mind Friday night's jamboree. What the hell is wrong with me?* Rob had never been admitted to the hospital before. He'd injured a knee playing high school football and fractured a cervical vertebra playing in college, but neither required hospitalization. He had no previous medical crisis. Usually, it was Diane in the hospital bed. She had suffered heat stroke during their honeymoon in Bermuda. She had given birth to Jennifer; she had miscarried twice.

Now, with the roles reversed and Rob in the bed, Diane was very strong. She masked her inner turmoil, kept herself in control and dealt with the situation. Everything else shut down. She had to consider school, but nothing was more important than what was happening to her husband. Diane would spend all day at the hospital and get home late. By then, news of Rob's condition had made newspapers across the state. Phone messages would be blinking on the answering machine, 16 one night, 30 the next. Some callers were just wishing well. Some required a return call. Diane would provide the daily updates then collapse into sleep.

She was also helping take care of Rob's dad, who was living downstairs in an in-law apartment. The stroke Bob Szymaszek had suffered 10 years earlier was so severe it had deprived him almost entirely of the ability to move and speak. Health care aides came in on a daily basis. Diane helped with meals and medication along with Rob's two sisters, Sharon and Jan, who visited regularly from out of state.

Neighbors lent a hand, too, helping take care of Mr. Diffley. One of the neighborhood children made Rob a card. She drew Mr. Diffley on the cover and inside she wrote, "Mr. D., come on. Good boy, Mr. D. You want to go for a walk? Yes? No? You miss Daddy? Most of the time. Well, Mr. D., everyone does. So do I, Mr. D."

Testing went on. As infectious diseases were ruled out, a brain tumor became more likely. This is where Yale-New Haven neurosurgeon Joseph Piepmeier, the doctor who would become like a god to Rob, got involved. Piepmeier recognized where the symptoms were pointing. The first indications of a brain tumor are often seizures or headaches. All but 10 to 20 percent of brain tumors show up with no advance warning. Here was Rob Szymaszek, age 51, in good health, and he'd suffered his first seizure.

At least Rob assumes he had his first seizure on that fateful September 1, but he can't be sure. How would you know a seizure—and we're talking small ones, here—if you'd never had one? Diane and Jen suspect Rob had one earlier that summer. They'd just come back from Mexico and Rob had just returned from the national high school coaches' convention in Fargo, North Dakota, where he was one of 12 finalists for national coach of the year. Diane and Jen were telling him about their trip, or trying to tell him. They'd long grown accustomed to Rob's frequent lack of attention during football season, when his mind was on X's and O's and he'd sometimes go through the motion of listening without really hearing anything. This went beyond that. Rob was off in space, utterly unresponsive.

So now the suspicion was a brain tumor. There was only one way to be sure: a tissue sample. Dr. Piepmeier scheduled a biopsy for Monday, September 10. Rob was put under, and all he remembers of the procedure was the pain as the anesthesia wore off. It was the most extreme pain he'd ever encountered.

The fact it confirmed was equally painful. Diane and Jen were the first to learn it. Jen had been emotional during the week of testing, while her mother had borne up, taking care not to get Rob alarmed. Now the roles reversed. When Dr. Piepmeier broke the news, Diane broke down. Even though she suspected it was a tumor, the reality of it, the actual saying of the word, was crushing. The full weight of the situation, the very real possibility of losing her husband, hit home. Jen went to her mother's aid. She felt stronger now that she had the concrete answer. That's their relationship. When one needs the other, the other is a rock. Throughout this ordeal they were a mutual support system. Diane would need it, starting right then and there. Fear seized her. Would she be told her husband had only months to live?

Diane and Jen went up to Rob's room. By then he suspected the truth, too. The look on Di's face confirmed it. For the first time since Rob had been admitted to the hospital, she couldn't mask her emotions.

"Are you telling me everything?"

"It's a brain tumor, Rob."

The family later learned the specifics: Oligodendroglioma, one of nine different kinds of primary brain tumors—as compared to secondary brain tumors, which are caused by the spread of cancer from another part of the body. Primary brain tumors are named for the cells from which they develop. With oligodendrogliomas, it's oligodendrocytes, which produce the fatty covering of nerve cells in the brain and nourish them. These tumors are typically found in the white cerebral area of the brain, mainly in the temporal and frontal lobes. Rob's was in the right temporal lobe. It was three inches long. And it was shaped like a football.

How did it get there? When it comes to primary brain tumors, medical science doesn't really know. Brain tumors are detected most often in patients ages 40-60, yet are rare, occurring in only 6.6 of 100,000 people per year. Unlike other cancers, the causes aren't clear. Risk factors have not been identified. There are theories. High doses of radiation in treatment for other cancers can lead to a brain tumor, but only as a secondary cancer. Living near power lines or using cell phones have been suggested and researched, but not proven. Rob's sister Jan wondered if all those years of wearing a headset on the sidelines had something to do with it. Doubtful, Dr. Piepmeier said.

Nor have genetic links been found to cause brain tumors. Rob has his suspicions, though. He's reminded of a story he heard from Steve Filippone, a Connecticut high school coaching colleague. Filippone was having a picnic at his house. One of his guests, a doctor, was eating hot dogs, smoking, drinking. Steve, who has had some heart trouble, was watching what he ate, not smoking and not drinking.

"Hey Doc, what's the story?" he finally asked. "I'm doing the right things and I look over at you and you're doing all the bad things and I'm the one with the bad heart."

"I hate to tell you this," the doctor replied, polishing off a hot dog, "but it's the genetics."

Genetics: Those from Rob's maternal side of the family are not good. Cancer is everywhere. Rob's grandfather died of liver cancer. Rob's mother, Millie, died of liver cancer in January 1997 at age 71. Of Millie's 12 siblings, five died from either prostate or liver cancer. Uncle John and Aunt Grace had liver cancer. Uncle Stanley and Uncle Lenny had prostate cancer. Uncle Ted also died of cancer. Aunt Sophie died of congestive heart failure. A cousin, Greg Kosienski, had prostate cancer, though he survived. Genetics from the paternal camp weren't much better. That side was riddled with hypertension. Dad had a stroke and so had one of his sisters.

There was no history of brain tumors on either side of Rob's family, but he refuses to believe genetics can be ignored. Not with such a prevalence of cancer in one family. Moreover, a woman named Andrea Mann, whom Rob would befriend in Yale-New Haven's brain tumor support group, had a virtually identical family background—cancer on the maternal side, hypertension on the paternal—and she wound up with an oligodendroglioma in her right temporal lobe, too. There should be a study of people with our kind of background, Rob and Andrea often agreed. Is there a propensity for brain tumors?

Doctors say there is no proof of genetic brain tumor links, at least not currently. There are hereditary defects in certain regulatory growth genes, but these are rare, and people who are predisposed to cancer usually develop it elsewhere, not in the brain.

Whatever the cause, there it was, and Rob and his family had to deal with it. Because brain tumors grow in brain tissue and are not encapsulated, the World Health Organization considers them malignant by default, though some prove benign if they don't spread. The critical issue is how aggressive they are. Some oligodendrogliomas are slow growing—Grade 1 and 2 varieties, with Grade 2 having a higher risk of spreading. Other tumors are faster growing and likely to spread. They have cells that, under the microscope, look very different from normal brain cells. Those are classified Grade 3 and 4 and they are more severe.

Rob's was a Grade 2.

In the case of a slow-growing tumor like that, there's no way of knowing how long it's been around. Who could tell how long Rob's had been gathering? The seed of it might have been there since birth.

Also uncertain was what future course the tumor might take. The Szymaszeks wanted answers. Some just weren't available. "I can't tell you what the future is," Dr. Piepmeier told them. "I can tell you, 'this is what we need to do, this is the next step and this is how we get there.'"

Indeed, there was an upside. Oligodendrogliomas are highly treatable because they're so operable. Surgery is the No. 1 treatment. Surgery would be Rob's first step.

Given the residual pain, Rob was wishing Dr. Piepmeier had just taken the damn thing out during the biopsy. But it was just a biopsy, not a major operation. It was sort of like a scrimmage, Rob thought. It gave Dr. Piepmeier an idea of what to expect when it came to the real game. In the meantime, the pain was bad. Rob had staples in his scalp and he was looking square at another operation, one that would be more invasive. *But we have to get it done, so let's get it done.*

The strategy was clear: Remove as much of the tumor as possible. From there, the tissue could be analyzed. What's the morphology, the vascular structure of the cells? What sort of blood supply was feeding that sucker? Were the cells proliferating? From that information, the doctors would determine the follow-up treatment. The Szymaszeks would have answers eventually, some lay of the land.

Rob was ready to move forward, yet it was such a fearful new landscape: a brain tumor, with brain surgery in the immediate future for a guy who was always healthy, who never liked to even take aspirin, who did 100 push-ups and sit-ups a day.

A world turned upside down.

On the day after the biopsy, all Americans experienced that emotion with the terrorist attacks of September 11. Rob had been in the intensive care unit, but was hustled out because Yale-New Haven was readying to receive any victims who might be brought up from New York City.

Even as the Twin Towers crumbled and the Pentagon burned, Diane and Rob felt a distance from the devastating events unfolding on live television. "I remember that morning," Diane said. "You remember where you were that morning. We were in the ICU. Obviously, what was happening on TV was horrible and scary, but it was different for us."

It was different. It couldn't help but be different. Yet the core emotional pull of September 11 was the same for all Americans as it was for this recently diagnosed brain tumor patient and his family. You and I, Rob and Diane and Jennifer, we were dealing with a new reality so unprecedented, so unthinkable and so suddenly thrust upon us that it permanently shook our sense of security. It was not merely the windows of a warm, well-known home that had cracked. It was the roof, the floor, the foundation, the very earth beneath.

How would we rebuild?

CHAPTER 3

Spartan Pride: No. 82

EVEN WHILE HE was in the hospital, undergoing test after test, Rob could not forget about the team. How could he? Maloney football had been his life for 30 years. The coaches' office was his second home, the practice field his backyard.

That field sits at the bottom of a steep hill behind the school. From up top, in the parking lot, looking east, you can see the interstate highways that pass north-south through town and, beyond that, the East Side ridges. Down on the field, all this is obscured by trees. There are no views of cliffs glowing in the sunset, no views of fast-flowing traffic heading in and out of town. You see two goalposts and a cleat-torn, 100-yard grid that lies between and steadily turns to bare earth down the middle as the season progresses. You hear the crunch of pads and the whistle that stops the drills and starts them again. You smell dirt and the unmistakable scent of sweat in football pads.

In the summer of 1965, heading into his sophomore year, Rob joined the Maloney football culture. It started with a preseason practice. The senior captains ran it. Yet there, up on the grassy slope, in the shade of a tree, smoking a cigar, was the legendary coach, Ed McGee. Physically imposing, with broad shoulders and massive hands, Coach McGee looked the part and he had lived it, too. As a player, he was a standout guard at Temple University and was drafted by the New York Giants, spending a year with them. He was coaching in New Hampshire when he landed the Meriden job in 1955 (this a few years before the city split into two high schools) thanks in part to a letter of recommendation from his superintendent that read, "I hope that you will not take him."

McGee had put in 10 seasons behind the bench—three at the old Meriden High and seven at Maloney—by the time 15-year-old Rob Szymaszek came along in the fall of '65. The kid looked around the field, looked over at McGee, looked around at the senior captains—one the quiet, hard-nosed lineman Mike Falis—and thought, *Wow, I'm part of Maloney football. No more just watching on the sidelines, no more just singing the Maloney fight song. Now I'm on the field, wearing the green and white helmet. No more plain white shirts of the junior high school team. Now I'm Number 82. And there's the legend.*

McGee rooted the team in tradition and made it feel like family. He was the original architect of "Spartan Pride," the concept Rob would make the Maloney mantra when he became coach. McGee made so much out of so little. His teams were always considered contenders for their work ethic alone. Years later, when Rob read books on Vince Lombardi, he felt he already knew the Green Bay great. Coach McGee was so much like him.

McGee had a tremendous influence on Rob. So did his father. Rob was Bob Szymaszek's only boy, born between two daughters who still tease him about being treated like a prince. Sharon, three years older, was the sibling Rob grew up with, the one first exposed to Rob's competitive nature and the one who doted on Rob. His mother Millie and Sharon were both protective of him, especially when he was sick. Jan, five years Rob's junior, was the one Rob protected, the kid sister who idolized her big brother. Sharon was a beauty queen, Jan an athlete and brilliant student.

Szymaszek family photo.

Jan Szymaszek (center) celebrates her first birthday with Rob and Sharon.

The family was Polish on both sides and it was large and extended. Most relatives lived in the Meriden area. There were sprawling reunions at local parks and regular gatherings at the Szymaszek homestead, which was tucked in a leafy subdivision of modest ranches, capes and split-levels on the East Side. Their split-level had a fireplace on the main floor and three bedrooms upstairs. The fridge was always stocked; the visiting policy was always open door. Through open windows drifted strains of Polish songs sung at parties.

Bob was a Meriden cop, Millie head of a middle school cafeteria and later a telephone operator. The Szymaszeks weren't well off, but they were comfortable. Summer vacations were spent at Lake George in New York, then at Lake Pocotopaug in eastern Connecticut where Bob and Millie bought a small camp. Bob and Millie spoke Polish when they talked about money, so the kids never knew how the family stood financially. They never lacked, but Bob worked plenty of extra shifts and had holes in his underwear before he'd buy a new pair—a transaction Rob would speed along by tearing the holes beyond repair.

Millie's forte lay in the kitchen. Every day she made breakfast. On game days, she'd feed Rob and a few teammates steak and eggs. Kielbasa was waiting after games. With Millie, "every day was a holiday and every meal a feast," as her nephew Greg Kosienski put it. Her plates and bowls were oversized and she expected you to finish, because there was more where that came from. People wanted to be around Millie and she wanted them around her. After the first Thanksgiving game he coached with Rob, Mike Falis stopped in with his family and was not allowed to leave.

"Where you going?" Millie demanded as Mike tried to shepherd his wife and three young kids out the door.

"We should go. You people are having your Thanksgiving dinner."

"You stay right here. We got a seat for you. Sit down."

Bob had been a staff sergeant in the 9th Armored Division in World War II. He was 20 years old when he was drafted in 1942—the youngest from Meriden up to that point—and his tank was among the first to cross the Remagan Bridge over the Rhine River during the Battle of the Bulge. He got a Bronze Star for that. After putting in a few post-war years at the International Silver Company, the backbone of Meriden's silver industry, Bob hooked up with the city police force. That was 1955. Ten years later, he was promoted to sergeant.

Rob was a teenager by then, and his greatest desire was to please his dad. Dad was a police officer; Dad could never be embarrassed. Bob didn't demand that. Rob demanded it of himself. He could not hurt the guy he loved and respected so much—and these were the 60s. Talk about counter-culture: Rob was a straight-laced kid in the Age of Aquarius. There was no defying authority, no drugs, no long hair. Rob didn't even have his first beer until the night of high school graduation. The following fall at Southern Connecticut, Coach Ron Carbone met a freshman defensive back from Meriden who seemed to have dropped into New Haven from another era. Coach liked to use big words and "anachronism" was the word he used to describe Rob. After the first day of practice Carbone, who had played his college ball at a small school in Kansas, went home and said to his wife, "Rose, I just met the All-American boy."

Not that the All-American boy didn't need disciplining growing up. Millie broke a lot of spatulas—either her paddle of choice or what she always seemed to have in hand—across Rob's backside. With Bob all it took was a look of disapproval to keep the boy in line. So even when he was wayward, Rob never strayed far, like on the day he ran away. This was way back; Rob was no more than four or five years old. It was on a Good Friday, a serious holiday in Millie's home. No radio, no TV. A parish priest came over and blessed the food. Everybody had to be clean and quiet. No place for a restless kid. That house was just too solemn. So the little man took off to play in a nearby sandpit. When he didn't get home in time for church, Millie reached for a spatula and it wasn't to flip pancakes.

Well, that made Rob's mind up. He'd run away from home. Stating his intentions, he grabbed his toy Ferris wheel—a favorite, he'd just be lost without it—and hit the road. Millie was amused, but Bob, arriving home from work shortly after, was upset.

"You let him go?"

Millie chuckled. "He'll turn around. He'll come back."

Come back? Rob and that Ferris wheel were rolling. He wasn't exactly sure where he was going or what he was going to do with the Ferris wheel, but he was a determined sucker.

"I'll teach Mom. She can't scold me on Good Friday. I can play in that sandpit as long as I want."

He got all of eight houses down the street by the time Bob rolled up in his police car. The window was rolled down.

"Get in this car."

Rob got in the car. Bob just had to look at him.

"Where you going?"

"I'm runnin' away from home."

"Hmm."

Father and son rolled down the street in silence until Bob pulled into the parking lot of a neighborhood drugstore.

"I feel like having a soda," he announced.

"Can I have vanilla cream?"

"Sure."

Father and son went in and sat on those circular black stools you used to find at drugstore soda fountains, Bob in his police uniform and Rob with his Ferris wheel. Rob wrapped two hands around a glass of vanilla cream. Bob took a few sips of his.

"So," he said. "You're running away from home?"

"I guess."

"You've got to be careful, you know. You've got to watch for cars. You're young. Kids get picked up by cars."

They took a few more sips and Bob said, "Your mom's really upset with you. You've got to respect your mother. I want you to apologize to her and I don't want this to happen again."

It was quiet, but it was firm and it was an order.

Glasses emptied, Rob collected the Ferris wheel and Bob drove them back home. Rob was antsy. He figured Millie was going to lay into him with another spatula. There never seemed to be a lack of those spatulas. Millie was waiting, all right, waiting with a big smile and a hug. Rob would feel the sting of a few more spatulas down the years, but says he's the better for it, and Millie's doting TLC was a more than ample counterweight.

As Rob grew up, Bob was his greatest motivator. Rob would cut the lawn and Bob would come home in the cop car and say he'd never seen anybody cut a lawn so well, so fast. They'd be driving home—say, from football practice—and Bob would say, "last time you cut the lawn in five minutes; think you can break your record?" What a motivator. Millie: She was more about quality control; she could be critical. She'd point out the spot he missed by the tree. From that, Rob learned a lesson he would apply to coaching: Coach "on the up." Complement good work and players will want to please you and they will deliver. Constructive criticism is fine, but it can't be constant or nit-picky. Players will get turned off.

All the motivational techniques Rob acquired from his relationship with Bob found their way into his coaching. He wanted his players to love him, yet perform for him as well. That's a fine line, one walked by instilling a little bit of fear and a lot of love. Coach McGee instilled it. When Rob was tired in the fourth quarter, all he had to do was look at his coach's face to muster up the energy needed to soldier on.

As a Spartan, Rob was a defensive back and offensive end. Coach McGee employed a running attack, but there was one day in '66 when Coach put the ball in the air and No. 82 piled up 261 receiving yards. It was a state record at the time; 40 years later it still ranks in the top 10. At Maloney, it remains the school record. Ironically, Rob hurt his knee in that game. Quarterback Pete Panciera also got hurt. Rob tried coming back the following week, but re-injured the knee. As a result, he missed the Thanksgiving Day game of his junior year against Platt. All-League honors and a 35-12 Maloney win over its rival were his consolation.

The next year Rob and running back Dan Hatch were named senior captains. This was the start of a lifelong relationship. They would coach together at Maloney nine years later. More than 30 years later, including the fateful 2001 season, Rob would coach Dan's son Patrick. In the summer of '67, in the days before the organized off-season workouts that are now the norm in high school sports, Rob and Dan gathered the team for weightlifting sessions in Rob's driveway. They were always well-attended. Sharon had everything to do with that. "Rob had a good looking sister," Dan still says to this day. "I think some of the guys hung around to get a good look at her."

The senior season opened with a classic Maloney win. The Spartans were up against the Catholic school Xavier. It's always a tilted numbers game when private schools meet public. Parochial schools draw students from a wide geographic range. Public schools draw from defined borders. Xavier had the numbers and the size; Maloney had the win, 8-6. Hatch scored the touchdown. Rob hauled in the two-point conversion pass.

The Spartans got rolling, winning five of their first six games to move into first place in their league. Then they stalled, going 0-2-1 in their last three games. One ended with Hatch stopped shy of the end zone in a bid for a winning touchdown. That was in West Hartford against Conard High, the one time Rob felt the wrath of Coach McGee. Coach had his motivational techniques. One was to go around the locker room and look each player in the eye. He wanted to see who was ready to lay it on the line and who needed to be fired up. Coach was old school. He had no filter. He didn't soft-pedal criticism; he was never shy about lacing into a player. Some resented him for it. Rob couldn't understand why. Sure, some players heard it all the time, but you had to take a good look at yourself: Why am I in Coach's doghouse? He never jumped on you unless you deserved it.

Rob had never heard it from Coach. His teammates would ride him for it. "Coach McGee never yells at you." That day in West Hartford, he did. McGee just ripped him. He wasn't the only one singled out at halftime and there were mitigating circumstances. Rob wasn't giving 100 percent because he wasn't at 100 percent. He had strep throat. Two days earlier it caused him to miss practice for the only time in his Maloney career. Still, Rob felt the sting of reprimand in front of the team and vowed it would never happen again. McGee was like a second dad; Rob didn't want to let him down. He and the Spartans played better in the second half, but to no avail. Late in the game, bidding for a comeback, Rob caught a pass inside the 10 only to be dragged down at the 4. Maloney failed on four tries to get into the end zone. Dan was stopped on the last. "I could see the goal line," he said. "I just couldn't get to it. There was too much weight on me."

The season finale was the crusher: a 35-26 loss to Platt on Thanksgiving. Actually, the game was played four days after the holiday due to a series of rainouts. Meriden's Ceppa Field drains poorly—did back then, does today. The '67 Spartans and Panthers played in heavy mud. It was a bitter end to Rob's Spartan career. Maloney had lost to Platt for the first time in five years. But the defeat would later serve him well as a coach. He knew what it was like to lose that last game of the season to the cross-town rival, so he was doubly motivated to win on Thanksgiving, a fervor he instilled in his players.

In the meantime, Rob still had some seasons in him as a player. He went on to Southern Connecticut and suited up for head coach Harry Shea. Home or away, even if the games were out of state, Bob Szymaszek was a fixture. He'd be waiting with a hug and a handshake for his son after each one, just as he'd been when Rob played high school ball. Knowing Bob was in the bleachers was powerful motivation for Rob. He'd spot his dad the minute he entered the stadium. He'd be looking for him. The assistant coaches could spot him, too. They all knew him. One Saturday the team was playing down on Long Island against Hofstra and, as kickoff approached, Bob hadn't shown.

"I don't see your dad," said Ray DiFrancesco, one of the Southern Connecticut assistants.

Rob began to panic. Dad didn't miss games unless he had to work. He wasn't working that day. He was coming to the game. "Something happened! There must have been an accident."

"Relax. He probably got lost. It's easy to get lost around here. The traffic is crazy."

The first half came and went. No Bob. When the team came back onto the field after halftime, Rob and DiFrancesco scanned the crowd. Bob still wasn't there. Rob tried to focus on playing, but was awfully worried. He didn't find out until the team got back to Connecticut that Bob had gotten down to Long Island only to get lost. After endless circling, he'd turned back home.

"It was the most frustrating ride of my life," he told his son. "Jesus Cah-rist! So how'd you guys make out?"

Rob played defensive halfback. It's a tough position to play. Make a mistake and everyone sees it. Linebackers, defensive linemen: Their mistakes aren't so visible. Miss a tackle in the backfield and, well, 10 other guys let that guy get to you, but everybody sees the defensive back miss the tackle that leads to the touchdown. You're covering a receiver one-on-one or in zone coverage and he beats you, everybody sees that, too.

At Southern, Rob was a terrific competitor. "Rob gave everything he had and he did it willingly and constantly," Coach Carbone said. "Not all players did that." Rob thought it was the only way to go. He wasn't overly big or overly fast, but could lay a good lick. He hit so hard he sometimes hurt himself. There was a hit at Gettysburg College in Pennsylvania that left Rob sniffing smelling salts on the sideline. Late in his junior season Rob laid into a guy who had caught a pass on him. *"You beat me on coverage, but I'll send a message. You won't want to catch another ball in my zone again."* Rob lowered his head, delivered the hit and wound up fracturing the seventh cervical vertebra in his neck.

Amazingly, the injury wasn't diagnosed right away. The team trainer was going through some "personal issues" at the time, as Rob prefers to put it, and he wasn't at the top of his game. Rob's health could have suffered drastically for it. He practiced Monday, he practiced Tuesday—and he was hitting people. Finally, he confronted the trainer.

"If you don't send me to the hospital, I'm going to go myself. I can't keep my head off my shoulders. This thing is throbbing all night."

"Well, you can go if you want," the trainer said.

Rob got a ride from a roommate. X-rays revealed the fracture and Rob was put in a protective collar.

The season finale with Central Connecticut State was four days away. Central was a rival. The year before, at Central's homecoming, Rob had a big game and Southern won. Sharon wasn't too happy about that. She was not only a student at Central, she was that year's homecoming queen. It was like the Cowboys and Indians they'd played as kids in the sandpit, when Rob always had to be the Cowboys and Rob always had to win. "KID BROTHER SPOILS BIG SISTER'S BIG DAY," sang one headline.

Rob wanted to have another big game. He sized up the newly fitted collar.

"Doctor, can I play in it?"

"I don't think you understand what you're dealing with," the doctor said. "Another blow to that area and you could become a paraplegic. Do you know what that is? It means not having the ability to make love for the rest of your life."

That was an effective way of putting it to a young man.

"You telling me I'd be paralyzed from the waist down?"

"Yes I am. There's also a chance you could be a quadriplegic if you got hit the right way. Quadriplegic: Do you know what that is?"

Rob stopped asking about playing on Saturday.

The doctor did say he would be OK to play the following year because the vertebrae would fuse as it healed and actually become stronger. Rob did come back, but he wasn't the same player. He was gun-shy. *Quadriplegic: Do you know what that is?* Rob did a lot of exercises to build up his neck muscles, but in his heart he knew he wasn't the same player. He'd played Pop Warner football, junior high football, high school football and college football, and now he wasn't the player he always was.

At age 21, a playing career was over.

A career in football, though, was just being born.

CHAPTER 4

Spartan Pride: Coach Smaz

THERE IS A picture in the 2001 Maloney High School football yearbook that shows the team yukking it up for the camera. Helmets on backward, tongues wagging: a whole bevy of showboat poses.

It was August 30.

The shot was taken by Bill Lischeid, whose two sons had recently played for the Green and White. As Bill later remarked, little did the Spartans know what the next few weeks would bring.

Spartan Pride, the staple of the Szymaszek coaching philosophy

The Spartans expected to do some winning in 2001. They had a good senior class, some size and speed, and they were solid at most positions. They had their "11," a philosophy Rob had established over the years that held the 11 hardest working guys were going to play, the 11 who would go all out on every play until the whistle blew. Rob and his assistant coaches naturally put stock in speed and strength, but most of all they desired heart. The Spartans had to have the kind of "wide-eyed, fanatical effort," as Rob put it, to compete against all those bigger schools on their schedule.

Heading into the fall of 2001, the Spartans had their 11, and then some. Momentum was building. Weightlifting coach Pablo Valentin had overseen a strong off-season program. Rob liked the way he achieved chemistry with the team, the way he could push players in the weight room, making them work harder than ever while maintaining a sense of fun. Spring practice went well, as did the summer camps at Syracuse and Southern Connecticut. Participation in a summer passing league kept the secondary sharp and fine-tuned the offense's run-pass and sprint-out packages.

The team was also tightly knit. Bryan Smith, a rookie assistant coach, noticed the family atmosphere right away, from the upbeat attitude on the field to the bin of extra shoes and equipment in the locker room for players who couldn't afford them.

These were characteristics of a program Rob had forged over his 26 years as head coach, the first eight with his former senior co-captain Dan Hatch as his top assistant, the next 18 with Mike Falis as his right-hand man after Hatch stepped down.

How far Maloney football had come since Rob was hired in 1976. The Spartans had taken a nosedive after Rob graduated in 1968. Ed McGee retired following the 1969 season and over the next seven years the Spartans won 10 games, lost 57 and tied one. They lost 22 straight in 1970 and 1971, and that was under a coach who would go on to win state titles at another school. Spartan Pride was dead. Who would revive it?

Rob had been steadily gravitating back to Maloney since graduating Southern Connecticut in 1972 with a bachelor's in physical education and health, and a minor in history education. He and Diane, dating since high school, married that summer. He was 22, she 21, still an undergrad at Southern. They rented the top floor of a three-family home in Meriden's north end owned by a Polish family that knew Di's parents.

Teachers just out of college take jobs where they can get them. Rob's first was up in Winsted, in the extreme northwest corner of Connecticut, 100 miles round trip from home. Every day he made the haul with the principal, Bill Papallo, who also lived in Meriden. Bill had taught at Maloney when Rob was a student. On the long drives to and from Winsted, Rob would pepper Bill with questions, pencil and notebook at the ready. "How would you handle this situation if you were in the classroom? How would you handle that?"

The commute got considerably shorter the following year when a physical education job opened up at a Meriden middle school. That's where Rob was, with a Master's in health education and a six-year degree in counseling by then in hand, when the head football coaching job at Maloney opened up in the summer of 1976. Initially, Coach McGee had been brought out of retirement to turn the Spartans around. Rob was slated to be one of his assistants. But when McGee learned he couldn't pick his own staff, he resigned on the spot. The season was just three months away. Time was tight. McGee urged Rob to apply.

"Coach, I'm not ready to be a head coach," Rob protested.

"If you don't," McGee said, "I'm concerned about what might happen to the program."

So Rob applied. There were several other candidates. It was up to the Board of Education to decide. Rob had an ally there. One of the members, Dr. Bob Montemurro, was a friend Rob had known since his playing days at Maloney. Doc taped up players before games. He was also Bob Szymaszek's physician. One time Bob took his son to see Doc because Rob had a big callus on his heel. It was the day before a game. Doc heated a scalpel and sliced it off. It hurt like hell, but Rob wasn't going to show it. "I'm going to play," he said, and Doc liked that.

The two bonded, and Montemurro proved as big an influence as Bob Szymaszek, Coach McGee and Coach Carbone. Doc hired Rob the summer after he graduated Southern Connecticut to install a pool and help with other work around the house. As each summer day wound down Doc would call out, "Hey, Smaz, come on in here and have some dinner."

He was an unbelievably good cook.

"Doc, you've got to give me this recipe."

A passion was born. While Millie was a great cook, Rob never had the urge to learn from her. That was woman's work, right? Now here was Doc Montemurro, a tough old Italian who loved sports, who sliced away calluses as if they were potatoes and looked you in the eye and liked it when you didn't flinch. This guy was cooking. That dispelled Rob's hang-ups. Doc showed him how to cook and there was nothing sissified about it. They started with linguini and white clam sauce, moved on to red sauce. Rob wrote everything down on index cards. He drew from multiple sources. There was another Italian, a guy named Dominic who owned a bar on the other side of town, and Rob picked up tips from him.

"Ah, my linguini and clam sauce is better than Doc's. Does he put this in it?"

The Polish kid tapped into a deep Italian pipeline.

"Hey, Doc, I put some onions into my linguini and clam sauce."

When it came to the head football coaching job at Maloney, Rob told Doc not to stir the pot. "Advocate for me, but don't play politics. If I get the job, I want it on merit."

But did Rob's resume have enough muscle? He'd spent two years as a volunteer assistant at Maloney and another two as a volunteer at Hamden High, where Coach Carbone had gone after leaving Southern Connecticut. It was a thin football resume. Nonetheless, Rob was the man for Maloney. Doc called at midnight the night the school board voted. Speculation was reality. It was time for the novice to leave the feet of the masters. Rob returned the phone to the receiver. "Diane," he said. "What have I done?"

* * *

Rob hadn't lied to Coach McGee. He was unprepared to be a head football coach. He believed the other candidates had to have been better qualified. He was only 26! In time, Rob discovered he was no greener than most high school coaches when they take their first job.

Still, Rob hit the ground scrambling. His first call was to Coach McGee. Anyone who goes into coaching often does so because he was inspired by a coach he once played for. Coach McGee was that guy for Rob. Only nine years before, he'd been on that Maloney field, wearing No. 82, huddling up and taking a knee when Coach started practice. The Spartans would look up and Ed McGee would look them each in the eye. On the day after his appointment, Rob cast another glance McGee's way.

"Coach, what should I do?"

The look back was baffling.

"Bobby, I've been hurt an awful lot by a lot of former ball-players. I don't want to be hurt again."

For all his bluntness, Coach was sometimes hard to understand. Rob would never figure out where McGee was coming from with that statement. After all, McGee had urged him to apply. Now he was declining to help for unexplained reasons. Maybe he didn't want Rob operating in his shadow. Who knows? Out of respect, Rob accepted his answer and pushed no further.

His next call was to Ron Carbone. It would not be the last. Over time, as Rob strove to uphold McGee's "Spartan Pride" traditions, he found himself blending the best of McGee and Carbone into his own coaching style, just as he had blended the best of the old Italians into his cooking. There was much to draw from. Their pep talks were inspirational. Their energy was tireless, particularly Carbone, who was still coaching. You could find him any day down in his basement office working on football. Carbone's preparation and attention to detail had rubbed off on Rob when he played for him at Southern Connecticut and coached with him in Hamden. So did Carbone's philosophy. "Players will work hard for you," he'd say. "Your obligation is to have them prepared." Such preparation is its own reward and Rob would come to relish it. En route to games, he thrilled at the thought of his team, so well conditioned and so well prepared, about to put hours of work on public display.

Yet in that summer of '76, as America celebrated its bicentennial, Rob was the greenhorn. Dan Hatch was the first guy he brought aboard. The former co-captains had made a pact when they learned they were both going after the head job. Whoever didn't get it would be the other's assistant.

Their first objective was re-instilling the attitude that had shaped their playing days. A losing mentality was unacceptable.

Photos by Bill Lischeid

Left: Rob and his mentor, Ron Carbone.
Right: Rob and his first assistant coach, Dan Hatch.

Never mind the 10-57-1 record of the past seven seasons. The Spartans were going to do everything as if they were established winners. The reality was the Spartans were established losers and attitude adjustments don't happen overnight. Yet in a way, those seven years of losing made '76 an easy situation to walk into. Dan and Rob were young, but they were energetic and intense, and the kids bought into it. They were ready to win. *Rocky* was the hit movie of the summer; it was the season of the long shots. Bumper stickers proclaiming "The Pride is Back!" started popping up on the East Side of Meriden.

While Rob was a home-grown product and now a guidance counselor at Maloney, he was an unknown commodity for most of the football team. Only wide receiver Tom Gaffey, the latest No. 82, knew much about him. Tom ran track and Rob had taken up the coaching reigns (largely because no one else wanted them) the previous spring. On the first day of track practice Rob gathered the athletes, a more forlorn losing lot than even the football team, and told them to meet him at the municipal golf course to run the next day at 6 a.m. About 20 kids showed and ran with Rob. From there, the numbers quickly dwindled until it was just Rob and Tom Gaffey, running early each morning on an empty golf course with their Irish setters.

Now the football team wanted to know what it was going to be like under Coach Szymaszek.

"It's going to be different," Gaffey promised.

And it was. At the first captain's practice, the new Spartans workout included rolling *up* the hill where Ed McGee used to stand.

Rob worked that first team hard. He worked all his teams hard, but he was also compassionate. When he had to come down on a player, the policy was to be constructive. "We're talking about 15, 16 and 17-year-old boys here," he once explained. "If we tore a kid up in practice, we patched that player back up before he went home. Players must be treated with love and respect."

Positive reinforcement was the byword. While watching film, if some players clearly hadn't gone all-out on a play, Rob would rewind the tape and point out not those players, but the one who was hustling.

"If you don't have the same effort that he has, then you've got to ask yourself why. He's doing it, why can't you? If we can get 11 guys who are playing like he is, we've got something."

The best 11: Some seasons it would take longer, but the Spartans would find their 11. That first year, senior quarterback and captain Scott Sundberg was one of the 11. In preseason he got used to seeing Rob's car pull up in front of his house early each morning, either for a run down to Hamden to tap into the wisdom of Ron Carbone or to go to Rob's house to study game film. By then Rob had purchased his first house, a

Cape on Reynolds Drive. They'd hole up for hours in one of the small rooms upstairs, poring over the film to find what little the Spartans did right amidst so much wrong. If they paused the machine for too long, the tape would heat up and start to burn through.

That's what Rob wanted. He wanted the Spartans to catch fire. He had no interest in a long rebuilding process. He wanted to win right away. On opening day, the Spartans traveled down to the shoreline to play Guilford. Rob had prepared like a madman, yet a critical detail was overlooked: The Spartans forgot to bring footballs for warm-ups. Rob walked across the field, thanking God each step of the way that the Guilford coach was a former teammate from Southern Connecticut. Other than that, the Spartans executed. They scored a touchdown and they were making it stand up with shutout defense. But then, late in the second half, Guilford punched in a touchdown. Rob was standing next to Sundberg on the sideline with a hand resting on the back of the quarterback's neck—an unconscious habit of Rob's that a long parade of Maloney quarterbacks would come to know. When the extra point sailed through the uprights to tie the game at 7, Rob squeezed Sundberg's neck hard. Very hard.

"We're not going to let this happen!" the rookie coach screamed in fury. *"We're not going to let this happen!"*

Pained, startled, and then caught up in the fire, Sundberg roared right back, "This ain't happening! *This is not gonna happen!"*

Sure enough, the Spartans, aided by some improbable fourth-down plays, responded with the winning touchdown. The exuberance on the bus was incredible.

"Coach, thank you so much."

For what? Rob thought. They'd only won a first game. Then

Rob's typical reaction to a "can't do" attitude

he realized these Spartans had never experienced victory on Opening Day. They had grown too accustomed to losing.

Rob and Dan kept flying by the seat of their pants that first season, picking the brains of older, established coaches. But they were determined to re-instill the "Spartan Pride" that had shaped them, a pride steeped in hard work. Their goal was to finish their first campaign better than .500. They did. By beating Platt 24-6 on Thanksgiving, the '76 Spartans came in at 5-4-1.

Rob never forgot that first game, though. How could he? Since that September Saturday in 1976 a game ball has sat on a shelf in his house, encased in glass, reading Maloney 13, Guilford 7.

* * *

It was raining Friday, Sept. 14, 2001, the national day of mourning for the 9/11 terrorist attacks. The country still lay stunned. The sky was eerily silent, empty of airplanes. President Bush went to mass at St. Patrick's Cathedral and then went down into the World Trade Center wreckage where rescue crews continued to comb through the smoldering ash and rubble.

It was rainy and dismal in Meriden, too, but the landscape of Rob's personal crisis was not so stark. Fruit baskets and flowers sent by well-wishers were piled everywhere in the dining room at 76 Oak Ridge Drive. Rob had come home from Yale-New Haven on Wednesday the 12th. His surgery was in exactly one week, on Friday the 21st.

Rain beat against the windows. Maloney's season-opening game at Ceppa Field against neighboring Berlin had been postponed 24 hours to Saturday night. Diane was at school. Jen was at college. Mr. Diffley slept. The house was quiet. Rob read through some of the new plays Mike Falis had drawn up, but it wasn't easy to focus on such a dismal afternoon . . .

The doorbell rang. That was me, standing in the rain out on the front stoop with a bouquet of flowers. "Would you go to the prom with me?" I inquired.

The idea of this book was still years away and I was stopping by not just to wish Rob well, but to get closer to the story of the city coaching legend who had suddenly and shockingly been diagnosed with a brain tumor. I had been to Rob's house only once before. I did not yet know the best way in was through the garage, where the door is always open.

"Hey, you want some fruit?" Rob asked as we passed through the dining room. "I've got plenty. I'm thinking of opening a produce market."

We sat at the kitchen table. It was strategically placed where the kitchen gave way to the living room—there's no wall between the two—so while you eat you can glance over the couch and watch TV or glance out the back windows and admire the fine hilltop view facing west across the city.

A towering stack of plays on the table caught my eye. Rob indicated one play, his blue eyes widening behind his glasses. "If Berlin puts eight defenders in the box," he explained while sizing it up himself, "we can pull this tackle and try to open up running room over here on the outside."

A rash of injuries had forced Mike Falis to revamp the Maloney playbook. It was all such foreign and unwelcome terrain to Mike, who had been running the team since Rob was hospitalized for the first 11 days of September. Mike was an ideal lieutenant. Since Hatch had stepped down after the 1983 season, Mike had been Rob's right arm. But he was a reluctant general. He had been like that in high school, too. Mike played guard and linebacker and had little to say, but he was the most respected player and was named team captain because of the example he set. He often played in pain. Once Mike was urinating blood before a game and still wanted to play, but Coach McGee wouldn't let him.

Who could forget tough-as-nails Mike Falis? Rob didn't. Several years into his coaching career Mike approached him at a picnic asking about helping out. Mike was plant manager at Meriden Manufacturing, and when a position opened up on Rob's staff upon Hatch's departure, Mike's boss, Les Maloney, allowed him to adjust his schedule so he could get to the school in time for practice.

A dynamo was unleashed. Mike just inhaled coaching. The Spartans went to camps and Mike's offensive line would come home running Syracuse University blocking schemes. Mike could have been a head coach at any school. Rob made him aware of openings. But like Rob, Mike had found his niche. "I enjoy doing what I'm doing," he'd say. "I have no desire to go further. I'm content here."

In the summer of 2000 Mike had been an uneasy coach-in-waiting when Rob was on the verge of becoming head of Maloney High's guidance department, where he'd been working since becoming football coach in the fall of '76. With the promotion, Rob was looking at a $10,000 raise and a related boost in retirement benefits. There was a catch, though. Meriden has a policy, albeit unwritten, forbidding department heads from coaching, the theory being coaching distracts from administrative duties. Rob appealed to the Board of Education: "Let me do both, even if for one year only." That would provide time to get the next coaching regime in place. It was mid-summer, after all. The 2000 season was fast approaching and Mike wasn't sure he wanted to stick around after Rob was gone.

He never had to make that decision. By a 4-3 vote the school board said no.

Now Rob had a decision to make: football or a promotion? Initially, he took the guidance job. A lot of people called up to congratulate him. Others weren't so thrilled.

"I'm angry to see someone like you getting out of football," said Tom Dunn, the coach at Rockville High in Vernon. "I hope you have a good reason."

Rob Cersosimo, the coach at Conard High in West Hartford, got a speeding ticket rushing down to Meriden to try to talk his old friend and college teammate out of it.

Their words echoed. So did those of Richard Neils, Joe Ferreira and the other Maloney players who had spoken before the Board of Education. "He's built what Maloney football is today," Ferreira had told board members. "I don't know if you guys are fans of football. We take great pride in what we do on the field and off the field due to him."

Joe and the other players spoke in vain. They knew it before the vote was even taken. They read the scene. They knew minds were made up. "Coach, they weren't even listening to us."

Was Rob listening?

About a week after taking the guidance director's job a coaching manual he had ordered from a clinic he'd recently attended arrived in the mail. Why bother, Rob thought, yet still flipped through it anyway that night in bed. In between play diagrams, Syracuse associate coach George DeLeone wrote about the essence of coaching, about the impact coaches have on their players. He mentioned the old bit about the grass on the other side of the fence. Rob tried to read George's words aloud to Diane, but he choked up.

He went downstairs and for the next few hours drew up a list of pros and cons for becoming head of guidance. One side of the paper ran much longer than the other. The one pro was money. Financially, it was a no-brainer. Taking the new job made Rob and Diane much more secure. Yet money had never motivated Rob in the past. Why should it drive this decision?

He stared at the list. *What did the Lord put you on this earth to do, Rob?* He pictured himself with other guidance directors. They were good guys, but they weren't football coaches.

He stared at the list. He'd been pretty lifeless since making the decision. He'd lacked enthusiasm. *What energizes your soul, Rob?* The kids.

The kids.

Rob met the next morning with his principal and superintendent. His new administrative title was shed. He was back in his old skin.

"I'm happy I recognized the mistake before it went on any longer. I realized it was something that was not as well-thought out as I thought it was," was his quote in the Meriden *Record-Journal.* "I've never felt so good in my whole life."

And now, a little more than a year later, Rob was staring at brain surgery. The rain beat down and we surveyed the plays stacked on the kitchen table, studying the X's and O's, the curving arrows. Everything so tidy, everything so well designed, but everything dependent on the execution of teenage boys to go according to plan. A coach always wants to be in control, and he usually is, until the ball is snapped. Then it's out of his hands— just like when a patient gives way to a surgeon, who has his own game plan, his own set of X's and O's.

Rob stood up, paced a bit, sat back down.

"Boy, I tell you, if the kids can win tomorrow night I think they could start 4-0. After Berlin they have, let's see, Hall, um, Rockville and, uh, Bristol Eastern."

Those were games he would not see. At least not in person.

Rob got back up, paced some more.

"They could be 4-0. Wouldn't that be something?"

We could hear the steady patter of the rain on the windows; we could hear the ticking of a clock. It was awfully dark outside, awfully dark for one o'clock.

"Boy, just think," Rob said. "One week from today I'll be under that knife."

Rob and Diane with Mike and Linda Falis at the 2002
Connecticut-Rhode Island All-Star game

CHAPTER 5

Together We Can

THE SPARTANS HEADED into 2001 thinking playoffs. All too quickly the objective became survival. As defensive coordinator Steve Hoag said, everything good that was supposed to happen went in the opposite direction.

Maloney's star-crossed year actually began in January, when Mike Falis' son Ryan, an assistant coach, died suddenly from heart failure. He was 29.

The heart failure stemmed from a kidney transplant. Ryan had been born with a deformed kidney. He hadn't been able to play football. He was able to coach, though. He was good with computers and he brought Maloney's playbook into the high-tech age. The kids loved him. He was like one of them. He knew all the video games.

Ryan was a big Syracuse football fan, too.

"Dad, did you see that play by Donovan McNabb?"

Ryan and Mike Falis got very close through coaching.

"Dad, I never understood why you loved this so much. Now I do."

When Ryan's one good kidney started to fail, he was in need of a transplant. The best match was his mother, Linda. She gave one of her kidneys to her son. The operation went well, but insidiously put a strain on Ryan's heart. No one knew until a Saturday afternoon in January 2001 when Ryan was stricken at the local shopping mall. MidState Medical Center was right across the street. It was still too late.

Mike had just lost his father and one of his brothers to heart disease. Now Ryan was gone. All in a matter of months. After Ryan's wake Rob stopped by Mike's house. They put their arms around each other.

"This just isn't fair," Mike said.

Ryan left a wife and young daughter. His initials "RF" were put on a patch and sewn onto Maloney's uniforms. Rob talked to Mike about whether he wanted to continue coaching, ready to make any concession. If Mike could only be there a few days a week, that was fine.

"Mike, you tell me what you need to do. If you can't do this, somehow we'll make it work."

Mike resolved to stay. "That's what Ryan would want."

This was the weight that Mike, by then Rob's associate head coach, took into the 2001 season. Now it was compounded by Rob's medical crisis. Yet in those long first weeks of September, as testing continued at Yale-New Haven and it became clear Rob wasn't going to return any time soon, it was equally clear who had to take charge. As reluctant an heir apparent as he'd been the previous summer when Rob wrestled with the guidance director's job, as aggrieved as he'd been by the loss of his father, brother and son, there was no one better equipped and better trusted to take up the reins of Maloney football than Mike Falis.

"You've got to do the things now that I normally do," Rob told Mike at Yale-New Haven one afternoon. "You've got to talk to the kids about school. Make sure they do their homework. Make sure they are on their best behavior in class."

That was easier said than done. With Rob out of the picture, no one on the Maloney coaching staff was in the school during the day. The players were accustomed to Rob's guidance office door always being open, and his presence in school helped resolve academic or disciplinary problems as soon as they arose. In the latter regard, Rob's absence would soon be felt.

In the meantime, Mike kept the kids informed about Rob's condition. He'd start practice having them stretch and run the hill above the field. Then they'd take a water break and Mike would give them a daily update. "How's Coach?" they wanted to know. "Will he be gone the whole season?" There were a lot of rumors floating around, a lot of doom-and-gloom stuff. Mike made sure the kids got it straight.

"Look, I'm telling you, I've talked with Coach Smaz. This is what's going on. Don't listen to anybody else. Don't believe any of that."

All the same, football went on haltingly without Rob. Mike had held up his cell phone after that successful Labor Day scrimmage against Lyman Hall and the kids had yelled out to Rob in unison, but they were dead quiet on the bus ride home. It was a team without its leader.

"The first day he wasn't here we felt it," tailback Christian Roman told the Meriden *Record-Journal*. "We knew something was different, but there's nothing we can do about it. All we can do is pray and just play."

The Spartans prayed. Raised Roman Catholic, Rob had been involved off and on in the Fellowship of Christian Athletes. The intensity of his devotion ran hot and cool, so faith had a cyclical influence on his teams. When hot, Rob took the team to mass. When cool, the Spartans still said the Lord's Prayer before games and did volunteer work at the Franciscan Life Center on the other side of town.

The 2001 squad was steeped in prayer more than most. There was 9-11, Ryan's passing, Rob's illness. There was also the addition of Hoag, a devout Christian who, even before Rob fell ill,

Rob and the Spartans kneel in prayer before a game.

suggested re-establishing a chapter of the Fellowship of Christian Athletes at Maloney. He carried a small green Bible in his back pocket. When Rob was in the hospital he led the team in prayer after each practice. Psalms mostly, nothing heavily denominational, nothing tying Rob's situation to the team winning or losing. They were prayers for healing.

Unfortunately, the prayers went unanswered. The health of the team rivaled Rob's for news flashes. Christian Roman, the latest in Maloney's long line of feature tailbacks, was out with a hamstring injury from spring track, and the injuries piled up behind him. Center Shawn Gardner, a senior captain, broke his left hand in the first scrimmage. He would continue to play wearing a big cast. In the final scrimmage, the Friday night jamboree at Ceppa Field, another senior captain, guard Danny Ferry, was lost to a knee injury. He would miss almost the entire season. Senior tight end Aaron Goldberg also hurt his knee in the jamboree.

There were landmines off the field. Flanker Steve Mandeville turned his ankle while skateboarding and would miss a month. The new quarterback, Eric Riddle, got in trouble in school and was suspended for the season opener.

And, of course, the Spartans were also missing their head coach. Lying in his hospital bed at Yale-New Haven, Rob sometimes forgot what that meant.

"You getting everything done in practice Mike?" he'd ask during the daily update.

"No, we didn't get to a few things."

"Why not?"

"Rob, we're down one coach."

On Wednesday the 12th, the day he came home from the hospital, his head still aching from the biopsy the day before, the date of his surgery on the calendar, Rob got a desperate call from Mike. The season opener against a heavily favored Berlin High was looming and the situation in Spartans camp was not good.

"Rob, we need you," Mike said. "We're practicing like crap. The kids aren't the same. They're just off. They need a pick-me-up."

Diane urged Rob to go. "It would be good for you, too."

She drove him to practice. Down on the field the players were going through their paces, the green M on the white helmets vivid in the slanting sun. Rob could see big No. 70: his veteran lineman, Patrick Hatch, Dan's son. Patrick was a senior captain just like his dad had been with Rob when they were teenage boys and moved so effortlessly through autumn afternoons. The boys were no more than 100 yards distant, yet it was strange for Rob to see them from even that remove. His place had always been down on that field, in the middle of it all.

Mike spotted Rob and Diane right away. He looked up as they got out of the car, and as Mike looked each player in turn stopped what he was doing and looked, too, heads swiveling like dominoes. Diane helped her husband down the concrete stairs. Thirty-three steps: three sets of 11. Rob descended slowly, overcome with emotion. It was the first time he was seeing the kids on the field since he'd left them after that September 1st scrimmage. Practice had come to a complete halt. Rob knew they were all looking over. Some people were walking and jogging on the all-weather track that rings the field. Kids and dogs and moms and baby carriages going round and round, but in the middle the team stood still, watching.

You've got to look strong, Rob told himself. *You can't give out any hint of being frail.*

But that's exactly how he felt. He had lain in a hospital bed for nearly two weeks. The right side of his head had been shaved and cut open. There were staples in his scalp. He wore a thick gauze pad to cover them and had also wrapped gauze around the right arm of his eyeglasses to prevent friction on the incision.

Rob slowly crossed onto the field, the grass just starting to wear thin along the hashmarks. Mike was welling up as he gathered the boys. Their faces were glued to Rob's. He could feel one intense collective stare. He could also feel their concern. It just emanated off of them, and it was a palpable step in healing, he later said, much like the American flags that were sprouting in windows and on car antennas in the wake of 9-11. "It's just like a homecoming," said Pete Sini, an old Meriden youth football guy who had hung around the Spartans so long and so religiously that Rob made him a volunteer coach and dubbed him "Papa Pete, senior advisor." Pete was 80 years old, and as he watched Rob walk onto the field he felt his soul stir.

The team's too: Mike could see Spartan spirits lift. The enthusiasm they'd been lacking came bustling back after Rob spoke a few words, trying to ignore the throb in his skull. Funny, but nobody remembers what was said that afternoon. They just remember the effect—"the presence more than the words," as Patrick Hatch said. Just the fact that Coach Smaz was somehow there and not laid up in bed mystified and moved the Spartans. He had a biopsy the day before. He had just come home from the hospital that day. He was facing major surgery in a little more than a week and *he* had come to pump *them* up? What player would not dig down and give his all after that?

What the Spartans did not know was they did more for Rob than he did for them. He trudged back up the 33 concrete steps, the three sets of 11, but he left feeling pretty good and strove to maintain that upbeat attitude. All the same, Rob got on his knees that night and prayed for everything to work out. The Master Coach upstairs: It was in His hands.

* * *

Mike and Rob had talked about Saturday night's game. Should Rob go? Nothing was planned. It was left up to how Rob felt.

"I don't know if I can physically be on the field," Rob said. "Maybe I could be up in the stands."

"Rob, you do whatever you can do. I don't want you to hurt yourself or have a setback."

Throughout his career Rob got caught up in the energy and emotion of the game and at times could get agitated. Yet he was composed on the sidelines, not a raving maniac like some coaches can be. Only rarely did he lose his sense of decorum. When a questionable touchdown call in the closing seconds cost Maloney a 1999 game against New Britain—a conference rival, one of the biggest schools in the state and a team Maloney always struggled mightily to beat—Rob stormed to the far end of the field to have it out with the officials. First, he made a detour past the New Britain team huddle.

"Congratulations, New Britain! Good game!" Rob bellowed. "YOU PLAYED YOUR ASSES OFF!"

Then he took up the issue with the refs, who'd ruled New Britain had creased the end zone when Rob believed Maloney had held.

"How could you make that call from the back of the end zone? HOW COULD YOU POSSIBLY MAKE THAT CALL?"

He didn't stop until he was flagged for unsportsmanlike conduct. One more flag and Rob would have been suspended for the next game.

The loss hurt the Spartans. After going to the state playoffs in 1998, Maloney finished the 1999 season at 7-3. At 8-2, the Spartans might have made a return trip to the postseason. They were 7-3 again in 2000, but again fell just shy of the playoffs.

Now they were opening the 2001 season against a Berlin team that had gone 10-0 in 2000 before losing in the state semifinals. Berlin had most of its top players back and was expected to make another run at a state title. The Spartans, decimated by injuries, their head coach diagnosed with a brain tumor, were a big underdog.

But part of "Spartan Pride" was belief. Rob never went into a game expecting to lose. Records and odds didn't matter. In 1989, the Spartans reached Connecticut's Class M final and they were long-shots against St. Joseph, a Catholic school in Trumbull that had already won six state championships in the 1980s. It was the first postseason appearance ever for the Spartans since a formal state-wide playoff system was adopted in Connecticut in 1976. On a chalkboard in their locker room at Strong Stadium in West Haven someone had written "Maloney Who?"

Rob didn't have to give much of a pep talk that day, and with the clock winding down in the fourth quarter Maloney was leading the No. 3 team in the state. Where were the Spartans ranked? No. 20, 21? At the moment, they were up 7-6 and they had the ball.

Under Rob, the Spartans were an I-formation running team, and with St. Joe's on the ropes they were grinding it out, working the clock. Facing a crucial third down, Maloney ran its bread-and-butter play, the toss, and it gained a first down at the St. Joe's 35.

No, wait. A flag: holding, Spartans. The first down was negated.

"I hope when I watch this film I can see a holding penalty!" Rob shouted at the official who made the call.

The Spartans were eventually forced to punt. St. Joe's took over at its own 8-yard line with scant minutes to play. Armed with a deeper roster and fresher bodies, the Cadets went to a running formation with multiple tight ends and multiple backs and pounded away. Four yards, five yards, four: The first-down chains moved with the clock. On a third down St. Joe's reached the Maloney 1.

Fourth and goal, under a minute to go: One play would settle it all.

A chant of DEE-FENSE! DEE-FENSE! swelled from the grand-stands behind the Maloney bench. All of Meriden seemed to be up there, people from both sides of town, even Platt fans who had rooted against Maloney only a week earlier on Thanksgiving. There, in an out-of-town stadium, a city so often fractured was united. Rob got down on one knee, turned his back to the field and made a sign of the cross.

Dear Lord, if I hear this side of the bleachers stand up and scream, we just won our first state championship. If I hear a cheer from the other side, we've lost.

The ball was snapped; the play set in motion. Rob didn't get the roar he'd hoped for. St. Joe's won 13-7.

Later, scrutinizing the key holding penalty with his coaching staff, Rob yelled at the projection screen. "Show me! Show me where he grabbed some jersey!"

Nothing.

"He had to have been a Catholic referee," joked Rob, who holds firmly to his own Catholic beliefs, and to this one as well: that referee probably had more to do with Maloney not winning a state championship than anybody. Even if the Spartans had failed to punch in an insurance touchdown on their last drive, he argues to this day, they would have at least drained valuable time off the clock. Instead, Maloney punted and St. Joe's took over, and Rob gives his opponent credit. St. Joe's drove 92 yards with the clock winding down without making a single mistake. A championship team does that.

Now, 12 years later, the Spartans were starting a new season against another team with solid championship aspirations while their own horizons had grown as dark as Friday's rain. The weather cleared Saturday, but it wasn't looking good for Rob. For much of the day he did not feel well. He napped only to wake with a headache. He felt weak. But he also felt resolve. Off came the sweat pants. On went white pants, a white shirt and a green sleeveless vest. On the left breast a football was outlined in white, with "Maloney" written in white block letters above it. Rob was going and he was going for the duration. To show up only to go home early would defeat the purpose.

"Diane," he said, "I'm committed to seeing it through all the way."

It was a lovely late afternoon. A September sunset painted the ridges. The view of the West Side cliffs is particularly good from the parking lot at Ceppa Field, which is tucked in a hilltop

68

neighborhood not far from the center of town. Rob arrived just as warm-ups ended and the Spartans were heading into the low brick building that houses the concession stand and cramped locker rooms. Mike and Rob embraced.

"Is it OK if I come into the room and talk?"

"Are you kidding me?"

Rob strode into the locker room. Patrick Hatch was in the face of one of his teammates, getting him fired up to play. Hatch turned and saw Rob's green jacket and the white gauze on his head and the emotion on his face.

How many times had Rob strode into that locker room and brought out the brimstone, the words so readily at hand? Yet on this occasion he could not find the words. Perhaps it was because words could not hope to capture the emotion. Perhaps it was because words were not necessary. There's a bond between coaches and players, a complex connection woven by daily contact, toil, disappointment and reward. The boys responded by just seeing Rob there. They gathered around him. First-year assistant coach Bryan Smith noticed some were visibly shaking.

"I don't know what's in store for me," Rob finally began. "Let's go play some Maloney Spartan football. Let's have people walk away from here saying that was a Maloney Spartan effort."

"One thing, Coach," Mike said. "We play with 12 every snap. You're with us on every snap."

And that was all. They took a knee in that small room, the ceiling so low. Rob was having such a hard time with words he was hoping he wouldn't forget the ones that came next.

"Our Father, who art in heaven . . ."

The Spartans said their prayer and finished with a quiet "Amen." Then they rose, and with a rousing "TOGETHER WE CAN!" the rallying cry they'd adopted for 2001, charged out of the locker room, out into a glorious September afternoon.

Mike and Rob embraced again.

"How'd I do?"

"Rob, you did fine."

"You think they're going to be alright? Are they ready? *Are they ready?*"

"They're ready now."

The Spartans *were* ready. The Berlin Redcoats would average 43 points in winning nine games in 2001, but at halftime there was still a 0 on their side of the scoreboard while Maloney had a 7. Late in the first half Alfred Williams, a shy unassuming senior filling in at quarterback, threw a pass to Mario Avocato in the back of end zone from eight yards out.

Mike had made the play call. On the other side of the ball, it was all in Steve Hoag's hands. The diminutive and bespectacled defensive coordinator, who worked for the state Department of Education and wore a tie and black high-top cleats to every game, had devised a "recognition of tendencies" plan based on reading formations and backfield sets culled from watching countless hours of Berlin game film, starting back before spring practice. His game plan was 30 pages long. When Steve produced it during the summer, Rob skimmed through it.

"Do you believe in this?" Steve asked.

"I believe in you," Rob replied.

Now, set into motion, it was working to perfection. Despite having a 230-pound fullback and a gifted tailback who would play Division I college ball, the Redcoats struggled to move the ball.

"What do you think, Coach?" Steve asked Rob at halftime.

"I don't know what you're doing Steve, but it's working. Keep doing it."

Rob was just a cheerleader that night. He was up in the press box, supposedly helping call plays, but Mike had put together his injury-altered offense and Rob was having a hard time following it. Finally, he told Mike to call the game.

The game slogged through the third quarter. The vaunted Redcoat offense had managed to get across the 50-yard line into Spartan territory just once. Linebacker Alexi Beltran was all over the place, making plays. Punter Porry Noonan's high booming kicks kept Berlin pinned down, facing long fields. Noonan was punting quite a bit. The Spartans, their injury-thinned ranks more telling as the game wore on, weren't able to move the ball either and they clung to their 7-0 lead.

In the end, as it had against St. Joe's in 1989, as it had against New Britain in 1999, the game came down to another goal-line stand. Mounting their first sustained drive, the Redcoats pushed inside the Maloney 10 with several minutes to play. Alexi Beltran made a stop on first down, Christian Roman on the second, Shawn Gardiner on the third. But with each snap the Redcoats ground closer to the goal line. By fourth down they were inches away, literally in the shadow of the Ceppa Field scoreboard that showed 2:36 left to play.

The Redcoats broke their huddle; the Maloney linemen dug in. At one end was Patrick Hatch. Earlier in the game, chasing down the Berlin quarterback, he dove and landed awkwardly on his left shoulder. The pain sent him to the sideline. A sprain? A tear? His shoulder throbbed as the game continued without him. But with the Redcoats at the gate, bidding for the tying score, he'd charged back onto the field. If he blew out the shoulder, he reasoned, there would be time for it to heal, time on the other side of 2:36. The third-down play had gone away from him. Now, on fourth down, there was a gap in the Berlin line on his side and Patrick honed right in, locking his eyes on the small crease of space amid the red helmets and the white shirts smeared with grime, harnessing the adrenaline, hearing the cadence of the count, the sharp clear numbers above the distorted roar of the crowd, waiting, quivering and then releasing the instant the ball was snapped. A 260-pound arrow: Hatch laid into Berlin's big fullback and it wasn't close. The big back went down heavily behind the line. Hatch had made the play; the Spartans had held.

The Redcoats did nail Alfred Williams in the end zone for a safety and did get the ball back for one last chance, but their high tide had come and gone. Berlin went four-and-out and the Spartans, underdogs though they were, had the win they knew they were destined to have.

"Coach has been on our minds since the first day; he's our main inspiration," Patrick told me in a post-game interview. "We knew we weren't going to lose after we saw him."

As the game had rolled along Rob felt faint. He promised Diane he'd stay in the press box, but as the clock wound down and the goal-line stand was mounted he couldn't resist the pull of the sidelines. His role had been strictly inspirational, but as anyone there knew, it was indispensable. In such a close game, it had given Maloney the edge.

"We were playing against a spiritual and emotional force beyond anything we could handle," Al Pellegrinelli, Berlin's veteran coach, told Rob amid the post-game handshakes.

"Coach, I had nothing to do tactically with winning this football game."

"I realize that. Your presence there is all those kids needed."

It hadn't been his presence alone. "I think we were actually playing with two extra men," Mike Falis told the sportswriters. "My son Ryan up in heaven—thanks, Ry—and Coach Smaz up in the press box."

The Maloney Spartans were in no rush to leave Ceppa Field.

They basked in victory in the long purple twilight of September. There were many well-wishers. One came up quietly. Rob didn't see him until he grabbed his hand with both of his and shook it steadily. Rob's chief rival, Platt coach Tom Ryan.

Tom: the moody, dark-haired Irish-Catholic from central Massachusetts who had been in Meriden since 1980, yet always felt like the perpetual outsider, especially alongside Rob, the fair-haired native son. Their relationship had always been more off than on. They were both good coaches. There was much they respected in one another—the dedication, the preparation, the passion. But cross-town rivalries are always intense, often nasty. Players come and go across district lines. So do accusations. Fans measured stories in the newspaper to see if the rival school was getting more ink. Thanksgiving was always emotionally charged.

And so, too, was this moment. Somehow, Tom and Rob were isolated amid the post-game tumult. They occupied a quiet private pocket on Ceppa Field, the field that so easily turned to mud and where they'd stood on opposite sides and waged so many Thanksgiving battles before thousands of fans who ringed the fences and filled the bleachers. This time, there was an audience of one.

"What a great competitor you are," Tom said softly.

Rob struggled to speak. It was touching and awkward, and more touching for being awkward. I could tell Tom wanted to say more. I could tell Rob wanted to fill him in on his condition. All it would take was the right word, the right gesture and so much would come rushing down along the course of seasons and decades, wives and grown children, careers spent on almost identical practice fields and basement locker rooms on separate sides of town.

Where do you start? Sometimes what says more are just hands shaking over an old battleground after the battle has been redefined.

"What a great competitor you are," Tom said again.

And then he turned and left as quietly as he'd come.

* * *

Rob went to practice on Thursday, September 20, the day before his surgery. Again, Mike thought the guys needed a spark. Despite Saturday's big win, the Spartans weren't practicing with intensity.

Rob wore a baseball cap over his half-shaved head, but had taken off the big piece of gauze. The staples were now visible, curving around the top of his right ear and then turning upward and disappearing underneath the hat. The right arm of Rob's eyeglasses remained bandaged to keep it from rubbing against the staples. He looked gaunt and careworn, but found it easy to muster enthusiasm for the practice. It bothered him that many of the players did not.

Bill Lischeid was snapping pictures for the football yearbook. Two years earlier he'd had his own bout with cancer. It had come out of nowhere, just like Rob's. Bill went from seemingly perfect health to having eight inches of his colon removed. He'd been healthy since. Pete Sini, as always, was at practice. He, too, was coming off a battle with cancer. The year before he had a huge piece of his intestine removed. Now it was Rob's turn to go on that table.

As practice wound down he gathered the team at midfield. This time, words came easily.

"This is the last time I'm going to see you guys for a while. Tomorrow's the big day for me. Tomorrow's my big game day. I can't wait to get it over with and get back out here with you.

I just want to, ah, I gotta be honest with you. I want to make a little observation on what I see out here today. I don't see a bunch of hungry Spartans wanting to get better. I see a few guys wanting to get better, but on the whole I don't see a lot of Spartans wanting to get better, and that's been a trademark here."

Unless this team picked up, it would not follow the Berlin upset with wins that should be forthcoming against the next few opponents. The Spartans weren't necessarily practicing badly, but the enthusiasm was lacking.

"Enthusiasm is contagious," Rob continued. "It's not fun to practice with lethargic people around. There are a lot of lethargic people out here. We need somebody to come out here and start hollerin' and whoopin' and get excited. I got excited on a couple of plays that you guys just ran out here. I got real excited

"Guys, you never know. I learned that. And tomorrow when I wake up out of that surgery they may say, 'Coach Szymaszek, you're all done.'" Rob talks to the Spartans the day before surgery. In the background is Pete Sini.

because if you practice and run those plays on Saturday, those are big plays . . . but you can't play this game without enthusiasm and without emotion. You've got to come out with the idea that you're going to get better every day. Don't take a play off; don't ever take a play off. And you've got to believe."

Rob would take that attitude into surgery. Belief: Would it be enough? He didn't hide the uncertainty.

"Tell you what, you never know. Guys, you never know. I learned that. And tomorrow when I wake up out of that surgery they may say, 'Coach Szymaszek, you're all done.' I—I enjoy myself. God dang it, I enjoy myself. So don't take anything in life for granted. Make the most of every opportunity."

Cars were passing out on the north-south highways, unseen beyond the trees. People were heading home from work. Twilight was coming sooner with the onset of autumn.

"All right, I want to come out of anesthesia sometime tomorrow night. Maybe it will be Saturday morning. I want to hear from my wife that the Spartans won it that day."

The boys were quiet. The boys—the boys were sons. They had to be. The coach who improves his boys as football players without improving them spiritually and mentally as young men is a coach who has failed. Bear Bryant believed that and so did Coach Smaz.

He looked around the huddle. He saw the eyes locked on his.

"All right, I love each and every one of you. I'll be back here as soon as I can. OK? Let's get it in here."

The boys leaned in, jostled to get closer. Hands fell upon hands. A tower of hands, Rob's at the bottom, his voice and the voice of the Spartans rising above the hands and up and out of the huddle. "One, two, three—TOGETHER WE CAN!"

CHAPTER 6

Game Day

ROB WAS UNAFRAID going into the operation. There just wasn't any doubt in his mind. He never thought in terms of life and death. His confidence in his surgeon was that complete.

"Who's doing your surgery?" nurses and receptionists at Yale-New Haven would ask.

"Joe Piepmeier."

"Oh, he's the best."

Piepmeier was a top gun in Yale-New Haven's neurology unit. He'd been with the hospital since coming out of the University of Tennessee's School of Medicine in 1975. He'd won top awards for his work. He wrote extensively. He was editor-in-chief of the *Journal of Neuro-oncology*. He was chairman of the American Association of the Neurological Society. He'd been a visiting professor at medical schools around the world. Rob felt he had the best guy in the world. Piepmeier's appearance and air of quiet confidence were enough to convince Rob of that. The surgeon stood over six feet tall, trim with an athletic frame, sharp blue eyes and a fringe of gray hair. He somehow seemed all-business and laid-back at the same time. If he played football you'd put him at tight end. You just knew he wouldn't flinch over the middle. And he had those proven hands.

Shortly before the operation, Piepmeier got a visit from Richard Diana, the former standout running back at Yale who had gone into orthopedic medicine. Rob had coached Diana when he was a high school player in Hamden, back when he was just out of college and a volunteer assistant for Ron Carbone.

"A special person came to see me today and said I had to do a better than usual job," Dr. Piepmeier told Rob. "So I'm going to do an extra special job."

Maybe Dr. Piepmeier said that to all his patients, but it put Rob at ease. "The guy who is going to be operating on my brain, the guy who is one of the best in the business, is telling me he's going to go above and beyond. Talk about pre-game pep talks. I'm ready to go."

Unfortunately, the surgical team was not. An emergency procedure on another patient delayed Rob's surgery, which had been scheduled for Sept. 21 at 10 a.m.

An hour passed.

Lying on the gurney, he had plenty of time to think. He thought about football. He thought about what he'd done with his family, the trips they'd taken.

Millie and Bob Szymaszek in the brief golden years before Bob's strok.

"Rob, enjoy the time of your life right now with your wife," his mother had told him. "Don't ever hesitate to go anywhere or do anything while you have your health."

Millie said that when she was healthy and her husband was healthy. Rob thought of the years they'd been cheated of. Bob retired in 1984 after a 30-year police career. He and Millie spent a few winters in Florida, but less than six years after retiring Bob had his stroke and landed in a wheelchair, barely able to talk. Millie took care of him and, after seven years, it wore her out. Strange bruises began surfacing on her arms and legs. She tried to ignore them, tried to keep them from her kids. It was liver cancer, the scourge of her family, and in 1997 she was gone.

Whenever Rob was in Florida and saw elderly couples out to dinner or walking, he'd think about how his parents had been cheated. No, the golden years weren't what they were cracked up to be. "Enjoy yourself," Millie said, so Rob took it to the extreme. If he was reading the travel section of the Sunday paper and saw a good deal on a trip or a cruise, he'd call John or Ed Siebert down at Meriden Travel behind his wife's back. "I want to surprise Diane for her birthday" or "I want to surprise Diane this summer." It's not that they always had money in the bank. It's not that they always had money in their checking account. But they did have American Express, and off they went.

All that they had done, all that they had seen—cruises, Santa Barbara, Sedona, St. Martin—Rob revisited them all lying on that gurney as noon came and went. *Thank God I took Mom's advice and didn't wait for the so-called golden years. I feel I've lived a good life . . .*

God forbid, but if this was going to be the end of it, there would be no regrets. *None. Some people get on their deathbed and have a lot of regrets. I don't. If I'm meant to go, then I have no regrets*

Rob and his one and only, Jennifer

on how I lived. I had a wonderful wife, a wonderful daughter, a great career with kids . . .

Another hour passed. Millie and Bob, Diane and Jennifer, Sharon and Jan, friends and fellow coaches passed through his thoughts, passed through again. Finally, around 1:30, it was go-time. Rob was wheeled down the hall to the operating room and there, at the door, at the last possible spot a person could stand without actually being in the operating room, stood Jennifer.

Jennifer: My one and only.

There is a peculiar trait in the Connecticut football coaching fraternity. Many coaches have daughters, but no sons. Rob always wanted a large family, always wanted to have a son. He wanted to dress him. Millie had been an impeccable dresser and Rob always took pride in his clothes. Each season he ordered matching Sahara shirts for the coaching staff, always quality stuff. "Dress for success," as he told his players, and he wanted that for his son. He'd open up the New York Times Sunday magazine and see pictures of kids wearing polo shirts or suits and ties. He wanted that for his son. He wanted to dress him sharp and he never had the opportunity.

With Jennifer, Rob turned a lot over to Diane. They always had a strong mother-daughter bond. They knew everything about each other, they were so much alike. Jen was a photographer, artistic like Diane, not sports-minded like Rob. Jen and Di were liberal, Rob conservative. There were topics they'd long given up discussing. Sometimes it seemed to Rob that Mr. Diffley was his only philosophical ally in the house. But Rob would listen to Jennifer. Trains of thought he'd try to derail in Diane or in his sister Jan he'd let ride in Jennifer.

"She melts you," Jan told him. "You can take a tough line with me, you can take a tough line with Diane, but you're a real softie when it comes to Jen."

They'd always been close, Jennifer and Rob. Football commanded his attention, but he was there for her and always wanted the best for her. When Jen was little, Rob was over-protective. He'd get upset whenever she fell and got bruised or scuffed her knees. Diane did most of the running around for her, but Rob was not absent. A few days after a particularly crushing Thanksgiving loss to Platt, he dressed up like a clown for her birthday party. "I know you," an observant little party-goer giggled. "You're Jennifer's daddy." When she got to prep school and her grades started to slip, Rob was the one who grabbed hold of the reins.

It's not easy being the child of a football coach. They get so wrapped up in the game. Jen loved it when she was young. She grew up on Maloney football. She wanted to be at every game. She wanted to know the players. She wanted to be a cheerleader. As she got older, football became more of a nostalgic experience. Jen still liked coming home from Sarah Lawrence and going to a game, she just had a different perspective by then. She enjoyed watching her father do what he was so passionate about and successful at. But there was more. Rob was like a second father to his players. Compassion, Jen saw, is what made him a good coach. *I hope it made me a good father, too.*

The gurney wheeled on toward Jennifer and the waiting door. Rob saw quite a bit of himself in his daughter: the lively spirit, the drive to do your best, the commitment to work. The football books and posters in Rob's study weren't lost on her, though her outlook and views grew far beyond that. She learned to speak Spanish fluently and for her junior year of college went to Mexico, then ventured down to El Salvador, camera in hand. It was called an independent study trip. Some of the places she lived in had dirt floors.

Now here she was by the operating room door, the furthest you could go without putting on the scrubs or lying on that table. She was crying. She looked down on her father and Rob felt a flood wash over him.

"I was hoping you knew how much I cared about you and loved you."

Did she say it out loud or did Rob just pick up on it? He saw it plainly in her face, in her tears. The sight of his daughter, the look in her eyes, well, that was more calming than any sedative any nurse or doctor could have sent coursing through his veins.

Rob felt big tears well up and he felt them run down. And then he was wheeled into the brightest lights he'd ever seen.

* * *

Being a football coach, Rob had a game plan going in.

1. Get to the hospital on time.
2. Is my surgical team in shape?

Like any coach, Rob took pride in the conditioning of his players. The Spartans might not be the biggest, deepest or most talented team, but damn if they wouldn't strive to be the team that practiced harder than all others and be the team that had the steam to make the fourth quarter theirs.

Rob sized up Dr. Piepmeier's team. Those guys had just gone through an emergency four-hour operation. They had already put in a full game. As he waited in the hallway, Rob had envisioned slumped shoulders, blood all over the place from the last operation. There was no blood. The room was clean, sterile and so brightly lit. But what about those players? *They've got to be tired, and they're going to be working on my brain.* Rob spoke up as he was slid from the gurney to the operating table.

"Can I ask you a few questions?"

"Fire away."

"Well, I guess I have only one: Are you guys ready for the fourth quarter?"

The head anesthesiologist peered over his mask. He looked Rob in the eye. It almost seemed to twinkle.

"Coach, it's not even halftime yet."

And the whole place cracked up. The bright lights, Jennifer's love, the laughing: Rob was flabbergasted at how calm and confident he was. *I'm about to have my head cut open and I'm laughing. How many other patients go through that?* There simply was no fear. *I'm going to wake up from this. I have the best neurosurgeon in America operating on my skull. I'm going to be fine. I am going to be fine.*

Funny, in a way, because when you're a coach, it's all about having control: controlling conditioning, controlling offense, controlling defense. But it's the players who ultimately play the game. Success or failure rides with them.

The players now gathering in a huddle around Coach Smaz were in another league, and they were pros in their league. They were beyond his control, but it was OK. Rob felt secure.

You have autonomy over me.

Voices began to fade, green scrubs to blur, lights to whiten.

Complete autonomy.

Your league, your game.

Let's go.

* * *

Rob's tumor was in the right temporal lobe. Dr. Piepmeier knew from the brain scans what he'd find. Still, it was tricky. The tumor cells weren't much different in appearance from normal brain cells. There were some small vascular differences, a slightly different color, but only very slight. It was not black and white. Also, brain tumors don't have defined edges indicating where the tumor ends and where healthy brain tissue begins.

"When you reach a margin what you're looking at looks like brain tissue. It is, but there's a scattering of tumor cells in there," Dr. Piepmeier had explained. "The decision about how far we push the surgery will be dictated by what's going to happen if I proceed further. I'll take you as far as I can, but understand there's going to be some scattered tumor cells left in there."

"What's the risk if you try to get everything?"

"You don't want to go there. We're not going there."

Piepmeier would have been flirting with paralysis, brain damage—and even then there would have been tumor cells left behind. Delve too deep and the quality and length of Rob's life would be seriously degraded.

Dr. Piepmeier worked. One hour, two . . .

At Maloney, principal Gladys Labbas led the student body in a prayer.

Game Day

In the Yale-New Haven waiting room, Jen and Diane kept vigil and called family members to relay the periodic updates that filtered in from the operating room. The news was encouraging. Jen expected this. Her father had a fighting spirit that would get him through. He had a spirit, she said, that still had more to do.

A third hour passed . . .

Diane and Jen got something to eat and walked outside. They returned to the waiting room. There were other people there, people with rumpled hair and rumpled clothes, keeping the strained, slumped silence of vigil, waiting for news from other operations. Beyond the windows daylight shifted, sliding to twilight. A day out of order, rhythm, routine. Intercom voices and a TV droning. CNN. Stories looped, half-heard. And then news would come and the people would stir and sit with surgeons and shuffle out, half-numb.

Jennifer and Diane were among the last. After four hours, Dr. Piepmeier emerged, projecting calm, projecting certainty, distinguished even in surgical scrubs.

"Well," he said, "we really got it."

Diane and Rob with baby Jennifer

CHAPTER 7

Too Much, Too Soon

HE WOKE UP to pain, unbelievable pulsating pain.

Rob had had a little taste of it from the biopsy and thought that was the most excruciating pain he'd ever experienced. It was nothing compared to what he woke up with in intensive care following the surgery.

The nurses provided a morphine drip. Rob could hit the button so many times every half hour.

"Don't try to be a hero," they told him.

Hero? The guy who hated taking aspirin, who hated giving in to pain, was on a morphine drip, and you better believe he was hitting that button.

And still he was in excruciating pain. So the nurses provided Oxycontin and Percocet. "That was one pain-relieving cocktail," Rob could later joke. "When I had all those medications in me, I couldn't feel the pain."

At the time, there was no laughter.

"You've got to stay ahead of it," the nurses told him. "Don't wait till the pain comes."

It was difficult for Diane and Jen to see Rob in ICU. His head was bandaged and swollen. Tubes ran everywhere. The surgery had gone well, though. Dr. Piepmeier had removed about 90 percent of the tumor. The Szymaszeks weren't happy about the

87

other 10 percent being left behind, but as Dr. Piepmeier said, those tumor cells had been too risky to touch.

There was another repercussion. Prior to the operation, the word "cancer" hadn't been bandied about. The phrase was "tumor cells," not "cancer cells." But after the procedure somebody who had come down from the radiology department let the "C" word slip. That upset Rob. Up until then, he didn't think anything else would have to be done or that there was even concern it was cancer. Dr. Piepmeier was also upset the "C" word had been uttered. The surgery did confirm the tumor was a malignant Grade 2 oligodendroglioma, but the gradient was the key factor. Rob's tumor was low grade. In high grades, pathologists can often see cancer cells actively dividing or growing abnormal blood vessels. Low grades typically act benign and can lie dormant, though they can shift into high grade and become aggressive and require active treatment.

Based on Rob's gradient and how the surgery went, Dr. Piepmeier decided on a "wait-and-see" approach. There would be regular monitoring, but no follow-up treatment, at least for the time being. No chemotherapy, no radiation.

"You may have had this thing for 20 years, we don't know," Dr. Piepmeier said. "It could follow the same indolent course for the next 20 years. What we have to do is be prepared for all alternatives. The behavior is hard to predict. Fortunately, they're treatable; but we don't move to the next stage in therapy until we need that next step. Let's see what the remaining cells do."

Blood clots, a common complication after brain surgery, were a more immediate threat. Anti-clotting sleeves were placed on Rob's legs to help keep the blood flowing. They'd constrict, release, constrict, release. After being removed from intensive care and returned to a regular room the day after the operation, Rob would also be roused from bed for a stroll around the floor.

Get the blood flowing: He did one lap the first day.

"That's a good start," the therapist said.

"Let's do two," said Coach Smaz. "Let's push it."

Two days after the surgery Maloney had a game in West Hartford against Hall High. John Pettit, one of my sportswriter colleagues at the Meriden *Record-Journal*, called the hospital late in the afternoon asking Diane about Rob's condition. When Rob heard about the call, he phoned back for game details.

"Who won?"

"Maloney, 34 to 10," John replied.

"All right."

Rob was tired. His voice was faint.

"How you feeling, Coach?"

"It's tough not being with the team. I'm looking at the clock and saying, 'It's one o'clock; it's kickoff time.'"

Mike Falis called. Rob felt for Mike. His illness had put Mike in a tough spot. When a coach takes over a program, he gets at least a couple months to plan and prepare. There had been no time for Mike. Initially, it went well. Mike and Steve Hoag engineered the upset of Berlin. The win over Hall followed. The Spartans were 2-0. What pleased Rob most was hearing about how the team had played with the enthusiasm he had asked for the day before his surgery.

There were some drawbacks. Quarterback Eric Riddle had returned from his suspension and played well against Hall, but tailback Christian Roman re-injured his hamstring during warm-ups. Patrick Hatch learned he had torn his AC joint in the Berlin game. The injury kept the future Division III lineman out of the Hall game and the one that followed against Rockville. Five regulars were out for the latter contest and Maloney still won 34-7. Five regulars out and Coach Smaz in the hospital and the Spartans were 3-0.

"We will only get better as we get more players back," Shawn Gardner told the Meriden *Record-Journal*. "More importantly, we can't wait for Coach Szymaszek to return. We all love him and miss him."

Rob was visited regularly in the hospital. He had stitches in his head, but a smile on his face. He had always taken a positive approach to coaching football and he vowed to take a positive approach to coming back from brain surgery. *I will return to the guy I once was.* Ron Carbone would come in very somber and Rob would square him away.

"Every time I visit it's the same thing," Carbone said. "I come up here with a heavy heart and come out feeling ashamed for thinking thoughts you don't allow yourself to think."

The rookie assistant coach, Bryan Smith, came up one night. "Do me a favor," Rob told him. "Go home tonight and hug your parents."

Rob thought about Diane. He thought about Jennifer. He couldn't wait to get back home and compensate for all they'd done. Lying in that hospital bed, he was overcome with waves of unquenchable love. He wanted to be the best husband and the best father. He didn't want to just be the guy he was. He wanted to be better. He envisioned a bright horizon, a beautiful sunset playing off the ridges. He had no inkling dark clouds were hovering.

* * *

Rob went home from the hospital on Thursday, September 27, six days after the operation. By Sunday, two days after the win over Rockville, he was itching to see the team, so Diane drove him over to practice. It was a cold, gray, wind-swept day, but the Spartans were in good spirits. They were undefeated, their coach had pulled through brain surgery and they had eaten well a few nights earlier at a pasta dinner hosted by Dan Hatch. Rob chuckled looking at the pictures. His old co-captain and coaching partner looked pretty good in an apron.

And Rob was feeling pretty good, though he noticed his calves were unusually tight as he walked back up the hill from the practice field to the car. He also had what he assumed to be gas pains from the mushrooms and onions Diane had cooked up with their steaks the night before. The chest pains were not severe, at least not at first, but when Rob got back home, they worsened. It hurt to breathe. Diane suggested they go to the hospital. Rob said no.

Then, out of the blue, came a call from David Bona, a former priest and family friend who had moved out to California. Years back, when David was Father David at a church in neighboring Middletown, Rob and Diane had stopped in for a Saturday night mass. It wasn't their regular church; they were just ducking in on their way home from the beach, just getting the weekend obligation out of the way. But that night Father David based his homily on the New York Mets' rallying cry of "Ya Gotta Believe," and that sure hooked Rob. It became their regular church and Father David became a regular guest at Millie's house. Father David loved food and wine. He taught Rob everything about wine, and Millie liked having him at her table because Father David loved to eat. He was built for Millie's oversized plates.

Rob and Diane hadn't heard from David in about four months. Then came the phone call.

David said he'd heard Millie's voice.

Millie had been dead for more than four years. But the voice was unmistakable. It was Millie.

"David, call Rob because he's not going to listen to Diane."

His call came at the absolute right time. When Rob told him how bad he was feeling and explained his symptoms, David said, "this could be more than gas pains, Rob. That's why you're paying these doctors. Call them."

David probably saved Rob's life. Rob called Yale-New Haven. Dr. Piepmeier wasn't on, but Dr. Dennis Spencer, head of the neurology department, was.

"Get down here right away."

The tone in his voice was unmistakable.

"Diane, let's go."

By then Rob was having great difficulty breathing. On a level of 1 to 10, he said, the pain was around an 8-plus. It was an excruciating 20-mile ride to Yale-New Haven. Every bump in the road made the pain zoom from 8 to 9 1/2. Rob couldn't draw a breath. He feared he was having a heart attack. Diane feared she was losing her husband. This, they said, was the scariest episode of the entire ordeal.

Neurological and vascular teams were ready and waiting at Yale-New Haven. A nurse gave Rob a handful of aspirin. They put in an IV, but as he was being wheeled in the line snagged on something and ripped out of his arm.

Blood splattered. Rob lost his composure. He was hurting; he was upset. More pain, more tests: What more?

"COULD YOU PLEASE BE MORE CAREFUL!"

"We're sorry, Mr. Szymaszek."

An MRI was taken.

"Take a deep breath."

Rob was fighting for the smallest breath. "You-got-ta-be-kidding-me." He could barely talk.

Using a Doppler ultrasound, it didn't take long to diagnose the blood clots. The doctors put a gel on Rob's legs, and looking down at the monitor he could see the clots. It wasn't just one. Two had piggybacked and lodged in his left lung. And it occurred to him: *To get to the lung, those clots had to have gone through my heart. I could have died of a heart attack.*

"I do believe that was the closest I came to kissing this old place goodbye," Rob said later. "I was certainly in the gravest danger."

The doctors had to walk a fine line. They had to thin the blood because of the clots, but if they thinned it too much they risked undoing healing in the brain from the surgery. The recommendation was to insert filters in the groin area to siphon off any future clots.

"It's just a minor surgical procedure," Rob was told.

At the time, he didn't care how minor it was.

"I really don't have the energy or the patience or the desire to do any kind of surgical procedure."

They accepted that. The other option was blood-thinning medication and blood tests every two weeks. Rob took that option and was put on Coumadin. He was also put back in ICU. The instructions were strict: Complete immobility. The doctors were extremely cautious. They didn't want to send Rob home only to have him clot all over again.

Consequently, Rob spent 11 days in the hospital for the clots—five more than he did for brain surgery—and it was a bitch. Complete immobility meant being completely bedridden, peeing into a plastic urinal, not being able to take a crap on his own.

The first time Rob had to attend to the latter business—a story he told me amid gales of laughter, but only because three years had passed—he rang the call bell. A nurse came in.

"Hey, I gotta go," Rob announced.

"We'll be right back with the bedpan."

"No, no, no, I'm not doing the bedpan."

93

"Doctor's orders."

"I can make it to the toilet," Rob said through gritted teeth. "Believe me."

"Doctor's orders. You cannot get out of bed."

"I'm not doing the bedpan."

"Mr. Szymaszek, you've got to do the bedpan."

Well, the bedpan was brought in and Rob did a week's worth of business in that pot. We're talking a sandcastle. The pain medication had him pretty backed up. The castle added a few parapets and Rob was straining, straining with every muscle to stay above it.

"I'm not gonna touch it! I'm not gonna touch it!"

He arched, a bridge over rising water.

"And you won't take me to the bathroom?"

Rob had that call button on steady ring.

"I'm gonna throw a freaking clot!"

He all but levitated.

"I'M NOT SITTING DOWN! I'M NOT SITTING DOWN!"

And that's when he lost it, all around. Being in that bed, immobile, with that bedpan under him was flat-out the most humbling experience in his life, the most humiliating, the most degrading. He felt utterly powerless.

This was the start of Rob's "bad patient" phase. He'd gotten fed up. The bedpan came on top of the IV getting ripped out, which came on top of the clots, which came on top of the surgery, which came on top of the biopsy, which came on top of the MRIs and the spinal taps, which came on top of the grand mal seizure, which came on top of the handcuffs, which came on top of the accident.

One big shit castle: What the hell else was going to happen? Rob felt bad. He'd snapped at the Yale-New Haven staffers when that IV ripped out. Diane, however, would bear the brunt of his frustrations once he returned home.

Diane: Rob's high school sweetheart.

They met at Maloney in the fall of 1967. He was a senior, she a junior. It was the middle of football season and one night some of the guys were at Rob's house, doing homework and talking about an upcoming Four Tops concert at Central Connecticut State. "Who you gonna take?" Rob wasn't dating anyone. Football season was football season; he didn't date during football season. He literally led the Spartan existence.

Then Greg Simmons, the quarterback, piped up. "Hey, do you know Diane Nalewajek?"

"Yeah, I know Diane," Rob said. "She's cute."

In his mind, Rob carried a vivid snapshot of Diane. She was walking up the bleachers in the gymnasium with a boy she was dating at the time. A face framed by short blonde hair: She was so stunning. "There goes one of the true lookers at Maloney High School," he said to himself, but to himself only. He didn't actually know Diane. He had never spoken to her—or of her, until then.

Too late: Greg Simmons scanned through the phone book, picked up the phone, dialed and thrust it into Rob's hands.

"Oh, Christ—Diane? . . . Hi . . . This is Rob Szymaszek. Do you know who I am? . . . That's good . . . Would you . . . um . . . would you like to see the Four Tops this weekend?"

Diane had to ask her dad. She'd let Rob know the next day. They arranged to meet in the school foyer. Talk about your awkward meeting between awkward teenagers.

"Hi, Diane? I'm Rob."

"Hi Rob. I'm Diane."

The ice had been chipped. And here's the good part: The Four Tops didn't show. The concert got rescheduled, so they had an instant second date.

Diane's dad was the caretaker at one of the city's Catholic cemeteries. He was a strict, old-fashioned Polish dad and he enforced a strict, old-fashioned curfew. Yet for "Rob Shamashek," as he pronounced the name, old-country style, he let it bend.

Rob bent, too. Al Nalewajek freely spoke his mind, and his range of topics included Maloney football. Now, for all three years that Rob played high school football, his dad never criticized Coach McGee. On his second or third date with Diane, her dad started knocking the guy Rob loved as much as his own father. Rob bit his tongue. Hell, he wanted to date Al's daughter.

Within five years he'd want to marry her. On August 5, 1972 he did.

Over the next 29 years their marriage would grow through good times and bad. They started in that rented third-floor newlywed love nest in the North End, saved money and bought that cape on Reynolds Drive, in the East Side neighborhood Rob had grown up in. They went further east, out toward the ridges, in the late 1980s when the colonial with the in-law apartment for Millie and Bob was built on a hill at the end of a cul-de-sac. From their back porch, when the leaves were off the trees, they could see the Maloney practice field through binoculars. From their front stoop they could see the looming eastern ridges shimmer in the sun.

They worked together in the school they once attended, passed daily through the foyer where they'd said their first awkward hellos. Jennifer entered the picture on November 23, 1979, arriving the day after Maloney beat Platt 20-6 in the Stoddard Bowl. Rob smoked two cigars that year.

They weathered miscarriages; they weathered Diane losing her job due to budget cuts. They celebrated Diane relocating to one of the city's elementary schools and celebrated again when she got her high school job back a few years later.

Through all those seasons of football Diane supported Rob, even as her enthusiasm for the game began to wane and she developed independent interests. Primitive art and Native American pottery took a place on the shelf next to football memorabilia. The bond was strong. It had to be, because nothing tested it like that terrible string of events in the fall of 2001.

Simply put, Rob was a dreadful patient. His patience had run out. After surgery, he had dedicated himself to recovering and getting back to normal one small step at a time. Instead, he was suffering setbacks. The frustration exacted a psychological toll that was worsened by the underlying loss of physical well-being. For a coach and a former athlete, someone who prided himself on strength and vigor, this was particularly acute.

"You think you've got your body in control," Diane said. "This happens and you realize you're not in control of anything. He couldn't accept the fact that he's not in control. I don't think he ever will."

There was also the uncertainty. Diane noticed that in the hospital Rob was OK. It was comforting, after all, to have doctors and nurses around. That sense of security evaporated when Rob returned home on October 10. He'd just had the scare of his life with the blood clots. He was on blood thinners and he felt fragile.

Diane was nurturing, but Rob couldn't always see it. He remembered the way Millie and his sister Sharon doted on him when he was sick as a boy. Diane wasn't the same way. She didn't seem to be caring enough and it bothered Rob. He'd get annoyed at the smallest expression on her face, which was usually prompted by the way he was acting. He should have understood just how frayed her nerves were. That was the kicker: he knew Diane was on the verge of sainthood after everything she'd been through. He knew how much he owed her. *After the operation didn't I lie in that hospital bed and vow to be the best husband? Diane: My high school sweetheart. Damn it.*

Rob was frustrated twice over and that just made him feel worse. He wanted to be this great husband and he wasn't even being as good as the guy he was before. He knew he was hurting her.

"I'm an intuitive guy. I can read people. I don't have the sort of intelligence that scores highly on verbal and mathematical tests, but I do have sensitivity and compassion. I read a book about emotional intelligences and my emotional IQ was off the scale. Yet there was my wife, coming to tears so easily," he admitted.

Tension reached a pitch the day Rob suffered back spasms. He and Diane had a weekend getaway planned to Vermont, but Rob's back was acting up. Nothing major, just a little stiff, so he decided to get a therapeutic massage before they left. During the massage, however, it locked up even more. He couldn't drive. The owner of the business had to bring him home. The trip to Vermont was off.

That night, back spasms kicked in. Rob couldn't get comfortable; he was irritable. He got in bed and suddenly he couldn't move.

"I've got to get you to the hospital," Diane said.

"I'm not going to the hospital again."

She picked up the phone.

"What are your doing?"

"I'm dialing 911."

Rob hung up the phone.

"I'm not going to the hospital!"

The call was traced back. The phone rang and Diane picked it up crying and pleading. "My husband has got to go to the hospital."

An ambulance crew showed up. One of the guys was a former player.

"Coach, what are you doing?" he asked with a coy smile.

Visions of wild sex acts were undoubtedly dancing in a few heads, but it was no joke. Rob was taken out of the house on a flatboard. When he returned home, a hospital bed came with him.

He was at his worst during the back recovery. *What the hell else can happen to me?* He'd asked that question after the blood clots, and now here was the answer. For a while he needed a walker to get around the house. *What the hell else?* Rob loathed self-pity. Now here he was, guilty of it.

The road to recovery was running in the wrong direction. There were no gains. It was all loss: loss of control, loss of power. Rob's pride had been dealt a big blow, and he continued to feel he wasn't getting enough love and support from Diane. That's usually where the arguments started. They'd bicker over petty matters; they'd have big blowouts. Early in their marriage they had arguments from time to time, but took pride in being able to work anything out on their own. They could be thick-headed— Rob more so than Di—but never to the point where they went a day without talking.

"Rob, obviously I care and want to take care of you," Diane would say, "but it's hard to look at you lovingly and say, 'You poor thing' when you're being so difficult and so difficult so often."

With Rob so intolerable at home, Diane found refuge at school. It was her saving grace. She loves teaching and she loves her students. School enabled her to get away and forget the nightmare for a while.

Do you blame her? Rob didn't. He was being horrible and knew Diane had just about had it. "That bothered me. I know when I'm right and I know when I'm wrong, and when I'm wrong I'll admit I'm wrong. At that juncture I was asking myself, 'Why are you being ugly with the one you love?' "

Rob was down and he couldn't get out of it. Maybe it was depression. The American Cancer Society estimates about 25 percent of cancer patients suffer from it, sometimes even when they end treatments.

Twenty-five percent: Was Rob in that group? Someone suggested he get on anti-depressants.

Do I?

"No," he resolved. "I can do it myself."

In football, Rob went into every game believing his Spartans could win. Why couldn't he win now?

He could. He just had to get back to normal. He just had to return to the life he'd always known.

CHAPTER 8

Returns

GETTING BACK TO normal meant getting back to work and getting back to football. Getting back to normal meant getting the mind off illness. There had been too much time to dwell. Familiar routines and familiar faces would provide the best cure.

So back Rob went to the Maloney guidance department in early November, into an office stacked with paperwork and wallpapered with motivational posters. One featured an enlarged photo of a purple crocus pushing through ice and snow. It read: "Go over, go under, go around or go through, but never give up."

Rob worked half days at first. He helped students plan course schedules and file college applications. He wrote dropout reports, filled out crisis intervention forms. It was good to be busy. There's little down time on the job. The Maloney counselors had about 230 kids apiece, each student searching for a college or career path.

Rob's workday steadily grew longer. He built up his stamina just as he would a football team's level of conditioning. When he first returned to school he came in at 10:45 a.m. The next week it was 9:45. It was an hour earlier the week after that. Rob appreciated Principal Gladys Labas allowing him the latitude. Gladys brought in a retired guidance counselor to work part time with Rob until he got back to cruising altitude. The department secretaries, Brenda Chapman and Sharon Bellenger, also looked out for Rob, solicitous of his sleep habits, his work habits. They were very mothering. Millie was gone, but Rob had Brenda and Sharon.

Returning to football was another matter. Rob's medical setbacks during the first half of October had mirrored those befalling the team. After a 3-0 September, injuries caught up with the Spartans. The team became so decimated Steve Hoag said it was like starting from scratch. Players were moved to new positions. Some freshmen and sophomores were elevated to varsity. Rob never liked bringing up kids that young, but Mike Falis and the coaching staff had no choice.

Worse, the Spartans had a blowup in the middle of their October 5 game against Bristol Eastern. At halftime, quarterback Eric Riddle got in an argument with Mike. Eric tore off his helmet, shoulder pads and jersey, threw them down and stormed out of the locker room—all in front of his stunned teammates. Eric watched the second half from the bleachers as Maloney suffered its first defeat of the season, 28-6.

At the time, Rob was in the hospital with the blood clots, but he knew what was going on at Ceppa Field virtually the minute it happened. Pete Sini had called with halftime and postgame updates. The news about Eric disturbed Rob. He insisted his players be impeccably behaved both on and off the field. This was another aspect of Spartan Pride. "You're football players," he'd tell them at the first team meeting each season. "You'll be under close scrutiny. I believe football players hold a certain responsibility to be leaders in school. I pass out a list of your names to teachers and I encourage them to come to me if any of you misbehave."

It was more than that. Rob wanted his guys to have the

courage to stand up when a student was cutting up in class and tell him to knock it off. He wanted to instill honor and a clear sense of right and wrong. Kids can see through bullshit, Rob knew, so he strove to be honest and consistent with his message. Former players say that message resonated through a team that brought together kids from different racial and economic backgrounds. "In Meriden, a lot of kids weren't getting that at home," said Paul Scoffone, a lineman in the early 90s who went on to play for the University of Rhode Island. "A lot of kids learned it being on the football team."

Rob reproached himself for not being around to help Eric. He could have intervened before things erupted. Eric was a senior, but fairly new to Maloney. He had transferred from Platt a year earlier. He had tremendous athletic talent, but what did this incident say about his psychological makeup? Rob knew Mike Falis was in a tough spot. He was a plant manager, not an educator; a football coach well-versed in the finer points of blocking and tackling, not the finer points of adolescent counseling. Rob got in touch with Eric the day after his blowup and told him to meet with Coach Falis and apologize to his teammates. The players agreed to take Eric back. They voted on it. Eric had to apologize and serve a two-game suspension. Sadly, it was a fleeting resolution. Within a week Eric was arrested for having a stun gun in school.

"Eric made a very big mistake. Zero tolerance is the policy on weapons in school," Rob said, looking back on it. "It was a foolish move on Eric's part, but it also bothered the hell out of me that not being in my regular posts had had such a bad effect on one kid. When you coach, when you counsel, part of the job is turning bad attitudes into good attitudes. I could have done that for Eric."

Mike tried to keep team spirits up. "Coach Smaz is with us," he'd say. All the coaches tried rallying the troops each day in practice. They tried to parlay adversity into motivation: Let's defy it, let's defeat it. Steve Hoag reminded the players of the burden Mike carried. He'd lost his father, a brother, a son. He'd been thrust into a head coaching role he never wanted when his best buddy was suddenly stricken. "You are led by a man who deserves your admiration," Steve said.

Nonetheless, the Spartans had lost their edge, and over the next two weeks they took it on the chin from New Britain and Southington. They were the biggest schools and the best teams in the league, teams that had recent success against Maloney, but not like this. The Spartans lost 50-0 in New Britain and 43-0 to Southington at Ceppa Field. The latter game was over at halftime. Southington coach Jude Kelly, a friend of Rob's, spent the second half with a stopwatch in his hand, making sure his team used up every last second of the play clock before snapping the ball. The referees pretended not to notice when Southington went over.

There was an interesting parallel in that game. Southington was led by its senior quarterback, Doug Fink, who played four days after his father died from colon cancer. Before the game Maloney honored Mr. Fink, a West Pointer who had continued coaching American Legion baseball that summer even as he was dying. Kingsley Fink was a battler. He told his doctor if it came down to chemotherapy or coaching, chemo would have to wait.

A long moment of silence was observed before kickoff. Then Dan Hatch spoke over the public address system: "If we have learned anything over the past month it is that, as Americans, we can come together and mourn the loss of people we did not know, but who in going about their daily lives embodied the spirit of America."

After the game, the Spartans extended condolences to Doug. That pleased Rob. It was what he wanted his program to be all about. West Point had a code of conduct; Maloney had a code of conduct. It applied to how you played; it applied to how you behaved.

Still, coming away from the game, Maloney's third straight loss and second straight shutout, morale sunk even lower. A sense of helplessness was settling in. This was a program unaccustomed to losing by lopsided margins. And the endless parade of injuries grew longer. Chris Rodriguez was taken off the field on a stretcher with an injured ankle against Bristol Eastern. Fullback Alexi Beltran and his replacement, Steve Mandeville, were both hurt against New Britain. Manny Torres broke his arm against Southington. Captain Dan Ferry was still on crutches from his injured knee. Captain Patrick Hatch was in and out of action with his torn-up shoulder. Captain Shawn Gardner was playing with a big cast on his broken hand. Tailback Christian Roman's tight hamstring kept him in street clothes. Eric Riddle had quit the team in the middle of a game. Coach Smaz was in the hospital with blood clots.

"There's a black cloud over this high school," said Bryan Smith. "What the hell else can happen to this team?"

The Spartans were physically and mentally drained. Practices were listless. Enthusiasm had evaporated. "I could use a cattle prod," Steve Hoag quipped.

"I see 30 guys and as few as two coaches sometimes," said Patrick Hatch. "It's a sad sight, knowing what it's been like the last three years."

While Rob was recovering from the blood clots, Mike often stopped by and they'd go over game film. First it was in the hospital, then at Rob's house. Rob would see the mistakes and wonder if the team was trying to do too much.

"Coach, the kids need another talk," Mike said one night. "Their morale is low. They aren't practicing hard when you're not around."

Returning to football had always been part of Rob's game plan. Recovery depended on it. *When am I going to get back to being myself?* He focused on feeling a little better, a little stronger each day. The tumor was out, some cells were left, but that was OK. He was battling back. *So when do I get back to football?* No return date was circled on the calendar, but as the October 26 game with Newington approached, forces converged. Maloney was 3-3 with four games to play. Lose this next one and chances for a winning season would begin to fade. Rob hadn't mentioned anything to his doctors about returning to the sidelines, but Diane was all for it. The more involved he got in football, she reasoned, the better it would be for his health.

After the 11-day hospital stay with the clots, Rob's stamina had not been good. But as the week leading up to the 26th passed he felt stronger, and not just physically. Football is a mental game, both the playing of it and the coaching of it. You've got to get keyed up to go out there. That Friday, Rob knew the time was right. Diane's remark when she came home that afternoon sealed it.

"The kids have been coming up to me in school, Rob. They need you on the field tonight."

* * *

For the first time since September 14, Rob was back at Ceppa Field, under the lights, in the little brick locker room with the low ceiling, decked in the green and white. Newington's veteran coach, Dick Vida, a yearly opponent who ran a good program, was on the other sideline. Rob was happy to see him. And he was happy to see the Spartans. He could feel a swell of confidence among the kids. Coach Smaz was back. It was the booster shot they needed.

Rob needed it, too. His hair was growing back over the incision, but concerns about blood clots remained. Those bastards scared Rob. He was on the blood-thinner Coumadin and his primary care doctor, Jay Kaplan, had the medication well regulated. But the Maloney team doctor, Len Kolstad, saw how animated Rob got on the sidelines once the game began and was concerned.

"It's just so hard to be sedate on the sidelines of a football field," Rob said. "How do you do that? How do you not run up to the kids and give them a hug and jack them up and dish out high-fives? That's the way I always coached."

"Take it easy. Please, take it easy," Kolstad said. "You don't want to dislodge another clot."

Once Rob had that thought in his head, he toned it way down. On the field, the Spartans crafted a comeback for his comeback. Down by two touchdowns early, Maloney rallied with four unanswered scores to win 28-14. The three-game losing streak was over.

Oddly, the win doesn't stand out for Rob. He doesn't remember much; everything was such a swirl that night. He was back, yet still far removed from the weekly coaching routine he'd established over the years. He hadn't put in the requisite time and effort. He was happy to see the team present the game ball to Mike, who had filled the breach so nobly. Rob felt he had merely made a guest appearance. *Do I even deserve to be out here with these kids?*

Some could tell he wasn't the same Coach Smaz. For all the game film he'd watched, for all the conversations he'd had with Mike, Rob had been away from football for over a month with graver matters on his mind. Mike noticed occasional lapses on Rob's part. They'd be watching film and Rob would make a comment that made absolutely no sense. Mike let it slide. Knowing Rob for as long as he had, knowing what his friend had been through, Mike knew Rob just wasn't himself. Others in the Maloney camp believed Coach Smaz was forcing himself back too soon. They were amazed he was even out of bed. They admired him for caring so deeply about the team. But should he be calling plays in the emotional cauldron that is a football game?

Rob's return at least got Maloney out of its funk, if only for that week. On the following Friday night the Spartans were smoked 55-0 by Bristol Central, whose standout running back, Tim Washington, broke the state's career touchdown record at Maloney's expense. Worse, that record had been held by a Spartan, Rahshon Spikes, the star of the late 90s who had gone on to play at North Carolina State and in the pros.

Photo by Bill Lischeid

The fiery side of Coach Smaz

Everything about the Bristol Central game was embarrassing for Rob. He felt his fire returning.

"There are going to be changes made," he said in a post-game interview. "We are going to look like a Maloney football team by season's end."

The Spartans rebounded with a win over Bulkeley on a frosty Friday on November 9. It was Senior Night and Rob pulled out the old "Bill Curry" speech. This was a pep talk he'd gotten from Ron Carbone. It was so good Rob used it only once every three or four years. As the story goes, Bill Curry played at Columbia University for Lou Little, the "Maestro of Morningside" who coached the Lions from 1930 to 1956. Curry was a back-up who never played, even in his senior year. On the eve of his final game, the story went, Curry went to Little's house and knocked on door.

"Coach, this is my last opportunity to play some college football. If you get a chance, I'd like to know if you could put me in tomorrow."

"Bill, it's a big game, a real big game. But if I get the opportunity, I will put you in."

The next day, the game raged back and forth. Bill Curry was on the sidelines, trying at all times to keep within Little's line of sight. Late in the game Columbia trailed by six. Little caught Curry's eyes.

"What the hell? What do I have to lose? This kid has dedicated himself for four years; he hasn't missed a practice. Let me get him in."

So Curry went in at running back. On the first play, he rumbled for eight yards. The next play he dashed for 14. The clock was ticking. Again Curry's number was called, and on the third carry he cut loose for 25 yards. The crowd was going nuts.

Who was this Bill Curry? His name wasn't even in the game program.

There were 12 seconds left; the Lions were down by six. Another running play—no, play action, and there was Curry making an unbelievable leaping catch in the end zone!

Columbia kicked the extra point and won the game. Curry was mobbed by his teammates and by fans. The sportswriters wanted to know who this kid was, this Bill Curry whose name was not even in the program.

"What got into you, Bill? What made you play so well?"

That's when Bill told his story. "My mom died when I was born and my dad was blind. He raised me. He only asked for a couple of things. No. 1, that I get an education. Next spring I will graduate with high honors. The other thing my dad always wanted was to see me play football. Well, my dad passed away this week, and I know he's up in heaven now and I know he can see. This was my last game. This was his one chance to watch me play. That's why I played as hard as I played. I dedicated this game to my father."

Rob wept as he told the Bill Curry story that Senior Night. He always cried when he told it, and so did the Spartans.

"I want you to dedicate this game to someone you love," Rob said. "It could be your mom, your dad, a grandparent, a special friend, but I want you to dedicate it to someone you love."

Before the game, each senior was introduced and went out to midfield with his parents. Each father wore his son's white road jersey. Several frosty hours later, with just 38 seconds remaining in the game, Maloney's kicker, Porry Noonan, booted a 22-yard field goal to snap a 21-21 tie.

"I dedicated my kick to my mother," Porry said.

Before the game, it had been just Porry and his dad out at

midfield. Several years earlier, Porry's mom had died of pancreatic cancer.

It had been an up and down three weeks. An emotional three weeks. Now there was just one game left on the schedule: the Stoddard Bowl, the annual Thanksgiving battle with Platt. It was the biggest game of the year, every year.

And Rob decided it would be his last.

Millie and Bob Szymaszek at Ceppa Field

CHAPTER 9

Farewells

WHY DID ROB leave coaching? Three reasons: His health, his wife and his right-hand man. Mike Falis had already told Rob he wasn't returning. He said he'd read the signs that started with his son's death. Then it was Rob's illness and the halftime incident with Eric Riddle in the locker room.

"I don't think I'm tired of coaching or want to get out," Mike said, "but I wonder if my son is trying to tell me it's time to concentrate on other things."

It had been 18 seasons for Rob and Mike. Eighteen seasons on the practice field, in the team room, on the sidelines, at camps, in shared hotel rooms at clinics. Eighteen seasons of well-crafted game planning and victory celebrations. Eighteen seasons of disagreements and defeats. Mike and Rob would occasionally butt heads over strategy and plays. They'd get particularly heated whenever Rob thought Mike was doing something fundamentally unsound and Mike held his ground.

"What's going on there?" Rob would demand when one of Mike's schemes didn't work in practice against the scout team. "What's going on there, Mike? How come we can't make that double team?"

"So-and-so blocked the wrong guy."

"What do you mean so-and-so blocked the wrong guy?"

"So-and-so has got to block down here and we've got to get a kick-out there."

"Are you sure, Mike? ARE YOU SURE?"

"Yes Rob, I'm sure. I'M SURE!"

Sometimes Rob gave in, sometimes he overruled. He and Mike always ended such nights with a handshake.

"No hard feelings."

"Rob, I never have any. I understand. You're the head guy. You've got to demand things. If I'm not giving them to you, then let me know about it. Don't worry about hurting my feelings."

There were traits Rob looked for in assistant coaches. They had to be dedicated. They had to know the game. They had to be willing to work and make personal sacrifices. They had to be honest and mentally tough enough to think on their own and take initiative. Rob's various assistant coaches through the years had those qualities. Three of them—Dan Hatch, Don Panciera and Tim Gaffney—went on to become principals or assistant principals. Rob was secure in his own abilities as head coach to want the best assistants. Not all coaches are like that. Some feel threatened by quality assistants who might appear to know more than they do. Not Rob. His thinking was, "How do we make the program better?" And of all the assistants he brought aboard to achieve that end, none surpassed Mike Falis. "Without him, Maloney football never would have attained any heights," Rob once told me. "He was as responsible as I was for whatever success we enjoyed."

Now Mike's expertise and camaraderie would be gone. Stepping onto the field without him? Rob couldn't imagine it-not just for sentimental reasons, but practical ones. During their coaching career high school football had become a year-round operation. Keep up or get left behind. The hours were crazy and the strain all out of proportion to the stakes. But high school coaches everywhere had brought it on themselves, and once they went down the path there was no going back. Keep up or get left behind.

Then there was the tumor. What if it came back? What would happen if Rob had to start chemotherapy or undergo another operation and Mike wasn't there to keep the program going as he had been this year? Where would that leave the kids?

"I can't do it without Mike," Rob told Diane.

Diane factored into Rob's decision, as well. Early in her husband's coaching career Diane had been very wrapped up in football. She had been emotionally attached to the games and the players. That waned over the course of 26 seasons. She'd lost her enthusiasm for the game well before Rob was afflicted. It's difficult being a coach's wife. Think of the most beautiful summer day and think of missing it.

"Let's do something, Rob. Let's go the beach."

"Sorry, hon, I've got playbooks to get ready."

Di gradually adapted. If Rob was busy with football, she'd find something to do with her friends or with Jennifer.

Now Rob thought about how much he wanted to make up for the time they'd lost as a couple. He wanted to make up for all the meals she cooked and had to leave in the oven until he came home from practice, for the missed beautiful days, for all the years of football, for how he had behaved after the operation.

His course was clear. Driving home from practice with Mike a week before Thanksgiving, Rob made sure one last time.

"Mike, I have to make this public. I've got to let people know. Are you coming back next year?"

"No, Rob, I'm not."

"Then that makes my decision easy."

Rob went home and told Diane, then went downstairs to the in-law apartment and told his father. Bob Szymaszek had seen virtually all his son's high school and college games. When Rob was first hired as coach, Bob would stop by practice when he could work it around his job. He'd stay for quite a while, perched on a lawn chair up on the hill, under the tree where Coach McGee used to smoke his cigars. The seasons passed. Bob saw all the games Rob coached at Maloney until the stroke hit in March 1990. It happened down in Florida. Millie called that morning.

"Get down here. This is serious."

The stroke left Bob in a wheelchair and he never went to another Maloney football game. "He's a proud man," said Rob. "I guess he didn't want to be seen like that." It was terrible for Bob. He'd seen one of his sisters suffer a stroke and deteriorate. He didn't want to go through that. In his living will he had made it clear: Do Not Resuscitate. For a while after the stroke, he was angry. Rob and his sisters had to explain he hadn't been resuscitated, that he'd never flat-lined.

Bob Szymaszek remained very much aware of his surroundings and what was being said to him. He just couldn't talk back. Nor could he write. The brain can be a mystery. Bob could still sing, but his speech was reduced to three phrases: "Oh God," "Jesus Cah-rist" and, when mad or frustrated, "Fuck it!"

"Fuck it!" he'd say when Rob, Sharon or Jan took him out to dinner and tried to pay.

"Fuck it!"

"OK, Dad, you can pay."

Other than those three phrases, Bob could get out nothing more than "ah-ha," with variations on it that sometimes conveyed what he was trying to say. Other times it just ended in frustration. For the longest time Rob had re-occurring dreams in which his father was talking to him. They were so vivid, so real.

I've never seen anyone cut the lawn as good as you do. Then Rob would wake up. Shit, it was just a dream.

Bob had wanted Rob to step down for quite a while. He saw the stress and strain on his son's face long before the tumor surfaced in his brain. He knew Rob was up late at night, working to the point of exhaustion, getting ready for a game. Rob would go downstairs to the in-law apartment to visit and Bob would point upstairs, put his hands together and lay his head on them. Get to bed, son—and this from a guy who sometimes hadn't had a visitor all day. That's Dad, Rob thought. Everyone's welfare always came before his own.

Bob loved the great Maloney victories. He ached with his son in defeat. Rob tried to not wear the losses on his face. He tried to camouflage the disappointments. But he could no more hide it from Bob than he could run away from home that Good Friday so long ago when Bob fetched him in the police car and set him square with a soda and stern advice.

"Jesus Cah-rist!"

"What, Dad? You want me to get out of this?"

"Ah-*ha*."

"You want me to stop coaching?"

"Ah-*hah*!"

And then he'd grab his son and hug him tight. Over Bob's shoulder Rob could see the Norman Rockwell print he'd found up in Vermont. It's the one of the policeman sitting with a young kid at a drug store soda fountain.

"Dad, it's coming soon, but right now I'm not ready."

"Jesus Cah-rist."

On a November night in 2001, Bob got the news he was waiting for. After practice on November 12, Rob and Mike told the team after practice. It was in the newspaper the next day.

"In my heart and soul it's the decision I had to make," was Rob's quote.

Responses came quickly. Rob got phone calls. He read quotes in the paper from players and other coaches.

"I wanted him to coach me my senior year," said Alexi Beltran.

Alexi was a junior. Each day Rob was in the hospital Alexi would rush over the minute Mike arrived at practice. "Did you talk to him? Did you talk to him?" Alexi was one of those of players it broke Rob's heart to leave behind. Alexi understood what Coach Smaz had gone through; he could understand the decision. "But it's still going to be hard to look at the sidelines next year and not see him there," Alexi told the Meriden *Record-Journal.*

Over in Southington, Jude Kelly said he felt empty. "There will be a tremendous void. Something will be missing from the game."

Across town, Tom Ryan pointed to Rob's career mark of 160-90-13. No Meriden coach had won more games. "Rob Szymaszek is the greatest football coach in the history of the city. He is one of the premier coaches in the state."

Tom mentioned how difficult it is to win in towns with more than one high school. Talent is divided; state championships are a long shot. Since Connecticut began staging football playoffs in 1976, towns with one public high school have won 120 of 162 class championships. Catholic schools have claimed 23, magnet schools 3. Towns with more than one public high school have won 16.

Maloney had gone to one state final under Rob. Platt had gone to two under Tom. They'd both lost, but their programs were sound. By and large, they had successfully fought the odds. Now they faced one last go-round.

Thanksgiving Day football is tradition in Connecticut. Some rivalries date back over 100 years. Platt and Maloney's began the minute Meriden went from one high school to two in 1958. Their game is called the Stoddard Bowl. It is Army-Navy, it is Yale-Harvard and it is more. It is more intimate and intense because it transpires within the confines of one town. Rivals are in close proximity on a daily basis. It often passes beyond healthy rivalry. One Maloney assistant from out of town thought Ansonia-Derby the biggest rivalry in Connecticut only to discover nothing surpassed the Stoddard Bowl for intensity and nastiness.

The rivalry had an effect on the relationship between Rob and Tom. Rob had helped Tom get the job at Platt in 1980. Though a Massachusetts native, Tom had put in time at Southern Connecticut just like Rob. There were bitter moments as the

Photo by Bob Lupinek courtesy of the Meriden Record-Journal

Rob celebrates a Stoddard Bowl win.

seasons rolled by, but Rob had no regrets helping Tom out. They had their differences and they disagreed, but there were sides to Tom that Rob liked and admired. "I'd like to think those feelings are mutual. Tom would say he hated playing me on Thanksgiving because he considered me the best coach in Connecticut. I hated playing Tom because Maloney's M.O. was out-working opponents, and when it came to working, I met my match in Tom."

Rob's tumor brought them closer together. *"What a competitor you are."* The Platt Booster Club sent a fruit basket. Tom wanted to honor Rob in a pre-game ceremony at the Stoddard Bowl.

As the game approached, Rob thought of the classic Stoddard Bowls of Thanksgivings past. There was the 1978 epic, when the Spartans drove 82 yards late in the fourth quarter to win 29-24. They converted several times on fourth down and scored on a sprint-out pass play called "78Z-Out." Richie Shammock was the Z in the formation. He went up field, cut outside and caught the winning pass. "78Z-Out!" Richie still shouted whenever he saw Rob. People say it was the greatest Stoddard Bowl ever. It was Diane's all-time favorite game. It was so exciting and nerve-racking she couldn't bear to watch. On the winning play she closed her eyes and listened for the roar of the crowd around her. When it came, she knew Maloney had won.

The 1998 game was a great one, too. Platt and Maloney were both on the playoff bubble. The winner went on; the loser went home. Maloney won 28-6.

Although the postseason was out of the picture for both teams in 2001, there was still much on the line. It was *The Stoddard Bowl*, after all. The game trophy resided in Maloney's trophy case. The Spartans had won three in a row. They also had a winning record to protect. It was the last game for the seniors and, of course, it was the last game for Mike Falis and Coach Smaz. Rob tried to downplay that part of the story. Thanksgiving was all about the kids, the seniors. That's why, as much as he appreciated the gesture, he declined Tom Ryan's proposed pre-game ceremony.

The two weeks leading up to Thanksgiving marked Rob's full return to coaching. No guest appearances, no motivational ploys. He was involved from A-Z. He got his hands back in the playbook. Mike had done what he had to do in light of all the injuries. Now it was time to get back to Maloney's bread-and-butter I formation offense.

Preparing for Thanksgiving is always pressure packed. Players are sky high and a coach has to harness that energy and keep his team from peaking too soon. It's a long layoff in between games. If the kids are hitting too hard, you end practice early. Save it for game day. It's an emotional week, too, and that year it was especially so for Maloney. The loss of his son Ryan had weighed on Mike all year. The finality of Thanksgiving made it acute. He watched the team run its last series of Green Bays and got choked up. Tears came at almost every turn.

"I look at the kids. I look at the locker room. I look at my locker. I look at the locker that was Ryan's locker . . ."

Rob found himself apologizing for deciding to retire.

"Sorry? Get better. Don't apologize," Mike said. "You're afflicted with this goddamn thing. It's not your fault. It just happened."

Emotions peaked the day before of the game. Jen was home for the holiday, and she and Diane wept openly at the afternoon pep rally. Evening was given over to Alumni Night and a tradition Maloney called the "Burning of the Shoe." For Alumni Night, former players went into the team room and talked to the current players about the Maloney football tradition, a tradition they were now permanently a part of. This time, Rob spoke and so did Mike. Class of '68, Class of '66. Then the rest of the alumni got up. They talked about beating Platt. They talked about what Coach Smaz and Coach Falis had meant to them. And they talked about how much they wished they were the ones who would be playing in their last game. "This is Coach's last hurrah. You get to carry Smaz off the field. You are the lucky ones."

The Spartans went out into the night and down to the practice field for the Burning of the Shoe. Rob had adopted the tradition 15 years earlier from an assistant, Ron Luneau, who'd done it at Derby High School and at Central Connecticut State. It was called the Burning of the Shoe, but each senior could burn any article of clothing he wanted. As he did, he told his teammates what Maloney football had meant to him. The ashes were symbolic. They embodied past efforts, sweat that would be forever mixed with the soil of the field. That's how Bill Lischeid's son, Kurt, had put it in an award-winning essay.

Burning of the Shoe was an altar to confidences. It marked the passing of time. The Spartans paid tribute to the program, to what it meant and would continue to mean. It was a legacy passed to the next wave of players, who listened as the seniors spoke. What came out often reduced coaches and players to tears. That was never truer than the night of November 21, 2001. The fire was lit. The Spartans circled around. One player spoke about his dead father and how his mom had once gone to jail. After she got out, she and the boy moved to Meriden. He was an only child. He walked to school alone every day. That changed when he arrived at Maloney and joined the football team.

"I didn't have any friends when I came here and now I have 33 friends," he said. "I never had a brother and now I have 33."

Each senior took his turn. It was their passage. Perhaps for the first time they realized the inevitability of growing old. "Time does not stand still," Bill Lischeid's son, Kurt, observed in his essay, "even though sometimes we wish it would." Now it was a passage for Mike and Rob. Football had been a cornerstone of their identity. Mike was saying goodbye to even more. He burned his ratty old shorts—the ones with the holes, the ones he wore every day in practice, rain or shine, warm or cold. Weeping turned to sobs when he put his late son's Maloney football jacket on the fire. Mike had worn it all year.

"I never would have made it through this last year without you guys," Mike said, his voice cracking. "I love you guys."

It was Rob's turn. He stepped to the fire and threw in the shirt from Land's End. "It was the shirt I was wearing the day my personal nightmare began."

"My purpose in life was to be a high school football coach. I never had any aspirations to be anything else." Rob at the 2001 Burning of the Shoe.

One of the books Rob had read in the hospital was *What It Takes To Be No. 1*. It was written by the son of Vince Lombardi. "The book says that we all need a purpose in life. Well, I found my purpose in life. My purpose in life was to be a high school football coach. I never had any aspirations to be anything else."

Rob looked into the fire. As much as he believed he would persevere in his battle with a brain tumor, he spoke of the final destination that awaits all men. "If you could be invisible at your funeral, what would you hear people saying? Will they say that you were a man of character, that you were a man of integrity? Or do you want them saying, 'He was a character; he had no integrity?'"

The day would come. What would they say?

Rob looked up. Faces looked back, faces glimmering with tears and fire. Beyond them lay darkness, barely a whisper from the highways even through the naked trees.

Rob looked around. "I love each and every one of you."

And then he retreated back into the circle.

* * *

Maloney and Platt were both 5-4 heading into Thanksgiving 2001, but the Spartans were the underdog. Platt had a good team and all the injuries the Spartans had suffered had kept them from reaching their potential. Senior captain Dan Ferry, who had missed every game since hurting his knee at the preseason jamboree, returned to the lineup. So did junior tailback Christian Roman, who hadn't played since the season opener thanks to his hamstring injury.

Rob felt for Christian. He should have been the next in Maloney's line of great tailbacks. His older brother Edwin had been a good one. He'd set a few school records, but when he was through playing Edwin said, "My brother Christian will break all my records." Instead, injury undermined Christian's promise, both that year and in the senior season that would follow. Christian wanted to play in Rob's last game and Rob wanted him to play, too. That mutual desire led to a critical mistake. A few days before the game, Rob took Christian to see Dr. Bob Mastriani, a highly regarded sports therapist in the area. Christian had some cartilage buildup in his hamstring. Bob manipulated the leg, there was a snap, and Christian burst out, "Oh my God, coach, I feel like my old self."

They stopped for dinner on the way home. It was Maloney tradition for coaches to regularly take kids out for meals. It was a reward and also part of the molding process: Here's how you comport yourself in a restaurant. That day, Christian and Rob

Rob, Diane and Jennifer after the 2001 Stoddard Bowl

had something to celebrate. Rob got home and told Diane, "We've got a healthy Christian Roman."

Rob wasn't necessarily being overly optimistic. In practice Christian Roman was running like a healthy Christian Roman. But a player who has missed a lot of time doesn't get ready for a game in a matter of days. Like most schools, Maloney had a rule that held if a player didn't practice during the five days before a game, he didn't play. There are precious few who can miss practice and not stink up the place on game day. You play the way you practice, coaches say, and without practice you are not ready for peak performance. Rob knew that, and yet in his 274th game as a head coach, he broke his own rule. "I lost sight of it. I loved Christian. He'd had such a frustrating year. I wanted to believe Christian was healthy. He was, but he wasn't himself."

When Rob goes back and watches the film of the 2001 Stoddard Bowl, he gets angry at himself for asking too much of Christian. "I should have featured Alexi Beltran and given fewer snaps to Christian. I did a horrible, horrible injustice to those kids on that day." This underscored another truth: Rob wasn't at peak form either. How much time had he missed? "I should have done what we did in the Berlin game. I should have turned more over to my assistants. Instead, I took complete control. Hey, it was my last game to coach. I wanted to hang on to it. This was my game plan; these were my plays. I just didn't do the job."

The Spartans were OK for the first half. Porry Noonan put them up 3-0 with a field goal late in the first quarter. That lead held until Rob called for a fake punt at midfield and it failed— more self-reproach Rob would take away from his final game. The botched fake led to a major shift in field position, and Platt eventually pushed across a touchdown in the final minute of the half. In the second half it was all Platt. The Panthers scored four touchdowns. The Spartans could answer only one. Rob watched the clock tick away on a 35-11 defeat.

His career was over and it was a horrible feeling. There would be no next week, no next season, no chance to regroup and get 'em next year. The Stoddard Bowl trophy was hoisted on the other sideline, bound for Platt's trophy case for the first time since 1997. That cast of Panthers hadn't tasted Thanksgiving victory until that day.

Platt was gracious. During the game Rob had felt a good vibe coming from the other side of the field. Where there was often animosity, there was warmth. When Rob's name was announced during pre-game introductions, an ovation resounded. After the game, Tom Ryan told the media, "We won the game, but right now I don't feel like a winner."

The Spartans were distraught. Hadn't the alumni talked about how they'd kill to play in Coach's last game and be the ones to get the win and lift him up on their shoulders and carry him off the field into that Hollywood sunset? Shouldn't that have been the script? The kids felt like failures.

Rob gathered them at midfield. He always put great importance on the post-game Thanksgiving speech. It was the last communiqué as a team. These were the words that would linger through winter until next year's spring practice. Rob strove to be positive. Even in defeat, it was not time to yell or scold. It was a time to congratulate the boys for laying it on the line and thank them for the season and tell them you were proud. The speech was always about more than the game, this one more so than any.

Dan Hatch, Rob's co-captain in 1967, fellow coach in 1976 and father of a player on his last team, said times of trauma made you do one of two things: put your head down and feel sorry for yourself or battle. Athletics, Dan said, condition us to battle. That is what Maloney football 2001 was all about. The final record was 5-5, but what did those numbers measure? Perhaps everything. In life you win and lose, you succeed and fail. Many times you just break even, and when the odds are long, sometimes there is victory in just breaking even. The Spartans had faced such odds.

"There is a great lesson to be learned today," Rob told his players that Thanksgiving. "This game will serve you well in life. Adversity can be a great lesson. You faced it this year and never quit. You kept fighting right to the end and I'm proud of that."

More than 4,500 fans had watched that 2001 Stoddard Bowl. Many were slow to leave Ceppa Field. It was a beautiful day, quite warm for late November. Former players came out on the field and shook hands. Rob was interviewed by a local TV crew. He started fine, but ended up in tears. Diane and Jennifer found their way through the throng. Rob hugged them tightly. "I'm not crying because we lost," he said. "I'm crying because this is my last game."

Rob leaves Ceppa Field for the last time as head coach.

Diane and Jennifer had wept for much of the game. They cried because they knew how much football was a part of Rob. They cried, too, because they realized how much football was a part of them.

They were slow to leave. It was a beautiful day, quite warm. Rob looked toward the western end zone. The scoreboard read Home 35, Visitor 11. It read Quarter 4, Down 1, 10 To Go. It read Time 0:00.

Rob Szymaszek's coaching career was over. Twenty-six years. His final record read 160-91-13. But what do numbers say? Mike and Rob walked off the field to catch the team bus. One last ride. Rob lifted the spectator rope. Mike ducked under and Rob followed.

CHAPTER 10

Wait & See

WHEN THE OPERATION was over, Rob figured that was it. The tumor was out. It was done with. It was behind him. He'd heard words like "radiation" and "chemotherapy," but never considered his brain tumor a life-long affliction. He never thought he'd be subject to MRIs and anti-seizure medication and watching what he ate and drank. He never thought chemo would apply to him.

He was wrong.

Coming out of the operation, the future was uncertain. Diane craved answers. Where are we going with this? Is it over? Will it come back?

"I need some kind of reassurance one way or the other."

Dr. Piepmeier couldn't provide that. Doctors seldom can. Many cancer patients want to know about percentages. How many people survive this? How many don't make it? What are my chances? How long do I have? Numbers, even when grim, can at least provide a concrete hold when the world turns upside down. Numbers, though, define only so much. There is no infallible measure that applies to each individual case.

"We're honest," Piepmeier said. "What we don't know, we say we don't know. I hate to speculate. If patients push, I give them my best judgment. There's so much unknown about this. When patients really push you to quote numbers, those numbers are irrelevant. There are patients whose progress is so much better than what the numbers say. There are patients on the other side, too. Right now, we don't know why."

Rob wasn't going to get hung up on numbers. He was going to get better. He would control what he could control. In September he'd dealt with the task at hand: Taking the tumor out. Dr. Piepmeier had gotten most of it. OK, about two-thirds of the right temporal lobe went with it. OK, there were those stray cancer cells Piepmeier had deemed too risky to touch. OK, what's next?

"Wait and see," said Piepmeier. Rather than jump into chemotherapy or radiation, Rob would start with an MRI every three months. His brain would be scanned from every conceivable angle to chart the problem spots.

If nothing changed, maybe the MRIs would be pushed to every six months, maybe to once a year. OK, that was good news. Every day, every month and every year of clean scans would buy time, and time was an ally. Time, Piepmeier emphasized, meant medical advances. Chemotherapy and radiation, should they be needed down the line, would likely be better than they were now.

So Rob bought into "wait and see." It was a sound game plan. It had direction; it made sense. It also enabled life to more or less get back to normal. OK, let's get on with living. Life is still good.

Of course, there was no getting around the side effects of having so much of the temporal lobe removed. There was a loss in peripheral vision from approximately the nine o'clock angle to high noon. Memory, being a temporal lobe function, was affected. While brain tumor patients don't necessarily lose memory, they can struggle to retain new information. Rob was fortunate. His tumor had resided in his right, or non-dominant, temporal lobe. Still, he had problems with short-term memory. He'd forget a detail or repeat something he'd already said. There was also some slight residual lung damage from the clots, and for a while he'd shy away from anything he thought was coming toward his head.

None of that was unusual or remotely debilitating. By and large, the outlook was good as 2002 arrived. The post-operation hurdles had been cleared; Rob was stable. With healing, he became a better patient, especially when he went off the blood thinners in May. After that, he didn't fear clots. He felt less fragile. The tumor cells lay dormant; the MRIs were clean. They were taken at MidState Medical Center in Meriden, where Nate Cumberlidge, one of Rob's former players, was head of the radiology department. Although he wasn't supposed to say anything—the scans were ultimately reviewed by the doctors at Yale-New Haven—Nate would look them over and whisper a word on the side, "Coach, looks good."

Rob would take the brain scans back to his guidance office at Maloney, close the door and put the transparencies up against the window. He was looking at the white spots. The white spots were the tumor cells. Had they changed? Had they grown? He studied, studied, pulled the scans closer, held them at arm's length against the light. Beyond the window lay a sliver of the practice field. Rob could see no discernible change in the white spots.

Work hours were back to normal, and now that Rob was through with coaching, recognition followed for his career achievements. In 2002 he was inducted into the Southern Connecticut State University Hall of Fame and the Connecticut High School Coaches Association Hall of Fame. It happened quickly, especially in regard to the latter. There was none of the usual pre-requisite waiting time between retirement and induction. While no one said it, urgency could be read between the lines. Perhaps some people wanted to honor Rob before it was too late. But Rob wasn't going anywhere. He was feeling good, both physically and mentally, and the Hall of Fame inductions were more good medicine. They validated what he'd done with his life.

In December of 2001 came word that Rob was receiving the Dee Rowe Inspirational Award given by the Nutmeg Games, the state Olympics of Connecticut. The banquet, however, was scheduled for the week of February school vacation and it conflicted with a trip Diane and Rob had already booked to St. Martin. Rob figured he'd have to turn down the award. Bill Mudano, the head of the Nutmeg Games, suggested videotaping an acceptance speech. Rob's gut said no, he'd better go. He ran it by Diane. She wasn't too happy. They both needed a vacation. But Rob had this vision of everyone in the banquet crowd, most especially Dee Rowe, the former University of Connecticut basketball coach for whom the award was named, wondering why this Rob Szymaszek from Maloney High School didn't have the decency to show up and accept it in person.

It came down to cancelling the award or cancelling the trip.

"We're not giving the award to anyone else," Bill Mudano told Rob.

So Rob bagged the trip. At the awards banquet, Kenny Mayne of ESPN, the evening's emcee, filled everyone in.

"This guy cancelled a trip to St. Martin to be with us tonight. I want everyone to know he's still going to go to St. Martin."

Mayne looked over at Rob.

"The stipend I get tonight, Coach, I'm sending to you for your vacation."

It was $2,600, plenty for flight, lodging and cocktails at sunset. Rob, however, had a hard time accepting it. He gave Mayne a call at ESPN a few days later.

"I'm a good giver, Kenny, but a bad receiver. I'm going to donate the money to brain cancer research."

"Hell," Mayne said, "I could have done that."

In a way, Mayne did donate the money to the battle against brain cancer. The trip Diane and Rob eventually took to St. Martin worked wonders. They were on vacation in a magical place in their memory. The trip was just like all the others. Normal life had returned. *It's all behind us. I'm back. Who said I'd never be able to do this again?* Diane and Rob were getting sun. They were swimming, drinking fine wine, dining at waterside restaurants and watching sunsets. In the Caribbean warmth, the old flame of romance rekindled. Life *was* still good.

And yet it was different. There was no way around that. Back home, Rob was attending meetings of Yale-New Haven's brain tumor support group. People sat around a long table made up of smaller tables that had been pushed together and they told separate accounts of what amounted to the same story. They talked about their condition, what treatments they'd been through, the medications they were on, the side effects.

At his first meeting, Rob, as the newcomer, went first.

"I'm Rob Szymaszek and I had an oligodendroglioma, Grade 2. I was operated on. So far, doing well."

He sat down. The next person went.

"Oligodendroglioma, Grade 2, operation, round of radiation, round of chemo."

Rob took that in. The next person went.

"Oligodendroglioma, Grade 2, operation, second round of chemo, radiation."

Same tumor as me. Same exact tumor.

From across the table: "Oligodendroglioma, Grade 2, now Grade 3, on my third operation, radiation, chemo."

Rob had gone into that meeting feeling a little guilty because he was doing so well, so much better than many of his fellow patients. He'd had the operation. It was over. He was on his way back. Now he knew he wasn't out of the woods. The National Cancer Institute reported on its web site that brain tumors often recur, sometimes many years after the first. From that table came first-hand proof: multiple operations, rounds of chemotherapy, rounds of radiation, a Grade 2 turned to a Grade 3. *I could be any one of these people. This could be a lifelong affliction.*

One of the patients who caught Rob's eye at that first support group meeting was a woman from Hamden named Andrea Mann. She had an oligodendroglioma virtually identical to Rob's. Same place: right temporal lobe. Rob paid closest attention to her. On a subsequent trip to Yale-New Haven for blood work and an MRI consultation, he ran into Andrea. She was also there for blood work and a consult.

"You two should have lunch together," suggested Betsey D'Andrea, the RN who was the clinical coordinator of Yale-New Haven's neuro-oncology department and ran the support group meetings.

Good advice. From that point on, Rob and Andrea scheduled their appointments in New Haven for the same day and same hour, then grabbed something to eat. The alliance was therapeutic. Their cases were so similar: same tumor, same family medical background, same operation. They were a support group of two. A brother-sister relationship developed. Rob and Andrea confided in a way they couldn't confide in their spouses, who for all their love and compassion couldn't possibly understand the full ramifications of having a brain tumor. They'd kid around, like the time Andrea was on a steroid to counter the effects of radiation. One side effect of the steroid was a ravenous appetite, and Andrea had put on weight.

"How's that appetite doing, Andrea?"

"Can't ya see?"

"Ah, I would never notice."

They kept each other updated on their progress, their treatments. Then Andrea caught Rob by surprise. He showed up for a support group meeting and there she was, with an incision on her head much like the one he'd had after surgery.

Rob stared at the staples.

"What happened to you?"

"I just had another operation."

"When?"

"Two weeks ago."

"And you're here? You're really something."

Admiration, and yet the same inescapable reality: *Same tumor as me, same exact tumor.*

Rob was a regular at the support group meetings by then. At home, he logged on to a national web site for patients with oligodendrogliomas. After a while, though, he found the daily messages too depressing. Most people talked about conditions that had gotten worse. Some people suddenly stopped logging on. Rob later learned they'd died.

Publicly, Rob maintained his upbeat demeanor. He was the same ever-optimistic guy with the ready smile and cheery voice, a guy who brought a happy turn to your day. Privately, doubts inevitably bubbled up. Rob thought back to his playing days at Southern Connecticut. That fractured cervical vertebrae was a clear dividing line in his career. There was the pre-injury player and the post-injury player. In the same vein, could there not help but be a pre-tumor Rob Szymaszek and a post-tumor Rob Szymaszek? Andrea just had another operation. Was it inevitable he would have another, too? He thought, and then he dug in: *No, I'm coming back. I'm coming back with all the gusto for life I have.*

* * *

That fighting spirit helped Rob recover as quickly as he did. Rob believed it and so did those who knew him. Steve Filippone, Rob's coaching colleague down at Hand High School in Madison, was close friends with an oncologist in California. Every once in a while Rob would have Steve call the guy, just to make sure his doctors were being completely candid with him.

"What kind of tumor does he have?"

"Oligodendroglioma."

"Well, it's not good. No brain cancer ever is. But of all the brain cancers to have that's the best one because it's treatable. How's his attitude?"

"Are you kidding?" Steve said. "On a scale of 1 to 10, an 11."

"That's the secret right there," the oncologist replied. "I wish all my patients were like that."

Not everything was so rosy. Diane and Rob were still having issues. This isn't unusual. Many cancer patients and their spouses experience difficulties under the strain of so serious an illness. There's a contributing factor, and Rob learned its name the day he was at Yale-New Haven for a follow-up test and ran into Theresa, one of his nurses.

"How are things going?"

"Well, my wife and I aren't getting along that well."

"You should get a therapist. There are neurological therapists to deal with people who come off operations like yours. It would be real good for you.

"Rob," Theresa added, "you've got to come out of Survivor Mode."

It was the first time Rob heard the term. He didn't know what it was, and yet he was mired in it. Survivor Mode. When patients put themselves and their condition above and beyond all else, that's Survivor Mode. Nothing matters but getting better. There's no taking into consideration that maybe your spouse is having a bad day. It's complete self-absorption. In someone healthy, it's egomania. In illness, it's Survivor Mode.

Attitude aids healing, but there comes a time to shed Survivor Mode. Rob was slow to do that and it put a strain on his marriage.

Survivor Mode can be insidious. You're a patient trying to get back to 100 percent. Once you believe you're there, that you are the person you were before the illness, you can become extremely defensive toward anybody who suggests otherwise. This happened to Rob. He would come downstairs to breakfast, running late because he hadn't been able to find the right shirt or tie, and he'd see a look in Diane's face he interpreted as, "It took you longer to get ready. It took you longer because of the brain tumor."

Such is the hypersensitivity of Survivor Mode. It can make things tense. There is a high divorce rate in these situations. Sometimes it's a tragic trifecta: Brain cancer patients lose their jobs, lose their spouses and then take their lives.

The Szymaszeks were tested at a time when Diane and Rob had gone a considerable way down individual paths. Rob had football. Diane had her art. Moreover, Diane had embraced Native American culture and spiritual philosophies. Like Rob, she'd been raised Catholic. During the 1980s, when Rob was involved in the Fellowship of Christian Athletes, they were active churchgoers. It was a Sunday routine: go to mass, go to breakfast. They drifted away, and by the time Rob wanted to reaffirm his religion, Diane had grown disenchanted with the Catholic Church. She'd adopted a naturalistic view of faith: God is a part of everything and mankind is a part of that universal energy. Indian prayer sticks popped up around the yard. A three-foot-high "earth mother" doll took up residence on a stereo speaker. When a solstice arrived, Diane and her friends broke out drums. Rob's reaction to all this was mixed. Sometimes he was proud. One of the classes Diane established at Maloney, "Cultural Art & History," won an award. Other times his conservative eyes rolled. Diane, as well as Rob's sister Jan, now found him to be less filtered, less hesitant to speak his mind. "There's an edginess to him at times that I don't think he let out so easily before," Jan said. "I don't know if that's his release because he's had such a hard struggle."

Whether he approved or not, Rob never prevented Diane from exploring any avenue of personal growth. "It's just wrong, and you risk losing your spouse if you do," he said. "Besides, I love Diane too much. I wish she was more aligned to my political and philosophical way of thinking, but she's not. That's OK. Our love is strong enough to bridge the divide."

That love carried Rob and Diane. The bumps in the road were much bigger for Diane. For a while, Rob wasn't seeing the bumps as clearly as she was. He'd read the stress on her face, see unhappiness in her eyes, but instead of saying something, he'd just file it away. Diane strove to be strong, especially because Rob was trying to be strong. She had fears, but found it best not to share them with Rob. God only knew how he'd react.

Rob would see more clearly in retrospect, and his advice to other cancer patients encountering marital problems was unambiguous: Go to therapy and go right away. Problems will arise. Be ready. Your relationship will not be the same. It will be tested to a degree it has never been tested before.

Rob said this even though he never liked the idea of therapy and didn't particularly care for it once Diane got him to go. The therapist had Diane and Rob keep diaries in which they wrote about their arguments and conflicts, which meant they relived the fights when they met with the therapist. Diane would read her journal and Rob would read his and they'd go home angry at each other all over again. Sometimes they'd laugh at the irony, but mostly Rob thought it was counterproductive. It was like losing a football game, then watching the film over and over just to criticize the players over and over.

Ultimately, the therapist fumbled when she told Rob he had to learn to accept his limitations. That ticked him off. Accepting limitations ran counter not merely to how he approached his battle with the brain tumor, but to everything he believed in. Accept limitations? That was capitulation. That was the door to defeat. Accept limitations! After four months, that was the last Rob and Diane saw of any therapist even though Diane suggested they try someone else.

"We'll go to a guy this time, Rob. I think we could still use it."

Diane was there for Rob, but she also had her own support system in place. She had people to talk to—friends, her daughter, other family members. She carved a niche for herself outside of Rob's medical situation. By tending to herself, she was better equipped to tend to Rob. "You realize how lucky you are. You're the one taking care of the person, but you're the one who's healthy. That's when you realize health is the No. 1 thing you need."

Jennifer was mostly away at college. She didn't see the darker moments. When she came home, particularly in the trying months after surgery, Rob tried to be the dad she always knew. Yet she could tell he was hurting, and that was hard on her.

"Everything at the beginning seemed overwhelming. If it wasn't for mom, I don't know how I would have handled it. In a way, I've almost blocked out the time. All the little details of day to day I almost don't remember. I just remember doing what we had to do and being there for each other."

At one of Rob's brain tumor support group meetings, the wife of a patient, who by then was in a wheelchair, spoke of the sanctuary and strength found in the simple details of a day.

"Day in, day out I ask God to help me through the next hour," the woman said. "Make someone call on the phone and make me laugh. Put a good movie on TV; put something good in the mail. Surprise me with something that will get us through to the next day. And something will happen, and the next day will be a better day."

That's what cancer patients strive for: the next day. Some days are better days. Some days end with a clean MRI and a celebratory glass of wine as a sunset plays off the ridges. Some days end with a banquet hall toast and the honor of your peers.

And then there are days when you're suddenly seized by strange pulsations as if a dozen hearts are beating in your arms. Rob began having many of those days as 2003 rolled around. He was on seizure medication, had been since shortly after the operation, yet now his simple-partials were growing in regularity.

A dozen hearts beating: The days of "wait and see" were about to end.

CHAPTER 11

Game Plans

THE FIRST ONE came on in the men's room at Maloney High School. Sensory perception was distorted. There was a slight ringing in the ears. It wasn't like the seizure Rob had suffered that fateful September day driving to Westport. It wasn't nearly as strong. Yet it made him think. *If I pass out in this bathroom no one will know something is wrong. They'll just see two legs under the stall. I'll be in here all night.* Rob bolted from the bathroom and the seizure passed.

It wasn't an isolated incident. The sensations kept coming back.

"You know, something's happening that's a little bit weird," Rob told Dr. Piepmeier during a regular appointment.

"You're having what they call simple-partial seizures."

Simple-partials are fairly innocuous. It's just one neuron misfiring in the brain. But as the simple-partials add up, they can pave the way for complex-partials, even grand mals.

Rob began keeping track of them in a diary. He noted details. He wanted to find out what might be causing them. Situations and symptoms varied. He got one shoveling snow; he got one talking on the phone. Sometimes they'd leave a medicinal taste in his mouth; sometimes they wouldn't. Often there was a pulsating feeling, that feeling of a dozen hearts beating in his arms and legs, with one giant pulsation behind them all. There would be a swelling sensation. It would swell, swell and just blossom through his body.

Thanks to the diary, Rob got attuned to what set them off: lack of sleep, alcohol, stress, certain angles of light. Thanks to the diary, he could also chart their rising frequency. During the 2002 holidays he had one roughly every three days. Their number increased during February 2003. By March they were routine. He had four one day alone and counted 28 for the month. He'd get them at school; he'd get them at home. He'd get them reading or watching TV or cooking dinner. Most lasted for just a few seconds. Some lasted a few minutes. He could usually feel them coming on. There was an aura that preceded them. Sometimes he'd fight them. Sometimes he'd just let them swell and blossom.

By then, the doctors at Yale-New Haven were mobilizing, particularly one who was new to the story. In late 2002 a German doctor, Joachim Baehring, joined Yale-New Haven's neuro-oncology staff after completing his fellowship at Harvard. Baehring got involved with Rob as the seizures increased. The MRI scans had remained unchanged, but Dr. Baehring suspected the seizures were a warning sign. There was likely some activity in the tumor cells. So he ordered up a PET scan—a positron emission tomography.

Baehring was tall, reserved and spoke with a German accent, but he knew his stuff. "This test is not the best study. It lacks sensitivity and specificity, but it can help determine what's going on in a seemingly benign brain tumor."

The procedure was much like an MRI. Rob was placed in a tube and a slightly radioactive compound called 18 flourodeoxy glucose was injected. Active tumor cells would light up on the scan. The test went fine, but there was a delay in getting results. Rob had a hunch something was up when he and Diane were finally summoned to Yale-New Haven and they were sent not to the third floor as usual, but to the second.

"Isn't that the oncology floor?" Rob asked Diane.

His gut instinct was right. The PET scan revealed a "hot" area in part of the temporal lobe left behind from the surgery. The hot spot suggested tumor activity. The increase in seizures suggested the same. The combination of the two convinced Dr. Baehring to prescribe chemotherapy for a year.

Rob heard echoes from the support group meetings. *Oligodendroglioma, Grade 2, operation, round of chemo.* Now it was his turn. Chemo.

Dr. Baehring noted that the majority of tumors like Rob's were sensitive to chemotherapy. There would be results.

"Many times even if you don't see shrinkage, at least you accomplish better seizure control."

"Has Dr. P. seen this scan? Does he agree with you?"

Up until then, Rob had worked almost exclusively with Dr. Piepmeier. He was dependent on him; he trusted no one more. As much as the question may have offended Dr. Baehring—and as much as Rob felt bad about that—he wanted the Piepmeier seal of approval.

"This guy is bright," Piepmeier later told Rob. "This is a brilliant, brilliant move on his part."

There was the validation. It was OK to move forward with Baehring's plan. And the more time Rob spent with Baehring, the more he learned how accurate Piepmeier's assessment was. Rob had a hell of a tag team in his corner.

* * *

The bout was commenced March 27, 2003 with Rob's first dose of Temodar. The treatment cycle was five days every 28 days.

Temodar was a fairly new form of chemotherapy: pill form, well-tolerated, few side effects. It was accompanied by Zorfan, an anti-nausea medication. It was a little unnerving for Rob to think about chemotherapy. The operation hadn't been enough. It wasn't over. Yet he was encouraged to learn many people go on chemo and get rid of their cancer all together.

Rob also had a deep well of experience to draw from. At a support group meeting, other brain tumor patients had told him what to expect. Most of the people around that long table had already been on Temodar. Grab a chair and join the gang, Rob.

The first dose was the toughest, just from a psychological standpoint. The warning label on the package read, "Handle with care. Do not touch unless with gloves." *Wait a minute: I'm not supposed to touch this medication with my bare hands, but it's OK to put it down my throat?*

To neutralize the toxicity of the chemotherapy and limit its side effects, Rob went on a specialized diet. It was prescribed by Dr. Taryn Forrelli, a naturopathic doctor. She was based at the same clinic where Diane had been seeing a homeopathic doctor. It was a clinic that offered alternatives to conventional medicine—acupuncture, message, aromatherapy, Feng Shui, nutrition and herbal therapy. There was a whole bunch, mostly Eastern in origin. Their common thread was dealing with the underlying cause of a condition rather than focusing on the symptoms, to work in conjunction with the natural healing mechanisms of the body rather than against them.

The gap between alternative and conventional medicine is still wide. Those in the conventional community are quick to point out that most alternative medicines lack scientific proof and warn patients to proceed with caution. Frauds and scam artists are always looking to gouge the vulnerable.

"There are a lot of people out there who are more than willing to take your money and say that they can cure you, but if they could cure cancer, they'd be multi-billionaires," Betsey D'Andrea warned the support group. "I've been in oncology long enough to have seen patients get really bilked from some of these people who really take advantage of someone at their weakest moments. Concentrate on what you're going to do and look into the other alternatives as you go along, but don't go crazy trying to go in 10 different directions."

Dr. Baehring had no problem with Rob going on a naturopathic diet. It's not that physicians are totally opposed to alternative medicine, he said. They just want to know what their patients are taking. Dr. Baehring also said there seemed to be few interactions between nutritional supplements and standard cancer treatment, at least as far as it was known at that point. There had been no studies about it. Common sense, though, dictated some combinations to avoid, such as taking anti-oxidants while undergoing treatment. Anti-oxidants would tend to negate radiation or chemotherapy.

With chemo, Rob was concerned with the side effects of nausea, vomiting, fatigue, low white blood cell counts and the concomitant susceptibility to infections. The aim of Dr. Forrelli's plan was to boost Rob's immune system, maintain blood cell counts and decrease the immediate and long-term toxicity of chemo while increasing its effectiveness.

That's a mouthful. Here's what she had Rob taking:

1. Emulsified Vitamin A: To enhance the effectiveness of the chemo, five drops twice a day.

2. Aloe: Also to enhance chemo effectiveness and to soothe and heal the gastrointestinal tract, two to three ounces a day.

3. Anti-oxidant: To provide cellular protection, support the immune system and support liver detoxification, one capsule three times a day.

4. Green tea extract: To enhance the immune system and block abnormal cell growth, 275 milligrams, two capsules a day.

5. Ashwaganda: An herb to reduce chemo's toxicity, boost the immune system and keep platelet, hemoglobin and red blood cell counts normal, one teaspoon twice a day.

6. Marrow Plus: A combination of Chinese herbs to boost immunity and maintain white blood cell counts, three capsules three times a day.

7. HMF forte: A "good" bacteria to prevent infections and replace flora depleted by chemo, one capsule twice a day.

8. Eskimo 3: Essential fatty acids to promote the production of anti-inflammatories and suppress tumor promoters, three capsules a day.

There were some other items—seaweed, whey protein. Diane would blend them in a morning "smoothie." Making the drink palatable took trial and error. Some elements were modified, some watered down. The ones that Rob found unpalatable—aloe and whey, in particular—were scrapped all together. It made for a doozey of a daily diet, but it gave Rob comfort.

Along with the supplements, Forrelli recommended balanced meals, with as many whole and organic foods as possible. Processed and preserved foods were to be avoided. Sugar, too. That suppressed the immune system. Animal proteins were to be limited. Even after chemo, Rob continued following a naturopathic diet. He eliminated some items, but added Vitamin E and the anti-epileptic herb taurine. He also added shitake mushroom extract to boost natural killer cells—those cells that patrol the body and sniff out invaders. He cut back on green tea extract because it supposedly countered the effectiveness of his anti-seizure medication.

"It's nice to know I'm taking some herbs that are trying to neutralize the toxicity in my system," Rob told Dr. Baehring. "Mentally, I feel good about that, Doc."

The naturopathic diet was not Rob's only foray into alternative medicine. He also underwent acupuncture treatments once a month. Mr. Conservative, Mr. I-Formation, was ranging far and wide. On second glance, this wasn't so odd. Rob's approach to cancer treatment was like his approach to football. Hadn't he always picked the brains of other coaches? How do you stop this, how would you suggest running this? Rob had always sought input. Even as veteran coaches, he and Mike Falis would go watch playoff teams practice. How did they run their program? If it was successful, it was worth watching. Why limit the number of sources you drew from?

So when it came to his health, Rob was receptive to Jen and Diane's suggestion of alternative treatments. Jen had started researching as soon as the tumor was diagnosed. What kind of tumor was it? What are the surgical options? Are there natural therapies that could work? She compiled lists and questions. She learned surgery was often successful with oligodendrogliomas, but also learned reoccurrence was common. She figured Dr. Piepmeier understated that future risk for the sake of keeping Rob's spirits up going into the operation. You know, one day at a time, one play at a time. But each play had to form a whole. Rob couldn't help but notice Jen was just like him, developing a thorough game plan, undaunted by a formidable opponent.

"Let's go after it," she said.

Jen kept pursuing options even after the operation. After all, some cancer cells were still up there and those cells had a way of regenerating. So Jen's approach became preventative, and her further research into alternative medicine led her to a new way of thinking: cure the underlying problem, not merely the symptoms.

That's what led the Szymaszeks to Dr. Tom Tam.

A master in Chi Gong and Tai Chi, Tam was born in China, came to America in 1975 as a political refugee and started practicing medicine in 1982. Since then, he'd developed his own healing system. It was based on traditional Chinese medicine, but incorporated modern knowledge of the central nervous system—in other words, a cross between West and East. Diane liked that Dr. Tam's treatments were based on ancient methods. If people had been using them for centuries and were still using them, she reasoned, they had to be valid. Jen saw promise in the blend of conventional and alternative medicine, in the intersection of modern and ancient.

"If Western medicine and Eastern medicine can work together, why not?" Jennifer said. "It's more of a holistic approach. People can definitely get better results."

Dr. Tam is fairly well known. Some consider him a miracle worker. He has several offices in greater Boston and travels extensively to teach seminars. He treats everything under the sun, from allergies to cancer, from eating disorders to phobias. Cancer, however, became his prime target once he developed Tong Ren in 2001. Tong Ren: It translated as "bronze man." Dr. Tam described it as ancient Chinese Chi Gong healing blended with Carl Jung's theory of the collective unconscious.

Jen tracked Dr. Tam down on the Internet and made a phone call.

"What kind of tumor does he have?" she was asked.

"It's a brain tumor."

"Ah, that's good! Brain tumors are our specialty."

As a Christmas gift, Jen scheduled an appointment. The show of love broke down any resistance Rob might have mounted. He went willingly to Tam's office in the Chinatown section of Boston. En route, Jen and Diane explained acupuncture and Tong Ren. The aim was attacking the cancer cells by getting through any blockages in the body and releasing energy and blood flow to the brain.

Dr. Tam also explained it well on that first visit. The reason

Rob had the tumor, Dr. Tam said, was because there was a blockage in his "chi," the Chinese word for the power source of life. What resulted was a reverse domino effect. Chi blockage led to a deviation in DNA, which led to the abnormal cells, which led to the cancer. The key was to find that blockage, open it up and restore the flow of blood and energy.

OK, that made some sense. Then Dr. Tam brought out a little doll—the "bronze man" of Tong Ren. That was weird, Rob thought. It looked like a little voodoo doll, and Dr. Tam began running a small hammer over it.

"You feeling the heat, Bob?"

Somehow, that little bronze man was supposed to work in combination with Rob's chi and remove the obstructions in his system. Back and forth, back and forth went the little hammer.

"You feeling the heat?"

Rob was trying not to break out laughing. He didn't want to be disrespectful; he knew Dr. Tam was held in great renown. He'd cured people who'd been in ICU, who'd been on their death beds. But Rob was in disbelief. What the hell was with this doll and hammer?

"You feeling the heat, Bob?"

Rob was feeling absolutely nothing. Then it occurred to him: He'd better buy into the treatment or it probably wouldn't work. Hadn't they driven all the way to Boston? Hadn't Jen done all that research and made the appointment? Hadn't she done it for him?

Rob concentrated. The hammer moved across the doll.

"You feeling the heat?"

And damn if he didn't. Rob's face reddened. The heat: He could feel it. His chi was on the move.

Dr. Tam also gave Rob acupuncture treatments. When Tam opened an office in Northampton, Massachusetts, where Rob's sister Jan lived, Rob went to see him every month. Diane said Rob was more relaxed after he went to Dr. Tam and Rob noticed a difference, too. It was palpable. When he went to support group meetings, it seemed he was doing much better than everybody else. The other members of the group, when they looked at Rob, seemed to be thinking, "What is this guy doing here?" Rob didn't look like a brain tumor patient.

Rob did not escape his turn with chemo, yet he was a much better patient on it than he had been after the operation. Chemo was regimented and that fit Rob's personality. Five days every 28 days. Rob joked with Diane that they should synchronize his chemo cycle with her menstrual cycle so they could both be miserable at the same time.

Usually, Rob didn't sleep well the night before a new cycle. He hated having to wait. He hated knowing what he'd be taking in the morning. Once he got there, it was game time and everything was fine. The plan was in action. He started each chemo day with the setup pill, Zorfan, to head off the nausea. He took that exactly a half hour before taking the Temodar. Then he'd eat breakfast exactly an hour later.

Temodar, being a pill, was not as devastating a form of chemotherapy as an IV drip. It wasn't good, it wasn't fun; but it wasn't as bad as other cancer patients had it and Rob knew it. Sometimes he'd see patients on drip chemo at Yale-New Haven. They'd have their IV poles in tow and Rob would look in their eyes and see looks of horror. They seemed so lifeless. *Is that going to be me some day? Will I become one of them? No! I will be spared this awful treatment.*

Rob made it a point of pride to continue working during chemo. He liked being able to say he'd missed time only for the operation. On some chemo mornings he had to will himself into school. By the second or third day of each cycle he'd feel it most acutely.

"It's like I'm moving through molasses."

"Rob, you're staying home today," Diane would say. "You're staying home."

"I can't do that."

Rob would point to a poster he'd propped up on the bureau in front of the mirror. It showed a stick figure bearing a briefcase and big grimace, and it read "STAYING HOME IS NOT AN OPTION." It was the first thing Rob saw each morning.

Don't underestimate the power of a piece of paper.

"Diane, I can't stay home."

Diane admired the courage and tolerated the stubbornness. Rob locked into a mode of thinking that didn't allow for deviation. It was just like when he was a teenager and, out of love and respect for Millie and Bob, refused the temptations of the 60s. There could be no exception, no lapse. He'd get up, put his slippers on one at a time, fight through the molasses and get to the bathroom, shower and shave.

On bad mornings he crawled. Retreat was not an option. No matter how inviting that bed looked—and on some days it really did—there was that poster staring him in the face and that inner voice that insisted: *Don't give in, don't give in.* Give an inch and an inch becomes a yard that becomes 10 yards and a first down for cancer.

So like the best Maloney defenses he ever coached, Rob refused to give an inch.

CHAPTER 12

Game Faces

ONE SUMMER WHILE Rob was still coaching, his sister Sharon, paying one of her regular visits from Toms River, New Jersey, dropped in on a Maloney conditioning practice. The Spartans, she said, looked like the Bad News Bears—and that was during conditioning week, when no footballs are used. Later that same season Sharon saw the team play. The Bad News Bears had gone into hibernation and a formidable Spartan squad had emerged.

"You must have made them feel that there was nothing they couldn't accomplish," Sharon told her brother.

That was exactly it. Each year Rob imbued the Spartans with the belief that good results would follow work and dedication. That old Spartan Pride: Some scoffed; enough believed. Proof lay in 160 career wins.

Rob took the same approach to his brain tumor. Attitude wasn't just half the battle; it was more. There could be absolutely no room for doubt. He always strove to make his players believe and he, too, had to believe. Here we go: another Goliath for the Spartans to take down.

Dan Hatch thought long and hard about Rob's illness. When a close friend, someone your own age, someone with whom you were once young, is suddenly stricken, you think. Dan surveyed the span of Rob's life. He thought about their playing days, their coaching years, and he saw few fundamental differences between the old battles and the new. It was like Rob was going into the biggest game of the season. Even though he was out-manned, he wasn't going to be out-coached.

There's no question Rob the cancer patient drew from his philosophy as Rob the football coach: Everything on the up, everything in the positive. During the 2001 holiday season Rob bought the nicest tie he could find and put it away as a gift to himself for Christmas 2002. He had no doubt he would be around to celebrate it.

Rob drew from core values. Hadn't Millie and Bob raised him to believe nothing was out of reach, that the world was an over-sized plate? Hadn't Rob always lived that way? "He puts attitude ahead of facts," Ron Carbone said, and Coach was right. Positive thinking had always been Rob's staple. The will to win could sometimes outweigh the other team's 275-pound linemen or college-bound fullback. Now it would outweigh a brain tumor. Be it out-run or over-powered or just flat out out-willed, that sucker would be defeated.

Some believed Rob's thinking bordered on the delusional. I sometimes did, but mostly found Rob's unwavering optimism far preferable to the defeatism I too often encountered in other quarters, where the gripes were awfully petty compared to a brain tumor. Rob's attitude was all that was infectious about him. You'd forget he had a brain tumor.

I also agreed with Sharon's assessment: "If this is his way of coping with what he has to deal with on a daily basis, far be it for me to say, 'Rob, deal with reality.' Whatever he needs to draw upon to get over the hurdles he faces, how do I dare say, 'Rob, accept what you have to accept.' I applaud him. I admire him beyond belief. But I worry beyond belief, and I pray for him every day."

Rob gathered his allies where he found them. He employed imagery. Whenever he dropped a Temodar pill into his mouth he pictured B-52s dropping bombs on the afflicted area of his brain, just obliterating those tumor cells.

He borrowed from Lance Armstrong. Rob read Lance's book *It's Not About the Bike* when he started chemo. It was recommended by an acquaintance, Boyd DeBaradino. Boyd had cancer, too, and cancer would claim his life. Before he died, Boyd passed on a lifeline. "Here's a book you've got to buy." Rob just ate up Armstrong's blunt challenge to the disease: *You came into the wrong freaking body; I'll kick your ass every day.* Rob adopted it as if it were a new offense that seamlessly fit his team.

Positive, positive, positive: Always unrelentingly positive. There were doubts; Rob just kept them private.

"God, I have no idea how I would react if I was in that situation," Marce Petroccio, the Staples High School football coach, thought after getting off the phone with Rob one night. "I hope I would react like Rob has."

"It's not that he doesn't know fear," Coach Carbone mused. "He knows fear. He doesn't let fear conquer him. He keeps fear in control."

Indeed, that first brain tumor support group meeting had been sobering. It gave Rob a new understanding of the severity of his disease. There was no mistaking it, no escaping it. This was the hand he'd been dealt. But it also gave him a new appreciation for the value of life. *Life is precious. Let's make the most of it and thank God for every day.* That was his constant message to the support group, and he considered it his responsibility to offer a ray of hope to the first-timer who had just been diagnosed. He remembered sitting there that first time. Doom and gloom pervaded. He would have loved to have heard someone say, "I'm three years removed from surgery. I'm working. I had a little bout with seizures, I was put on some chemo, but that's it. Life is still good."

Rob had a great ally in Peter DeBona, a glioblastoma patient at Yale-New Haven. Peter's forecast had been dire when he was diagnosed. He was given three months to live.

That was 1994.

Peter's zest for life and his sense of humor hardly suffered for his illness. If anything, they grew. He handed out plain white business cards reading "Peter J. DeBona, retired, no business, no job, no title, no office." But he had a business: relishing life and spreading the word to other patients. Pete always showed up looking great, head clean shaven, robust, as if he just rode in off the set of *The Wild One* with Brando. His wry humor never ran dry. "Learn to enjoy your tumor," he'd tell the support group. "If you forget something, well, it's the brain tumor.

Humor and optimism sometimes fell flat across that long table. Some patients were bald from chemo or radiation. Some had developed speech impediments. Rob, well dressed and running in from work, chirping about life still being good, sometimes seemed out of place. Rob felt no guilt doing better than many of his peers. He did feel grateful for being spared. He was fortunate. His tumor had grown in a part of the brain that did not render him disabled. If it had been elsewhere, he could have been paralyzed. Not all brain tumor patients had the sort of second-chance opportunities he had. Rob recognized that and he clung to it. "Life is still good" wasn't some bullshit line. It was the truth.

Rob's philosophy wasn't mystical or complex. It was simply about returning to normal life and believing life was still normal rather than dwelling on the abnormality. Dr. Baehring recognized the inherent sense in this thinking. "There are many patients who struggle with a disease that may relapse," Baehring said. "Some of them desperately look for accurate numbers. They just want to know how to plan their life. There are no accurate numbers. Brain cancer is a pretty rare disease compared to other types of cancer. It's a disease many patients perceive as a lot more threatening than common diseases such as coronary heart disease or diabetes, which in certain situations will not have a better outcome than a brain tumor. It's just the label 'Cancer'—particularly 'Brain Cancer'—is so frightening to many patients that they cannot get their thoughts off the fact that they're suffering from one, even if it's one expected to have a protracted course or they may even be cured from."

Cliffs' Notes version: It could be worse; buck up and get living.

Rob understood this was easier said than done. The mental battle against cancer is waged on so many fronts. Consider MRIs. After surviving surgery and follow-up treatments, some patients have what's called "MRI anxiety." At first Rob thought this meant being claustrophobic about being placed in the MRI tube. He soon learned it meant being petrified the results will bear bad news.

Fear of relapse is natural and universal, according to the American Cancer Society. Rob vowed not to have that fear. It helped having a close co-worker who was also going through MRIs and other cancer tests. Six months after Rob's operation, Tom Carr, a counselor at Maloney, had a walnut-sized tumor detected behind his eye. He and Rob would share war stories. "How'd your MRI go today?"

In the early days, Rob gave Tom the boost he often needed.

"How do you feel, Tom?"

"Black: Everything is black."

"Yeah, that's right, black. I can remember going through that.

You keep fighting, Tom. Keep a positive mind and you can get through it."

Rob's attitude and perspective rubbed off, and good news did follow for Tom. Doctors did a biopsy, but deemed it best not to operate. Two years later, after a thyroid condition cleared up, Tom's tumor disappeared.

Rob would chuckle hearing colleagues whine over the smallest things. He'd come into school during a chemo cycle and maybe pass an administrator whose shoulders were already slumped and it wasn't even eight o'clock.

"Good morning!" Rob would muster.

"Oh my God."

"What's the matter?"

"I've already had five bad things happen and the day's not even 10 minutes old."

Just a walking rain cloud passing down the hallway. Rob kept to the sunny side.

"Hey, you have a great day."

Rob heard others complain about being tired. This both amused and annoyed him. *Hey, I'm the one on chemo. I'm not whining about being tired.* Self-pity grated in his ears. Even before he was stricken, Rob never had patience for "bitchers and bemoaners," as he called them. Now, negativity was simply intolerable. He never stood for it as a coach and he would not stand for it as a patient.

Was this a form of denial? Absolutely: Denial of defeatism.

"I think he feels as though it would not be virtuous, even in a hopeless situation, to capitulate," Coach Carbone said. "That's the way he's made. I don't know if he can operate differently."

He probably can't. The last visit Rob and Diane made to their therapist was the day the therapist said, "Mr. Szymaszek, you've got to learn to accept your limitations." In Rob's estimation, when you accept limitations you grab the crutch. It would be like going into a football game expecting to lose, accepting that you were going to lose and taking the beating.

Rob could play semantics on this topic, really split hairs. He'd say he could accept limitations, but only as something that needed to be worked on and improved. Short-term memory loss was a good example. Rob recognized that after the surgery he had a hard time remembering, so he was happy when Diane bought him a Palm Pilot. He hyper-organized his desk at work: high priority here, lesser priority here. This he considered only a temporary acceptance, because he believed he would completely recover. "Until I get back to 100 percent, I might have to make allowances, but there's no permanency attached." It was like in football, he'd say, when your offensive line went up against a bigger defensive line. For that particular game you accept the fact that you're not going to be able to base block, so you adjust and use combination blocks and traps. You've recognized limitations, but you haven't so much accepted them as found a way around them.

Or consider Bob Szymaszek. Rob's dad had lost his ability to write and almost all of his ability to speak when he had that stroke. So Diane made a picture chart that contained pictures of all the family members, as well as inanimate objects like food, a car, a toilet. The chart enabled Bob to communicate fairly well. A way had been found around the limitation.

Hair-splitting? "Maybe, but when that therapist told me to accept my limitations," Rob said, "I never went back."

Rob did have his reality checks. Andrea Mann was the best one. She wasn't negative, but she was realistic and what she said had resonance with Rob. She'd supply the gravity when he got too elevated.

"When am I going to be 100 percent back to normal?"

"What is normal, Rob?"

"I want to be able to go out and not worry about how much wine I drink. I want a good old-fashioned inebriated feeling."

"I don't want those any more."

"Why not, Andrea?"

"It's too similar to what my seizures are like."

Andrea always had the bigger view. She wasn't argumentative. She'd just put it plainly, sitting at a lunchtime table in downtown New Haven after their appointments at Yale-New Haven.

"The reality is we have an affliction we're living with and may have to live with the rest of our lives."

"I don't want to buy into that lifetime-affliction philosophy, Andrea."

"OK, Rob, if that's what you want to believe."

So their conversations would go. Andrea would ground Rob without deflating him. Rob listened to her. She spoke from greater experience. She'd had three operations. She'd had multiple types of chemotherapy. And there was Rob, dancing along, living in the positive, having undergone only one operation and one round of chemo. Sometimes he'd look at her and think *same family history, same tumor, same exact tumor: I could follow that path.* He'd followed her with the operation; he'd followed her with chemo.

Andrea's tenor changed slightly when she underwent radiation. Rob was peppering her with questions: Is it painful? How many days do you have to go? Will you lose your hair? What about that mask they put over your face?

Andrea cut him off.

"Rob," she said. "Why are you asking me all these questions? You're not following me, understand? You're not following me anymore."

"I could, though."

"Rob."

"I don't think I will. I don't think I'm going to have a relapse."

"Rob."

"I really don't."

"Rob, you listen: You're not following me anymore."

* * *

Mike Falis says Rob's ordeal reinforced his zest for life and living well. For his part, Rob saw no reason to change his taste for first-rate food and drink; but he was forced to watch what he ate and drank. Given the amount of medication he was on, particularly the anti-seizure pills, there was considerable strain on his liver to break down the toxins, and he was mindful of the liver cancer that had taken Millie's life. He had to be smart; he couldn't cut loose as he once did. But he also had to live, and every once in a while he'd indulge. If he was on vacation he'd say, "Screw it, I'm going to have a good week just like nothing ever happened. I can't lock myself up in a medicine cabinet."

Getting back to routine was immensely helpful. There were plenty of stresses inherent in guidance counseling, but there were plenty of highs. He loved helping a student solve a problem in school or at home. He loved seeing the looks of joy and relief. He kept a "warm fuzzy" file of letters and thank you notes from students, the kind of folder that was pleasant to turn to on an unpleasant day for a little re-affirmation.

"Mr. Szymaszek: I couldn't have asked for a more wonderful counselor. You are the sweetest person in that school and probably in the world. You have done so much for me just out of your goodness and heart. Without you the school and college process would have been much tougher. I always knew I could come to you about anything and you'd help me with a smiling face and easy confidence. You are such a special counselor and person and I wish you much happiness and good health in the future. I've never met someone who gives so much of themselves for others."

That note was from Lauren Uhlan, who graduated Maloney and went on to the Fashion Institute of Technology. For Rob, such reinforcement was priceless. Social contact sped his recovery. Kind words from colleagues and kids at school, awards and letters: They were all part of the comeback and they weren't to be had wallowing at home. "Don't lock yourself away," he said. "People look at you and have a sensitivity and appreciation for what you've been through. They're rooting you back." It was like hearing the old roar of the crowd on Thanksgiving morning, and it was better than any pill he'd ever taken.

Of course, the crowd never universally roars in one man's favor. There are always nay-sayers and doubters. Rob heard them as a coach and he heard them as a patient. He couldn't control the perceptions of others. Some of those perceptions, even if unintended, hurt and angered him.

Maloney's senior football advisor, Pete Sini, had faced it. A lifelong factory worker, Papa Pete had remained active as head of his retirees group. In 2000, when Pete underwent surgery, went on chemo and lost 40 pounds, his peers wondered why he still showed up to run meetings. "They were all worried it would do me in," Pete said. "People would ask me, 'What are you doing here?' They were worried next month I wouldn't be there."

When Rob first returned to work some people looked at him as the guy who had the brain tumor. They saw he was upbeat, but would still ask Diane, "Is he really doing as well as he seems and sounds?"

Rob found some people were sensitive to a fault. They would take care not to say the "C" word in his presence; they would treat him as if he were a glass figurine. Others would be a little thoughtless. One afternoon Rob returned to school from a blood test just as another faculty member was driving out. Rob started pulling into the parking space she had vacated.

"What are you doing?" she asked.

"I'm taking your spot."

"I'm going to be back in 15 minutes."

"Well, park somewhere else."

"Rob, why don't you park in the handicap spot?"

"Hey, I'm able-bodied. I will walk five miles before I park in a handicap spot."

Nonetheless, at home that night Rob asked Diane, "Do I look handicapped?"

Rob was constantly trying to get feedback from Diane. *Is there any indication I'm something other than the guy I was?* He couldn't wait to come off blood thinners so he could resume breaking up fights at school.

Rob hated being slack around the house. That reflected on him, too. During the summer of 2002 some kids he'd hired to cut the lawn weren't showing up and the grass was getting long. It was hot, the front lawn is steep and Rob should not have been out there. But what would the neighbors think of that pasture? Rob hauled the lawn mower out of the garage. On the first pass across the slope, he noticed the self-propulsion on the mower wasn't working. And he felt everyone in the neighborhood was watching. Watching and thinking, "There's Rob Szymaszek, the guy who had a brain tumor, trying to mow his lawn."

Rob kept going, one step at a time. That lawnmower was a bitch to push. He went at it just like Mike Falis used to teach drive blocking: plant, push, plant, push. *I've never seen anyone cut the lawn as good as you do.* Plant, push: painstaking step by step. Plant: Could he get off another step? Push: Could he get off another row? By the time Diane came home his face was beet-red.

"Rob, you asshole, just let it go. Who cares if a single row is showing?"

Rob pushed that goddamn lawn mower across once more . . . and then back again and back again until it was finished.

That's how deep the sensitivity could run, and it's one reason why Rob refused to take one day off during the chemo treatments. He didn't want it to be said a brain tumor had changed him or that he couldn't handle his job. He bristled when Lou Kapell, the part-time guidance counselor hired to help Rob when he first returned to school, was still hanging around the office.

"What are you doing here? I told you a week ago I don't need you."

"I'm doing some work for someone else."

"But people don't know that, Lou. They think you're here helping me."

Refusing to miss a day of work was also a preventive step. Rob did not want anyone to hold his health over his head. That may have happened anyway. Two assistant principal jobs opened up at Maloney. Rob applied for both and got neither. Diane believed Rob's cancer worked against him, even though the Americans with Disabilities Act makes it illegal to discriminate against people with health issues in virtually every area of employment.

During the interview for the second job, Rob put it on the table. "I'm undergoing chemo, but I want everyone to know I'm on top of my game. I've just finished eight months of chemo; I've got another four months to go. I haven't missed a day of school."

His total absences, dating back to Day 1 of the illness, were 37. That included the week of testing, the biopsy, the major surgery and the blood clots. 37 days. And it wasn't an easy job he'd returned to. Connecticut's recommended counselor-to-student ratio was 1-to-160. Thanks to budget cuts, Maloney counselors were handling twice that.

"I'm ready to take on the rigors," Rob told the assistant principal search committee. "I know it's on everybody's mind about my health."

Rob was later told he didn't have to do that. Rob saw it as a moot point. "Tell me it wasn't on their minds."

The search committee went with another candidate. "We were looking for a different prototype," was the explanation.

That bothered Rob. He wanted to put his family in a better financial situation for retirement. He also thought he'd make a good assistant principal. An assistant principal has to be a leader and a firm disciplinarian, two qualities that also made for a good football coach. "In some school systems, it's an instant marriage. They look for those kinds of people," Rob said. "Most football coaches won't duck issues. They've got backbone."

Having backbone can make you enemies. Rob wasn't afraid to take an unpopular stand. In 1998, he backed a student who was trying to return to school a year after leaving Maloney under threat of expulsion. The student, who once played football for Rob, made a comment to another student, threatening to kill a teacher for giving him a failing grade. The teacher had been within earshot. This was shortly after Columbine. Punishment was swift. The student was essentially given a choice: get suspended from Maloney or enroll in another school district. Rob found that inexplicable. As much as he deplored the student's action, he disputed the sentence. There shouldn't have been any bargaining, he said. It was like being accused of murder and told you could avoid jail by moving to another town.

The student chose Option B. He enrolled in another district, spent a trouble-free year there, then tried to re-enroll at Maloney only to be told he'd be immediately expelled for the threat he'd made the year before. The majority of the faculty did not want him back in school. Rob believed he'd paid the price and had changed for the better. He publicly backed the kid and was ostracized for it by many of his colleagues, who saw him as a coach who just wanted a football player back in the huddle.

Ultimately, the student was expelled for six months, then allowed to return to Maloney. He never played football again. The tempest died down, but not without residue. Like anyone unafraid to speak up, Rob was not the most cherished employee in the Meriden school system.

That penchant for telling it like it is, even when detrimental, Rob got from his dad. When Bob Szymaszek retired, one of his colleagues said, "He'd take the bull by the horns anytime, even if it was the chief holding the horns." Maybe that's why he was elevated no higher than sergeant.

"I guess if you want to get promoted from time to time you learn to keep your mouth shut and play the game," Rob said. "I knew some actions could come back and haunt me. I should learn to avoid conflict and confrontation, but I seem to be attracted to it when I believe my cause to be right."

So it was that Rob failed to climb the career ladder.

The battle with cancer, on the other hand, was going well. As 2003 passed into 2004 he was still on Temodar, dropping those B-52 bombs every time he dropped a pill. *You picked the wrong freaking body; I'll kick your ass every day!* When the molasses came, Rob put his slippers on one at a time, looked at the "STAYING HOME IS NOT AN OPTION" poster propped on the bureau, turned his back on his bed, got to that bathroom, showered, shaved and got to school.

He had just completed his tenth cycle of chemotherapy when

Dr. Baehring ordered a second PET scan. The results showed the "hot spot" had not changed. There was no decrease in size, but nor was there any increase. Also, the frequency of Rob's seizures had gone way down. Taking those two factors into account, Dr. Baehring pulled the plug on the year-long treatment two months early.

Rob and Diane went back to "wait and see" and went home to celebrate. The chapter with chemo, for the time being, was over.

CHAPTER 13

On & Off The Bench

WHEN IT CAME to coaching, Rob had been a reluctant retiree. Cancer forced the issue. Cancer was in his system. So was coaching football. The desire had never left.

Rob's proximity to the Maloney program pulled on the old strings of Spartan Pride. Unlike most retired coaches, he was not physically removed from his former team. He was still working at the school; he saw players every day. That would have been fine if the guys were experiencing some success. They were not. In the first season after Rob's departure, the program plunged.

A former Maloney player and assistant coach in his late 30s had been hired as Rob's successor in 2002. He was hand-picked, chosen with the endorsement of Rob and Mike Falis.

Support for the new coach was fairly universal in the Maloney football family. He was the obvious choice. At the time, he was across town, teaching social studies and working as an assistant coach for Tom Ryan at Platt. Returning to his alma mater, the new coach brought along wholesale changes, from the uniforms to the playbook. The offense was virtually identical to Platt's. Some unhappy players and alumni started calling the Spartans the "East Side Panthers."

But that's a new coach's prerogative. Rob recognized that. He also recognized the difficult terrain his successor walked. It's hard to follow the old coach. It's even harder when the old coach was successful *and* still in the neighborhood. What's more, a new guy wants to establish his own identity. He doesn't want to be regarded as an imitator or someone just winning with the old system. But as Bear Bryant once said, a new system makes everyone a freshman, and the Spartans of 2002 and 2003 seemed to be just that: kid brothers among bigger boys.

Arguably, a gradual shift from old methods to new would have produced better results. The results that did follow were not good. They were, in fact, awful. Mike and Rob felt they had left behind a pretty good nucleus, one that had the potential for a winning season. Instead, for the first time in 30 years, Maloney football failed to win a single game. The losing streak stretched to 20 games in 2003 before the Spartans snapped the skein. Their two-year ledger for 2002 and 2003 read 1-21.

There was a mitigating factor. A few years earlier the Spartans had lost a season of freshman football due to school budget cuts. A trickle-down effect was inevitable. Those Spartans were a year behind their peers. But who could have foreseen it being this bad? One lost season of freshman football couldn't account for all of it. Maloney was losing by an average of four touchdowns a game.

Publicly, Rob refrained from criticizing his successor. Nine weeks into the 0-11 season of 2002, I interviewed Rob for a newspaper article.

"What do you think of the Spartan downturn?"

"Well, I'll tell you, I went to the Bulkeley game on Friday night and I liked seeing how hard the kids hustled out of the huddle even when the game was lost. It reflects well on the coaching staff, because when you're losing it's hard to motivate players and hard to keep them on the team."

It was a major reach, but Rob chose to leave it at that. Privately, it killed him to see the program struggle so badly and it killed him to not be able to do anything about it. Players would stop by his guidance office and complain. Rob would cut them off.

"Hey, you've got to talk to your head coach."

He did what he could to be supportive, did what he could to help turn things around. He gave occasional motivational talks to the team, but kept quiet about them. He also tried to keep something else quiet. Following the first game of 2002, a Maloney loss on the road up in Berlin, the new coach swore at the driver of the team bus and the driver filed a police report. Rob asked me if there was any way I could keep it out of the newspaper, but of course there was no way a self-respecting newspaper would suppress something like that. And, anyway, the damage was already done. The incident got the new coach suspended for the next game.

There would be more along these lines. The new coach yelled at the band director and some band members on another night. He frequently yelled at players. Yet he wasn't a monster. The guy was married at the time, had young kids. I found him to be cooperative, candid and easy to get along with, but then again I was a writer, not a wide receiver. I'll give him credit. He didn't duck responsibility for the team's struggles. He only complained when he found the newspaper's reporting to be overly critical of his players. He'd call, we'd talk and it would be very amicable and professional.

"Hey, I know you guys have to do what you have to do. When you go to our games, you have to write about what happens. If we play bad, we play bad. That's fine. I just have a problem when it shows up on Monday and the kids have to read it all over again."

Monday Morning Quarterback: Our follow-up piece from the weekend's action. Sometimes it featured a great human interest story. Sometimes it was a collection of unused quotes or factoids. Some reporters were better than others at drumming up material. Some just fell back on rehash, so some weeks the Spartans read about their Friday night failings on Saturday and then again on Monday. An unnecessary deal, I agreed, for players who weren't pros, but teenagers.

"You make a fair point, Coach."

In hindsight, it seems it was just a bad fit. Maybe the guy was better suited to be an assistant coach. Or maybe, if he were head coaching material, he would have been better served somewhere other than his alma mater, following in the footsteps of the guy who had won the most games in city history and had just gone into the state Coaches Hall of Fame. The drastic change in coaching style didn't help either. Health issues were probably a factor, too. Several years later, Rob's successor underwent replacement surgery on both hips. Old football injuries from his playing days. While he coached, the guy was probably a hurting unit.

And so was Rob. Watching the team struggle just ate him up. He'd be in a restaurant and people would call him over to their table.

"Coach, you're looking great. When are you going back to coaching?"

He heard that wherever he went, and he knew he'd stepped down too soon. Rob shared his feelings with Mike, and Mike understood. Rob's decision had been prompted by a reversal of health, not passion. The team's struggles were only a fraction of the frustration.

"If you'd been healthy," Mike said, "you would have continued coaching even after I left, regardless of how many times we said we'd go out together. And another thing: If I was the head football coach and you couldn't be the head coach it would have bothered you, even with the friendship we had for all those years.

You have a bond with those kids and it bothers you not to be on the field coaching them."

It bothered Rob, all right. By not coaching he wasn't fully guiding student-athletes. He wasn't fully inspiring them. He wasn't doing what he had the gift to do. *What did the Lord put you on this earth to do?* So much of his identity had been put on the shelf. Induction into the state Coaches Hall of Fame made that literally true, but Hall of Fame status and a Hall of Fame ring did not compensate for the void he felt in his life. Even going on chemo in 2003 hadn't validated the health concerns that had factored into his retirement. He was handling the Temodar well enough. He was fortunate. He was taking a pill, not toting around drip bags on an IV pole. Chemo wasn't that bad. He wasn't missing school. He could have coached through it.

Yet when Rob had chances to return to the sidelines, he declined. In 2002 and again in 2003, he was asked to coach linebackers at Southern Connecticut State. It was a part-time position, but Rob knew he'd want to give it full-time attention, and high school and college schedules don't mesh very well.

He was asked to be the offensive coordinator at powerhouse New Britain High, where talent and numbers were never lacking, but he couldn't go there. The state's most successful and controversial coach, Jack Cochran, was New Britain's head guy, but that had nothing to do with it. Rob had often defended the unpopular Cochran. Rob was the one guy in the state coaching fraternity who tried to bring the young maverick into the fold, who tried to get him to tone down a hardball approach that led to many hard feelings and many a lopsided score. No, it wasn't that Cochran coached at New Britain. It was that New Britain, as a conference rival, played Maloney every year. "I couldn't possibly coach against Maloney," Rob concluded.

There were overtures from a new coaching regime over at

Choate Rosemary-Hall in Wallingford, the prep school Jennifer had attended, the school John F. Kennedy had attended. Every year it received talented players looking to put in a post-grad year before going to college. The coaching staff being assembled was a good one, too. It included several former high school head coaches. They were guys Rob knew and liked, but it seemed like a case of too many chefs.

In late 2003, Rob's old friend Al Pellegrinelli stepped down at Berlin High after 37 years. That job was enticing. Since retiring, Rob had thought about how if he ever returned to coaching he would go to a town with one high school like Berlin to avoid the divisiveness of a two-school town like Meriden. But he also recognized that Pellegrinelli's young assistant, John Capodice, had been groomed for the position and was deserving of it. There were unwritten rules in the coaching fraternity. You respected turf. Hand-picked successors were not to be challenged.

Rob phoned Al.

"Is John your guy?"

"Yeah, Rob. I'm pushing for Johnny Capodice."

"Then my application is not going in."

So Rob remained a retired coach well within earshot of the arena. *"Coach, you're looking great. When are you going back to coaching?"*

Heading into the 2003 Maloney-Platt Thanksgiving game, Mike Falis got a chance to go back to the old stomping grounds when the new coach asked him to help out. Rob's spirit stirred. He offered his services.

"How about getting us both back out there?" Rob asked his successor.

"Coach, I can't do that."

"Why not?"

"I think we have a chance to win this game, and if we win

everyone's going to say the reason we won was because of you and Mike, not me."

Rob got annoyed. "That's all ego, buddy. What about the kids? Let's get the kids the victory and worry about the egos second. I don't want any credit for this victory. I'll defer any credit I get to you."

"I can't do it, Coach."

It was a valid point. Rob understood. It still hurt like hell. And Platt won, 27-12.

* * *

The losing continued for a second year. The 2003 season at least saw a win, but it also saw an 89-0 loss to New Britain, and after that game Rob's successor said Cochran hadn't run up the score, that it could have been worse.

A merciful 89-0? When could things ever hope to turn around?

Maloney football was percolating toward a crisis, and the boiling point came in early June 2004, a few weeks before school let out for the summer. Spring football practice was under way. One player, in the midst of baseball season, was late with some paperwork. The coach got on the kid for it. Things escalated and he wound up swearing at the student. This didn't happen on the football field, but in a school hallway.

The student reported the incident to his guidance counselor. That guidance counselor was Rob. Required to report such an incident up the administrative chain, Rob told an assistant principal, hoping the matter could be handled quietly.

"Keep it in house. Give him a good ass-ripping. He's got to learn kids can't be treated like this. But, please, keep it in house."

Instead, it went further up the line, ultimately reaching the school district's central office. Punishment was swift and it was severe. The coach was suspended from teaching without pay for four days. As far as football went, he was through.

Rob was not happy. He did not want to see his hand-picked successor get fired as coach. Nor did he want it to appear that he was maneuvering to get back on the sidelines, but that's exactly what some people believed. The story hit the Meriden *Record-Journal* and accusations started flying. It made for a contentious, bitter summer. Spartan Pride was being torn apart from the inside and the fight was publicly waged. My newspaper ran quite a few stories at virtually the same time Rob and I sat down to begin working on this book. That, too, caused a stir. How could the *Record-Journal* possibly be unbiased when one of its writers was so intimately involved with Coach Smaz?

A fair question. All that really bothered me was the notion that Rob had deviously maneuvered to return to coaching. The "conspiracy theory" was illogical. It held Rob culpable for reporting the incident, yet turned a blind eye to the inexcusable act of a teacher swearing at a student—another example of whistle blowing being deemed the greater crime. It seemed pretty clear cut to me, but not to most. Quite a few people told Rob he looked like the bad guy. It bothered me that none of the administrative higher-ups came to Rob's defense. All it would have taken was one of them to say, "Yes, Rob wanted to keep it in-house and he didn't want the coach to get canned." Instead, they ducked reporters or declined comment.

Rob, meanwhile, was hurt. Over the past two years he'd often gone to his successor's defense—sometimes successfully, sometimes not—and now he was being accused of doing everything and anything he could to undermine him. Rob also felt badly because the guy had played for him, had been a captain for him, had coached for him. They were part of the same football family.

In working on this book, Rob had no reservations talking about his marital problems or talking about crapping into a bedpan, but he anguished over this chapter. He didn't want to identify his successor by name. He fretted about opening old wounds.

"Rob didn't want him to get fired, he didn't want the job taken away from him," Mike Falis said that summer as the cuts bled. "They were friends for a long time and I hope they remain friends, but this whole situation is ugly at best."

There were times it appeared the rift would quickly heal. On the night of Maloney's 2004 graduation ceremonies Rob's successor drove him home. They spent a few hours talking in Rob's driveway. It was a pleasant night—warm, the beginning of summer, with the moon coming over the eastern ridge. Maloney football was a solid tradition, they agreed, and nothing should tear it apart.

The bad P.R., however, wouldn't die. The task of hiring a new coach kept tensions high. Rob wanted it, and yet didn't want to seem too eager. He also had apprehensions. Diane had apprehensions. There was a reputation to consider. There was health. Rob had made it through chemo OK, but his condition had produced another near catastrophe. In January 2004 he suffered a complex-partial seizure while driving home from the airport after flying back from a national football coaches convention in Florida. It resulted in an accident that luckily was not any worse than it was.

First came the aura: the precursor to a seizure, the advance warning. Rob knew when they were coming and he knew this wasn't going to be a small one. *Get to the side of the road. Get to the side of the road right now.* There was a stream of traffic rushing up from behind, a long uninterrupted line of headlights in the rearview mirror, twin eyes in the black. *Get to the side.* But he couldn't. There was no opening. The line kept coming and the aura swelled, swelled. The cars streamed, rushing, indifferent, lights upon lights.

GET TO THE SIDE!

No room, no time. He couldn't get over. And then there was nothing until the next lights.

* * *

"Do you know you went through a red light?"

The question came from the far end of a piercing, probing beam.

A flashlight. A face behind it. A badge.

The policeman peered into the car, probing. Rob looked around, too, and saw the wreckage. His car had barreled up an exit ramp and barreled through the red light on the bridge at the end of the ramp. As the car zoomed through the T-intersection it had been T-boned by another car. Or so he'd learn. At the time, he had no recollection of it. Had seen nothing, had felt nothing, even the collision. But right then and there, coming to, he saw that if the other car not hit him, he could have careened off the far side of the bridge and plummeted back down onto the highway.

"Sir, do you know you went through a red light?"

This time, there wasn't any confusion, no handcuffs, no trip to a holding cell. Both cars were totaled. Rob's Acura Legend, the car that had survived the fateful crash of September 1, 2001, did not survive this one. Rob wasn't seriously injured. Nor was the woman driving the other car. They were taken to a nearby hospital and Rob was relieved when she was released from the emergency room first. (Nearly two years later, however, the woman did file a $15,000 lawsuit.)

The immediate upshot of the accident was the suspension of Rob's driver's license. He couldn't get it back until he went eight full months without a seizure. This put a new strain on Diane and Rob. Diane had to drive him everywhere, and the old football coach, the guy so accustomed to being in control, made for one bear of a backseat driver. He'd critique her driving and they'd bicker. *It would be easier if you kept your mouth shut,* Rob told himself, and yet invariably he wouldn't listen to his own advice. Jessica Sperry, one of Diane's friends in the Maloney art department, gave him blinders to wear—just like the one horses wear while racing. That just made the feeling of having no control even worse.

What helped was getting away to St. Martin during February school vacation. Rob and Diane were back in their lovers' paradise, dining on gourmet food at waterside tables. The sun would set, the nightlights would come up and Diane and Rob would talk about how close they'd come to losing the magic between them. "The trip really recharged our marriage," Rob attested.

It also reaffirmed his attitude. One day on the beach he met a guy selling reggae CDs.

"You got any good ones?"

The very first one the reggae man handed over was called "Living in the Positive." Rob made his purchase. The CD fit right in with his Life is Good shirts and hats and The Good Life cologne he'd started wearing. "It was just a complete immersion in positive thinking," as Rob put it. Back home a few months later he participated in a local American Cancer Society "Relay for Life" with his cousin, police Lt. Greg Kosienski, who'd beaten prostate cancer.

"Whoever thought when we were kids we'd grow up to walk around this track as cancer survivors?" Rob asked his cousin.

Now the question was whether this cancer survivor should return to coaching. Health was the prime concern—not so much the tumor, but the tumor's collateral damage. Rob's stamina and short-term memory weren't the same. The blood clots had left some permanent damage in his lungs. He had resumed exercising, but could feel a tender spot in his chest when he was done. Also, his left knee was pretty shot. The cartilage on one side had deteriorated and he was looking at using orthodics to put off the knee-replacement surgery he knew was waiting down the road. The tumor had nothing to do with that, but it was another ailment on the list.

What to do? Rob soul-searched. He turned to his family. Diane and Jen had reservations. His sisters Sharon and Jan had reservations. But they all supported him. Diane's support was most vital. Rob was well aware Diane would once again be relegated to the back seat during the season.

For Diane, Rob's well-being came first. "Coaching will be good for you," she told him. Since the illness Diane had expected Rob to get more in tune with the spiritual side of life. He really hadn't, so he might as well go back to coaching.

"That's what you do best. You're good for the kids. That's probably the best place for you to be."

Would his health suffer from the stress and added workload? Everyone in Rob's family knew he'd go at it full bore. Jennifer, by then established in New York City as a freelance photographer, worried that her dad would take on too much. And yet she also believed this: Better to follow your passion and die too soon than be a shell of yourself and live too long. "When you love something that much and you're that successful at it and you've touched so many people's lives, you have to do it," she said.

Rob's sisters worried about the risk not just to his health, but his reputation. "Why do you want to put yourself out there again?" Sharon asked. "Why do you want to be vulnerable?"

In April, Diane and Rob had joined Sharon and her husband Mike for a few days in Florida. They had talked about taking a trip together to lush Sonoma Valley in California. Sharon now resigned herself to seeing Rob mostly at old muddy Ceppa Field in Meriden.

"Selfishly, I would rather not have you do it, but I know you love it," she said. "You'd rather die on the football field than play it safe and watch on the sidelines. Whatever you decide we'll support 100 percent. I want you to be happy."

What would the doctors say? Tom Tam often talked about how crucial it was for cancer patients to get back into the normal flow of life. "Bob," he'd say, "you no coach, you die."

Rob visited Yale-New Haven in early July. Dr. Piepmeier and Dr. Baehring gave the thumbs-up. The big dividing line with oligodendrogliomas was between high grade and low grade. So far, surgery and chemo had kept Rob in the latter camp. Maybe attitude had something to do with that, too. Maybe football would feed that healthy fire.

"You have a unique, mature, refreshing perspective on life," Dr. Piepmeier said. "You've been to a place we haven't gone. You basically put your life on the line and put your trust in us. I don't know if we're done treating this or not. I don't know if it's going to be six months from now or six years or we're done. But what I do know is you're doing great, you're functioning at a very high level and you want to get back into life. You want to get back to doing what you like to do. Why not? I like that. That's a great attitude. Do it."

Dr. Piepmeier, being a sharp guy, knew Rob would probably push too hard. Rob would have to recognize the signs when he overdid it—fatigue, headaches, seizures. "They're not dangerous. Just use good common sense," Piepmeier said. "You're a logical guy—and Diane will be all over you, too."

Dr. Baehring mentioned that stress alone probably wouldn't bring on seizures, that stress in combination with alcohol or lack of sleep should be avoided. The excitement of being back on the sidelines? That shouldn't hurt, Baehring said. It might even help.

What Rob didn't tell Piepmeier and Baehring that day at Yale-New Haven was that during June, when the accusations and newspaper stories were flying and tension in Meriden was high, his seizures had returned. He had three in as many days: one at home watching TV, one in his guidance office and one in a restaurant parking lot when Jen came up from New York and took him out to lunch for Father's Day. They weren't much as far as seizures go, but they were Rob's first simple-partials in over a month. He experienced that same distorted view and the heartbeats all through his arms, all pulsing at the same time.

He was annoyed. Just when it seemed he had hit upon the right balance in medication, the seizures returned. He'd started with Tegretol. When he supplemented the pills with the anti-epileptic herb taurine, he went four weeks without a seizure. Then a seizure specialist recommended by Dr. Baehring supplemented the Tegretol with another anti-seizure medication called Keppra. That combination kept Rob seizure-free for over a month. Then came the turbulence of June.

Rob was at least handling the anti-seizure medication well. The stuff can be pretty heavy. One guy in the Yale-New Haven support group mentioned he was taking 600 milligrams of anti-seizure medication a day and couldn't keep his head off his desk at work, he was so drowsy. Rob was at 2,150 milligrams a day and doing fine. Baehring said the medication shouldn't affect his ability to coach.

And when it came to coaching, Rob knew he still had the touch. After school let out for the summer, he helped run a football camp at Southern Connecticut State. It was hands-on stuff. Each day he noticed his stamina improving. Diane noticed. Rob looked revitalized.

His memory was good, too, at least on the football field. It never seemed to have slipped. One coach was describing his new zone blitz package and Rob recognized it right away. He'd been running it at Maloney four years ago. Another day Rob forgot his script for the quarterback drills, but found he could recall the routine by rote.

He'd come home at night, meet with me to work on the book and recount highlights from long-ago games. His eyes would widen behind his glasses and lock on a point in space, as if the game film flickering through his mind was playing there for all to see. Or he'd describe plays—coverage schemes, for example. He'd stand up and assume a defensive back's ready position. We'd be in the kitchen and he'd back pedal, cut left into the fridge, cut right into the stove, come rushing up, collide with the table. Mr. Diffley would bark and snatch up his toy football.

In late June, Rob served as site coordinator for the Connecticut Senior All-Star team, which practiced at Maloney in preparation for its annual summer game with Rhode Island. Rob had always been active in the game; he coached the Connecticut team in 2002. Simsbury High's Joe Grace was the head coach for 2004. On game day Rob went down to the locker room at Rentschler Field in East Hartford at halftime. One player, a running back bound for a Division I school, sat apart from the team, sulking. Berlin's John Capodice, one of the Connecticut assistants, asked Rob to talk to him.

Rob sidled up. "What's the matter?"

"Man, I ain't getting' the freakin' ball."

Low, quiet, but seething.

"Hey, I thought first thing Coach Grace asked was for everyone to leave their egos at the door."

Louder: "I did leave my ego at the door, but I ain't getting enough carries."

Guess what buddy, you didn't leave your ego at the door. But Rob didn't say that. The last thing the kid needed was criticism or someone in his face screaming "get your ass over here!" He would have simply shut down. Kids are surrounded by too much negativity, Rob reasoned. This one needed some empathy and support.

"I understand what's going through your mind. Your parents probably bought more tickets than any guy on this team and you've got a lot of people from your hometown sitting in the bleachers and you're feeling all that, aren't you?"

Anger ebbed. "Yeah. I want to play, Coach."

"You know what? Coach Grace is too smart a coach not to get you into this game. Now, I can't make statements for Coach Grace, but I know he's a smart coach and he's gonna get you into the game. The best thing you can do right now is get over there with the team and show Coach Grace you're with everybody."

So the player got up and rejoined the team. John Capodice sidled up to Rob.

"Coach, you've got such a knack with kids."

That was always Rob's strength, and surviving a brain tumor made him feel even more empowered as a motivator. Who couldn't he inspire? At the 2002 Thanksgiving game Rob saw his former player, Alexi Beltran, just before kickoff. He saw a fire in the kid's eyes, knew the kid needed just a little nudge to go into absolute hyper-drive. "Hey Lexi," Rob called out. "The opening kickoff, you're taking it all the way. All the way, Lexi, ALL THE WAY!"

Lexi went all the way.

As for the 2004 Spartans, they would be a project if Rob ever got the chance to lead them. There was no illusion about that. Maloney football had fallen behind, and not just because the team had gone 1-21 over the past two years. Spring practice had been discontinued when the fatal swear words flew. The traditional Green & White intra-squad scrimmage had been cancelled. Now it was summer. Other teams were heading off to camps and playing in passing leagues. They were lifting weights and working on speed development. The Spartans didn't even have a coach. They were losing valuable time.

There was a silver lining. Maloney's conference had been realigned by enrollment. Starting in the fall of 2004, the Spartans were no longer going to be grouped with the biggest schools. No more Southington, no more New Britain. The state playoff system had also been expanded. More postseason berths were to be had. Rob had visions of not only one state championship, but a whole string of them.

Of course, nothing guaranteed immunity from a losing season, and Rob recognized the inherent risk in returning. He was already in the state Coaches Hall of Fame. His record was a winning one. His program was clean. There was never a taint of scandal. He never had a player suffer a catastrophic injury. All that went back on the line the minute he stepped back on the sidelines. He'd also be opening himself up to criticism and cheap shots. Lord knows it wouldn't be long before some smart-ass in the stands would yap, "Hey Szymaszek, how much of your brain did they take out?"

Let 'em, Rob thought. Life is a series of risks, and he still had the ability to do something positive for kids. The window of opportunity wasn't all that wide. Only a few years remained before he could retire from education. But the window was open.

And it isn't about my reputation, Rob reminded himself. *It's about the kids.*

Just before school let out in June Rob could feel an energy building in the school.

"Are you going to be our new coach?" the kids would ask him.

The place is about to explode. I can feel it. Maloney football can be revived.

A solid coaching staff would be necessary to pull it off. Rob had never done it alone and couldn't now. The first call went to Mike Falis.

"If I decide to take this job, will you come back?"

Mike was enjoying the summer, enjoying time with his wife and family, with his three young grandchildren. One was the daughter Ryan Falis had left behind. Mike and Linda liked walking the grandkids down to a farm by their house to see the horses grazing at sunset. They'd bring treats and the horses would amble over for a snack. No rush, no hurry: a big summer sun going down. Mike had a taste of what he'd been missing in all those years of football. Still, he was torn.

"I don't know. I don't know. I look at my grandkids playing and I want to still be able to do that, spend time with them."

Rob played with the telephone cord, gazing out his back window. In winter, when the leaves were off the trees, a slice of the Maloney practice field could be seen through binoculars. Right now, the trees were in full summer swell, with nothing to be seen beyond the back deck, the shed, the pool and the hot tub.

"Yeah, I know how you feel."

It took a few more calls. Mike knew what would be sacrificed if he went back. He also knew what could be shared again.

"All right, I'll go back," Mike finally said. "But I'm giving you one year and one year only. You better find some young kid I can fasten to my side and I'll teach him everything I know in a year."

When Mike told his wife Linda it would be just one year, she chuckled. She remembered Mike saying "just one year" when he first signed on with Rob in 1984.

Rob remembered, too, and he remembered all that followed. On the day Mike said "yes," Rob updated his coaching resume. He turned it in at the Board of Education office two minutes before the deadline to apply.

"I'm going for it," he told Diane as he headed out the door. "I think it's going to happen."

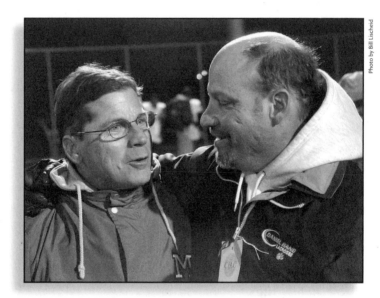

Rob and Steve Filippone

CHAPTER 14

Goal Line Stand

YOU'D THINK WITH Rob's resume in the ring, the Maloney coaching appointment would be automatic. It wasn't.

Not everyone was on his side. Not everyone was impressed with 26 years of coaching, a 160-91-13 record and a place in the state Coaches Hall of Fame. Not everyone was moved by the thought of a remarkable comeback story. Some people were furious with the firing of the previous coach, and the rumor was at least one highly placed politician on the Meriden Board of Education didn't want Rob back at all.

In regard to the latter, it may have been due to a fight instigated by Rob.

Amid the heavy newspaper reporting that followed the firing of Rob's successor in June, the chairman of the Meriden Board of Education, Frank Kogut, was quoted in the Meriden *Record-Journal* saying "I don't give a damn if this waits until August. I don't see any urgency."

Rob read that and raged. *August?* That would be too late. Even if hired immediately, the new coach would have to hit the ground at full sprint to make up for the time lost from spring practice and summer workouts, and even then he was under the gun. It would be impossible. Wait until August and the program would be crippled.

So on the night of the Maloney graduation ceremonies, when

Rob saw Kogut in the school hallway, he strode right up to him and it wasn't to inquire after the chairman's health.

"Hey Frank, that was the most irresponsible comment I have ever heard from a Board of Ed member," Rob said. "If I was the parent of a Maloney football player and my son got hurt, I would hold you personally responsible."

Rob strode away and didn't give the confrontation a second thought. In his mind, it was the right thing to say.

The gauntlet, however, had been thrown. Kogut wasn't one to just let something like that slide. He owned a large nursery business in town. In land-poor Meriden, it was like a fiefdom. He was the long-time school board chairman. He was the kind of guy accustomed to controlling the strings and unafraid to speak his mind.

Rob's first inkling that he had a fight on his hands came when the coaching search was extended outside Maloney. The position had been first opened up to employees in the school district. That's standard operating procedure in high school sports. Faculty gets first crack. Union rules typically call for it, and so does common sense. In-house coaches make for a tighter ship. Certification, communication and the reins of control are easier to manage.

The Maloney football posting netted two applicants: Rob and the guy who had just been fired. Mary Cortright, the school superintendent, spoke with Greg Shugrue, Maloney's first-year principal, and the posting went back up, this time statewide.

"The principal certainly consulted with me and we decided there should be a larger pool of candidates," Cortright told the *Record-Journal*. "I think it's always good to have a large comparison."

It was a principal's right to expand a job search, and Rob's health was a legitimate concern, but had Shugrue done it on his own volition or was someone else calling the shots? When asked about it by the *Record-Journal*, Shugrue was reticent at first, then angry.

"Lou Holtz didn't get this much press when he resigned from Notre Dame," he barked at a reporter. "Are you kidding me with this?"

Rob was hearing that Kogut was the power player and he took it as a shot across his bow. Let's flush him out, Rob thought. *If Kogut is going to chop my legs off behind the scenes, let's make him do it in public.* So Rob released a statement to the *Record-Journal* fingering the chairman as the guy pulling a power play behind the coaching hire.

"It appears Mr. Kogut can intimidate a lot of people. Since I believe he was responsible for having the Maloney football position re-opened because he felt there wasn't a qualified individual applying for the position (our differences are well documented). Well, he doesn't intimidate me and that is why I am speaking out. The kids and parents of our students deserve better leadership from their board president."

Kogut shot back, and in his denial he flat-out said Rob should not be hired.

"I'm very surprised that a guidance counselor and a past coach would make those accusations," Kogut told the *Record-Journal*. "I think it's very unprofessional and he should be ashamed of himself. He can say what he wants and he can make accusations, but they are not true."

"Does he think he intimidates me?" Kogut added. "He's got some nerve to make those accusations. He's making them about the wrong guy . . . I would never recommend him to be coach."

There it was, all out in the open, served up on the morning

of June 23 in black and white on Meriden breakfast tables. Hot days in a small city hornet's nest: The summer of contention buzzed on.

In time, Rob suspected he made a bad play here. He didn't calculate just how much heat Kogut might bring to bear—not on Rob, but on the people responsible for hiring the next Maloney football coach.

"I want you to be my football coach," Rob says Shugrue initially told him, and the principal was heading the search committee that would interview candidates, then pass a recommendation on to the school board for official approval.

Rob liked Shugrue. He was a football guy, had done some assistant coaching. He had just finished his first year at Maloney and Rob was looking forward to working with him. It looked good, but the landscape was shifting. Rob heard more rumblings. Word was Shugrue's job was on the line if the coaching recommendation had Szymaszek's name on it. Rob was not even to be interviewed.

Shugrue called Rob at home. "You're not a viable candidate."

"What does 'viable' mean?"

Shugrue wouldn't go into details. Rob hung up the phone in almost slow motion. Diane read his face, went to him, embraced him.

"Di, I could lose anything in life, I could lose the football position. As long as I have you, I'm going to be fine."

But Rob was a battler. The game wasn't over just because of one deep strike. The next day he met with an administrator in the school district's central office, who asked Rob if the brain tumor had ever affected his job performance. The guy knew the answer. Rob's personnel files were clean. He hadn't taken a single day off while undergoing chemo. He'd done it, aside from a matter of pride and principle, to pre-empt this very question. All of a sudden the talk was about job performance? If there were questions regarding job performance, Rob wondered, shouldn't they have come up sooner?

Strange. Rob had stuck it out through chemotherapy. He had not cashed in sick days. He had not retired early. He met the demands of his job. *Now I'm being kicked in the ass? Thank you very much.*

Forces were being mobilized from unclear directions. Rob dug in. Compared to a brain tumor, this opponent wasn't daunting. Compared to the fight back from surgery and the blood clots, compared to the 10 rounds of chemo, this fight was easy. Rob did resent having to fight it, though, and I didn't blame him. The situation was so straightforward, so logical. Rob was the guy to coach Maloney football. He had done it extremely well for 26 years. It had taken cancer to chase him from the field. Now a few well-placed opponents appeared to be doing everything in their power to keep the obvious decision from being made. Small-city politics at their worst, another mid-day train backing up traffic in the center of town, with eyes seeing nothing but the tracks.

Many of Rob's coaching colleagues were incensed. From Madison, Hand High School coach Steve Filippone, who was about to embark on a season that would culminate in a state championship and Connecticut's overall No. 1 ranking, wrote a letter to the *Record-Journal*. Steve began by mentioning he had known Rob for 25 years, through times of tragedy and triumph.

In all those years I have yet to meet a more principled, compassionate and hard working man. It is inconceivable that any list of candidates for this position could contain the name of someone who is better suited for this position. I suggest that the powers-that-be put aside whatever it is that compels them to take their current stance. Many school systems are experiencing difficulties related to the hiring and retention of qualified coaches. In this case, Meriden has a candidate whose career could stand as the basis for the training of young coaches all over the country. I should know because I have always been a student of Rob's philosophy both on and off the field.

A flood of letters would not have changed the tide. Rob was out. He had called Kogut out on the night of graduation. Was he now paying for it? Rob empathized with the people reportedly being squeezed, but he was also aggravated. When attacked, Rob prided himself on being a bulldog, especially when he felt he was in the right. Standing in Shugrue's office one July morning, Rob's anger rose. It annoyed him that this young, promising guy he liked so much seemed to be caving in. He wanted Shugrue to stand up, square his shoulders and say "Szymaszek's going to be my coach whether you like it or not."

But Rob also looked at the framed pictures on the principal's desk—a pretty wife, smiling young children. *His job is supposedly on the line over this?* Rob thought about his dad, how Bob Szymaszek would always take a stand, even if it was against the chief of police. He thought about the coaching staff he had waiting in the wings and what it could do for the football program, the positive effect it would immediately have. *We're going to keep all that from happening?*

No, Rob concluded striding from Shugrue's office, that wasn't going to happen. He was a candidate. He was *the* candidate.

* * *

On the morning of July 8, Rob got a phone call from Shugrue summoning him to the school. He was one of five applicants being interviewed.

None of the other candidates were at Maloney when Rob showed up. He sat down with Shugrue and Don Panciera, the assistant principal who was once his assistant coach. Also in on the interview was one of the team's two senior captains. The second captain showed up later, when the session was almost over. The school's athletic director, another first-year administrator, was not present.

Rob went in bustling with his usual energy and optimism. He laid out what he would do if hired. He'd meet with players and parents to explain his vision of where the program was going. He'd answer any questions about the mess Maloney football had just endured. He'd make it clear he did not undermine his successor. He'd make it clear this was a brand new day.

"How long would it take to turn around the program?" he was asked.

"I believe the future is now."

If hired, Rob would inherit a losing program just like he did in 1976. This would be a trickier deal. The 1976 team was ripe for a winning attitude. There was none of the discord that now surrounded the program. There had been so much wrangling in the press. On the field, Maloney's once-proud program was now considered among the worst in the state. In Rob's estimation, it was at an all-time low.

There was, however, precedent for an immediate turnaround. Ed McGee once went 1-7-1. That was in 1958, the year Meriden split into two high schools. The next year, McGee and the Spartans went 9-0. That 1959 team out-scored its opponents 228-26 and was still considered the best in school history. If Rob were coaching he'd dig that story up and trumpet it around the locker room and in every team huddle. *How about it? It's happened before. Let's go from worst to first.* That would be the rallying cry.

"Kids are looking for something to hang their hats on," Rob explained. "As a coach, you're looking for anything to make them believe in themselves."

He wanted to provide the same positive mindset he tried to

provide for himself while bouncing back from surgery and going through chemo. It was Spartan Pride's turn to go through recovery. That recovery could be quick and it could be complete. Rob told his interviewers he was coming back with high aspirations, returning with the same attitude Lance Armstrong took back to cycling. The Spartans weren't just going to be good, they were going to be great. Lance had just embarked on the 2004 Tour de France, which he would win for a record sixth time. Well, the Spartans would be going after Meriden's first-ever state championship in football and then they'd go back for more. They had that new league alignment. They'd be playing schools their own size. They had a good group of kids coming up, kids who had enjoyed success in youth football. They had a good coaching staff. What's the state record for consecutive wins? The Spartans would go after that. Just like Lance, if Rob got a second chance, he'd do it even better than before.

"Be prepared," he had told Diane. "If we go back this time it's going to be like nothing you've seen."

Rob got fired up as the interview moved along. He felt he answered all the questions well. Moreover, he was the only "in-house" candidate being interviewed. That worked in his favor. If there were problems with any of the players, be they academic or behavioral, he could jump on them right away just like he used to.

Leaving the interview room, Rob believed he'd hit a grand slam, that he'd touched every base. He'd soon realize that he struck out, that he was doomed to strike out before he even came to the plate.

* * *

The phone rang within minutes of his return home. It was Shugrue. He wanted to see Rob at school the following afternoon.

"I think we've arrived at a resolution," the principal said.

Was the job his? Rob tried to read Shugrue's voice, but it was noncommittal. Rob couldn't cipher what was up.

That same morning, Diane had been down at MidState Medical Center undergoing follow-up tests after a mammogram had revealed some suspect shadows. The tests went well and the concerns proved unfounded. Rob hugged Diane as she came through the door. She seemed to almost collapse from the released tension.

"Oh, man, that was scary," she said.

I was at Rob's house that morning and it annoyed me he hadn't been down at the hospital with Diane. Rob seemed to regret it, too, later saying how in the instant he held Diane he was again reminded that if he didn't get the coaching job, it wasn't the end of the world. Hadn't Diane been one of the reasons he had walked away in 2001? All those dinners left in the oven, the lost late summer days? And then all the hospital vigils? If Rob was fated not to return to football, Diane was more than ample consolation.

Diane lingered in Rob's embrace. Then she made a passing remark that immediately shed light on the coaching situation.

"While I was at MidState, I saw Bob Zito in the emergency room."

"Bob Zito?"

"Yeah, his son had gotten bit by a spider or something. I was joking with him. 'What, Bob, is this the closest hospital?' He said he was in Meriden on business. He asked how you were doing."

Zito was a long-time member of the Connecticut coaching fraternity. He had lived in Meriden for 20 years—for a while right down the street from the Szymaszeks—and his son had played for Rob. Zito had since relocated to the southwest part of the state, living in Derby and coaching at Weston High School. Prior to that he'd been at Newtown, where from 1990 to 1992 his teams went to three straight state Class MM championship games, winning two. He'd also spent a year in Stratford, at the same school where Shugrue had been a teacher before moving on to Maloney. In fact, Shugrue had been one of Zito's assistant coaches.

It was clear to Rob what Zito's business was in Meriden: an interview. If Shugrue was indeed under the gun, squeezed from above, or if he were concerned about Rob's health, it seemed logical that he had turned to a proven coach he knew.

Later that afternoon, while working the football camp at Southern Connecticut State, Rob's hunch was confirmed. A few of the coaches said Zito had applied for the Maloney position. "It wouldn't bother me to lose out to Bob Zito because the kids will be in good hands," Rob told the guys. "The kids are going to be coached up; the kids are going to have a good head coach."

There was more information forthcoming when he got home that night. Rob made a few well-placed phone calls. He had to know the exact lay of the land. Did he have any chance to get his job back? A member of the school board told Rob that Kogut had lined up enough votes to block his appointment. (Had he? Kogut didn't return phone calls for the book.)

Rob hung up and thought it out. Even if he could somehow reverse the vote and get the job, the resulting situation would be unbearable. Shugrue would be in the crosshairs and so would Rob. This wasn't farfetched speculation. The more I saw of the Meriden Board of Education, the more I was amazed at the degree of its meddling and micro-managing. For good or for ill, individual members got involved in personal crusades. Rob would be eligible for retirement in three years. Would he be walking on eggshells until then? Rob figured he'd be watched constantly. Any minute during the school day not devoted to guidance counseling would probably be duly noted and stockpiled in a personnel file. So would any slip-up. He wondered if he'd even suffer for going the extra mile. His guidance door was open to all students, whether they were his counselees or not. He didn't think twice about getting involved in social cases. Would he catch flak for seeing a kid not in his group, for getting involved in a family crisis?

Extra pressure would lurk at every turn. It was a stress Rob didn't need. It would not be good for his health; it would not be good for his family. He thought briefly about filing a union grievance, but then let it go. Too much carnage. Too much time, too. If Rob took that route the team would suffer, and the team had already missed valuable spring and summer preparation.

Besides, Bob Zito *was* a good candidate. Rob hadn't slung around any B.S. at camp that afternoon. He was comfortable having Zito coach at Maloney. In time, I came to believe Shugrue had found a workable solution to (if the talk were true) an impossible situation. Rob wasn't so sure and never would be. Kogut swore he wasn't pulling any strings to the same school board member who had told Rob about the votes. Did that mean Shugrue manufactured a smokescreen to get his man Zito in the door? Would a first-year principal really be able to pull something like that off? Would he have the audacity?

Many questions, few answers. Bottom line: returning to coaching was not meant to be for Coach Smaz. He rationalized: *Kick back and remember all the sacrifices Diane has made.* With that, it seemed very clear and very easy. He found himself relieved it was over. The emotions of the past three weeks had been draining, perhaps more so on Diane. She's tapped into the harmonies of life. She has no stomach or patience for controversy. She hated seeing Rob get so worked up, so agitated. What she liked was having Rob around the house. She liked doing things together. There would have been no time for that if Rob had gone back to football.

"I'm not disappointed," Rob told Diane. "This is good for our relationship right now."

Diane had long arrived at that conclusion. "If you had returned to coaching, you would have done it, but I think it would have taken a big toll on you. I'm glad the way it's turned out. I'm relieved. I'm just glad it's over."

Rob did want to walk out with dignity. As much as he respected and liked Zito, it was demeaning to lose out to another candidate for a position he once held longer and better than anyone in city history. That night, Rob sat down and spent hours working on a public statement announcing he was pulling out of consideration and endorsing Bob Zito.

The first draft he drew up laid the whole sordid story right out on the table. There was no soft-pedaling. Rob was going down swinging. A few friends deemed the draft too harsh, however, so he tempered it, and then sent it to the Meriden *Record-Journal*.

I have given 31 years of my heart and soul to this community. I have battled back from a life-threatening illness and haven't missed a day of work due to this illness in the last two and half years. Throughout these wonderful years my desire has been to serve the students at Maloney High School in every way I can.

The events of recent days have led me to regretfully withdraw my name as candidate for the head football position at Maloney. I am pleased to announce that there is a candidate who is competently qualified to return Maloney football back to its successful heritage, and that person is Bob Zito.

I regret that the selection of our football coach and my being a candidate for that position has resulted in such high emotions on the part of some people.

Decisions in the educational process are difficult enough without personal attacks and negative supposition. Certainly I do not wish to be the cause of difficulty and conflict in the high school where I have spent the best years of my life. My love for Maloney High School and football had prompted me to apply for this position, but those same feelings tell me that in the best interest of all concerned I must withdraw my application.

It is my most fervent prayer that the Maloney family, students, teachers, administrators and the community of Meriden support Coach Zito and together we will see the Maloney football program return to statewide respectability.

Rob liked the way it read. I did, too.

By then we were doing a lot of writing. We were working on this book, and we watched our fairy-tale ending flutter away.

CHAPTER 15

In His Corner

I've seen fire and I've seen rain.—James Taylor

* * *

THE STORY WAS played up big in the next day's Meriden *Record-Journal.* The headlines ran across the top of the lead sports page.

SZYMASZEK BACKS OFF GRID JOB
Withdraws name, promotes Weston's Zito for next Maloney coach

At Rob's house that Saturday morning, the telephone rang steadily.

"My son's in tears," said the mother of one player. "And the newspaper got the headline wrong. It should be, 'MALONEY LOSES BELOVED COACH AGAIN.' "

Alluding to the all-too-public infighting and politicking that had transpired, Rob explained to another caller how important it was to smooth the way for the new coach. Rob, of course, was also rationalizing to himself.

"I'm not disappointed; I'm not embittered," he told me that morning. "You know, it took a long way to get back to where I am. I feel like I made it. If I took on the job, the scrutiny they would have given me would have been unbelievable. I don't need that."

I commiserated and sympathized with Rob. I didn't want him to feel bad; I didn't want him to have regrets. But I was angry and so were plenty of others. A few days earlier I had spoken to Ron Carbone. As usual, Rob's wise old mentor saw the big picture. "I really get upset when I hear about people in power who are susceptible to all the human iniquities," Carbone said. "These people make decisions that affect a lot of people. You know who's getting hurt: the kids at Maloney High School."

As upbeat and assured as Rob sounded to callers that Saturday morning, you better believe he had mixed emotions. He slept badly the previous night. He watched the clock pass minute by minute from 3 to 4 a.m., the red numbers silently burning in the dark.

Rob was relieved the whole episode was over, but he was down. He knew Bob Zito would be good for the job—he had no doubt about that—but also he knew how good he would have been for the kids, how much knowledge and experience and passion he would have brought back to the field.

But what about the brain tumor? The tumor was always lurking. That morning, Rob was scheduled to have one of his regular MRIs over at MidState Medical Center. I picked him up and Rob took the newspaper along for the ride. The full text of his statement had been published. He re-read it and the accompanying story en route to the hospital. Early morning sunlight washed through the car, glinted off Rob's eyeglasses, played off the western ridges.

At the hospital SZYMASZEK BACKS peaked from the folded paper beneath Rob's arm as we approached the front desk of the radiology department.

"Name, please?" he was asked.

206

MRIs had become routine. Have a seat. Sign the form. Right this way. Remove shoes and socks. Remove belt and all metal. Place wallet, keys and jewelry in the tray.

"Are you metal free?" asked the nurse.

Rob slipped off his Hall of Fame ring.

"I am now."

A new technician—or at least one Rob hadn't worked with before—was running the show. His name was Mark, but Rob kept calling him Peter. A little bit of that short-term memory loss, maybe. Or maybe Rob was thinking of Peter DeBona. He'd be seeing him in a few days at the next brain tumor support group meeting down at Yale-New Haven. Good old Pete DeBona. *No business, no job, no title, no office.* Or maybe Rob was thinking of Pete Sini. "Papa Pete" had part of his lung removed when cancer recurred in 2003 and was now undergoing a new round of chemo. A spot had been found on his kidney. He was 84 years old and still battling—and still willing to help the Spartans. If Rob had returned to coaching, Pete would have returned as senior advisor. Rob asked him to.

"Yeah, I'll go back," Papa Pete had said. "Even the way I am, I'll go back. The chemo knocks the heck out of you."

"Are you going to have the strength?"

"Yeah, I'll go back."

"You can't keep good men down, Pete. You beat it twice; you'll beat it a third time."

Along with the newspaper, Rob had brought a James Taylor CD, the one he always brought to his MRIs. The room is equipped with a stereo and Rob would use the passing songs to keep track of where he was in the test. Despite the whiteness and bright lights of the MRI tube, despite the little overhead mirror that enables you to see into the control room where the technician is working, it's like being in a crypt—and you're in there for about

20 minutes. Rob had me try it out. I lay down and they slid me in. Pure claustrophobia: As calm as I tried to remain, breathing was quickly disrupted and I was relieved when the bed slid back out of the tube after a just a minute or two.

"Good news, Bry!" Rob called out. "You handled the MRI fine. Bad news is you have a brain tumor."

Learn to enjoy your brain tumor, as Pete DeBona had quipped. Listening to Rob's giggles, looking at his impish little boy's smile, I wondered, *Is this really true? How can it be? How can this guy be afflicted?*

But he was.

"I need you to lie completely still," Mark said when the jokes were over and it was time for the real test.

Mark was a nice, friendly guy. Rob gave him the James Taylor CD. Mark closed a headset over Rob's face and into the tube he went.

The music started up with the hum and drone of the MRI. The light touches of "Something in the Way She Moves" floated above the deep rumblings of the machine.

Rob said he's gotten much better at listening to lyrics.

"There's something in the way she moves or looks my way or calls my name that seems to leave this troubled world behind.

If I'm feeling down and blue or troubled by some foolish game she always seems to make me change my mind."

Rob used to sometimes listen to that song after a loss in football. Diane was always there. Those Saturday night dinners to take the sting away . . .

Rob thought about how it would be OK not to coach. Diane would not be put on the shelf August through November. There would not be that intense scrutiny on the job. There would be no added pressure threatening his health. Who needed it? Diane would be happy.

"And I feel fine anytime she's around me now; she's around me now almost all the time.

And if I'm well you can tell she's been with me now; she's been with me now quite a long, long time. And I feel fine."

Songs and minutes drifted. The bed slid out of the MRI tube. The first round of images had been taken. Now the tracing element—gadolinium—had to be injected for the second round. There's a lot of it; the needle is long. The gadolinium would collect around any cancer cells in Rob's brain and make them show up brighter on the scans, which would contrast with the batch of pictures taken before the injection.

"I know you can't say, Peter, but how do the pictures look?" Rob asked the technician.

"It's Mark."

"Oh, geez, I'm sorry."

They laughed as Mark tied the tourniquet onto his upper arm.

"Mark, you guys love my veins."

Out came the long needle.

"You'll feel a little stick."

Mark was smooth with the needle.

"Life is still good," Rob said as he closed his eyes, and then he disappeared back into the tube.

The machine's deep droning resumed.

I've seen fire and I've seen rain, James Taylor sang.

After the MRI was finished we picked up some coffee and poppy seed bagels at a little stand inside the hospital. The two girls behind the counter were Maloney students. One of them smiled and spoke right up.

"You were in the paper today, Mr. Szymaszek."

"Did you see that? I thought that was the best thing to do. What do you think?"

"I think it's good."

She handed Rob the bagels.

"Did you want to see me come back to coach?"

"I think so."

The girl getting the coffee spoke up. "I liked you as coach."

She sealed the lid on the cup nice and tight.

"Girls, you just made my day," Rob said, and we were on our way.

Rob had bought an extra coffee and poppy seed bagel for his dad. We would be passing by his nursing home. Bob Szymaszek had continued to live with Diane and Rob until his body deteriorated to the point where it was better for him to be in a nursing home. Fortunately, there was one right down the street from the house, no more than two minutes away.

We drove. Rob said he believed his dad was still happy. Bob was 82. Fourteen years had passed since the stroke, seven since Millie died. He'd had some pretty good years. Rob's sisters, Sharon and Jan, still visited from out of state at least once or twice a month. There was no longer any need to count pills or help prepare meals as they had done when Bob was at Rob's house, but Sharon and Jan still visited regularly.

"It's only natural," Rob said. "It's just out of love and respect for one of the greatest dads that lives on this earth."

Bob must have known we'd be stopping in early that day. He was in his wheelchair in the hallway outside his room, smiling, wearing shorts and the same buzz cut he had when he was a cop.

"Dad!"

"Oh, God, Jesus Cah-rist."

"How are ya, Dad?"

Rob kissed his father and wheeled him into his room and began preparing his coffee and bagel. Framed family photos

Rob with Bob Szymaszek

overlapped on the dresser: Sharon and Jan, their husbands, their kids, Diane and Rob, Jennifer, Millie and Bob. There was even one of Mr. Diffley. The picture board Diane had made was perched on a bedside table.

"You want a little creamer?"

"Ah-ha."

"Did you see the newspaper today, Dad? No? I took my name out. How do you feel about that?"

"Aagh," Bob rasped, but with an unmistakable inflection. There was no need to consult the picture board.

"You're happy, Dad?"

"Eaaghh!"

"Okay! You had some concerns?"

"*Aaagh*-ha."

"You did have some concerns."

"Agh-ha-*ha*."

"You didn't tell me, though."

211

"Ah-*ha*-ha."

"You were going to let me do what I wanted to do, huh?"

"Ah-*haa*."

Bob's eyes twinkled. I do believe Bob was busting Rob's ass, as if to say, *you're a big boy now, son, you don't need me driving after you when you stray from home . . . and this time you're buying the vanilla cream soda.*

Rob spread the butter. "But you feel good now that I'm not gonna to do it?"

"Ah-ha."

"And I'm gonna be able to spend some more time with Diane?"

"Aaagh-ha!"

"And I won't get sick? That's what you were concerned about, huh?"

Bob was chuckling and Rob laughed, too.

"You're a son of a gun. You didn't tell me. See what a great dad you are?"

They laughed. Bob wasn't going to tell Rob not to do it. Not Bob. When had Bob dictated?

"So it looks like I'll stay a high school guidance counselor. Just like you stayed a sergeant when you should have been chief of police."

"Oh, God, Jesus Cah-rist."

But Bob was smiling, laughing.

"You and me, Dad, we always tell it like it is, right?"

"Jesus Cah-rist."

"But you know what? We can look ourselves in the mirror."

"Aaagh."

"You know?"

"Aaaagh."

"You know that, Pops? And we can sleep comfortably at night, can't we?"

"Aaaagh-a!"

"I love ya, Dad."

"Aaagh."

* * *

Rob had tried to reach Mike Falis all day on Friday while he wrestled with the decision to pull out. They never made contact. As a result, Mike didn't get word until he read Saturday's paper. Even then, he couldn't believe it. Last he'd heard from Rob, the interview had gone well and things were looking good.

Rob went out Saturday afternoon. When he got home around twilight Mike was waiting on the back porch. They popped some beers. Rob felt himself getting emotional almost immediately.

"Is it true?" Mike asked.

"I'm not the candidate."

"You're not the candidate? You gotta be kidding me."

Mike's voice rose with his anger.

"What's wrong with these people? Can I give these people some film to watch? You take 25 to 30 kids and you look on the other sideline and there's Southington with 100 kids and New Britain with 90 kids and we battled them year in, year out. And you're not the best candidate? WHAT IS WRONG WITH THESE PEOPLE?"

Half the neighborhood had to have heard that. Once Rob explained the politics that drove the situation, Mike understood and calmed down, but only a little.

"You should have sent that first letter to the newspaper," he said.

Rob felt bad for Mike. Once he'd been swayed, Mike was as excited as Rob to return to football. Rob had called one night earlier in the week and Mike was watching game films he'd ordered from a coach they knew at Michigan State. "Hey, you get the job, Szymaszek, and I've got to brush up. I forget things easily."

Actually, Mike hadn't forgotten, hadn't forgotten a thing. All the endless practice and preparation: Every ounce of it so worthwhile once Friday night rolled around and the team gathered and the lockers rattled and the pads went on and the bus pulled up and the field lights went on.

Now their lights would remain dark.

Twilight was falling. The trees were full. The panoramic view of the city from Rob's back porch was lost.

"It looks like the Falis-Szymaszek reunion won't take place," Mike said.

Rob studied his partner.

"Hey, Mike, I can see the disappointment in your eyes."

He could see tears, too, welling up as readily as when Mike put his son's football jacket on the fire at that last Burning of the Shoe. *"I never would have made it through last year without you guys."* Rob felt himself choking up, his voice breaking.

"I let you down."

"Rob, you did what you had to do. You did the right thing."

"Thank you."

"I mean it. You were going to fight this thing and maybe not get it anyway and cause your health to get worse. All it was going to be was mud-slinging."

"I know."

"Who knows?" he said, "Maybe there will be another day."

Maybe.

It felt good to talk to Mike, but Rob was down as soon as he left. He felt like he'd just lost on Thanksgiving. *I should have hung in there and battled.*

He didn't feel much better Sunday morning.

"I should have sent that other letter. I should have called it like it was. I should have dared the consequences rather than live like so many spineless people who only worry about protecting themselves and their jobs."

"What about the scrutiny and the stress?" I asked.

"I would rather die of a brain tumor, fighting the good fight, than succumb to injustice."

Rob railed, he paced. He recited his favorite quote, the one from Teddy Roosevelt about how it's not the critic who counts, but the man in the arena, for even if he fails he has dared greatness. His soul will never mingle with the timid, who knew neither victory nor defeat. He talked about how the Lord put him on this earth to have the courage to confront injustice, to call it out, just like Bob Szymaszek had always done.

"Did I duck the challenge here?"

Did he?

Later, I talked with Steve Hoag, the defensive coordinator. Steve remarked that the coaching upheaval was probably harder on Rob than the brain tumor. He'd seldom been so criticized before. He'd seldom been so attacked. He'd seldom heard words questioning his performance. And who were his enemies and who were his friends? In the battle against cancer, that was never in doubt.

Doubts: They hounded Rob that summer. Whenever he succeeded in beating them down and was certain he'd made the right move, they came rushing right back at him.

Before Mike had left that Saturday night, Diane had taken a picture of him and Rob. You can see the tears in Mike's eyes. He was trying to smile, but his face looked like it was about to just burst and wash away. Rob had a strong, yet limp arm draped around Mike's shoulder, looking somewhat dazed as if he'd just smashed into a wide receiver and been shaken up on the play and needed help getting off the field.

"Rob, you did what you had to do."

Twilight filtered through the wall of trees behind them. The city was lost from view, and with it the practice field behind Maloney High School down at the bottom of the hill, down the 33 steps, down past the tree where Ed McGee had stood and Bob Szymaszek had sat, down to the field where Rob and Mike had played as boys and led as men until, on a cold November night, with scars so fresh and permanent, they had burned a jacket and a shirt and left the ashes behind.

But what was ever permanent? Did it have to end there?

Look at the picture. They are trying to smile, but there are Mike's tears, so very clear and forever welling.

F·R·I·E·N·D·S·H·I·P

**"Of All Blessings That Time And Earth Bestow,
There Is None So Precious As
One True Friend."**

Rob and Mike Falis, July 10, 2004

CHAPTER 16

Away & Home Again

"Hello, I'm Rob Szymaszek. September 2001 I was diagnosed with an oligodendroglioma, grade 2. One operation, one round of chemo. Life is still good."

* * *

In 2004, the National Cancer Institute and American Cancer Society were estimating 18,400 new cases of brain cancer would be diagnosed during the year. One new case was Noreen, a mother of two who paid her first visit to the Yale-New Haven brain tumor support group on the afternoon of July 13.

Noreen had been diagnosed the previous week and had already undergone surgery to remove a glioblastoma measuring two centimeters. The surgeons did a good job. They didn't remove any more of her shoulder-length brown hair than necessary. Thanks to some deft touches with a hair brush on her part, you couldn't tell Noreen had undergone any sort of procedure. Nor could you tell Noreen had cancer treatment looming in her immediate future, but she did.

Noreen was scheduled to start radiation, so she had plenty of questions for the support group that afternoon. These were the people to ask. There was Peter DeBona, just back from a fishing trip to Lake Champlain. Tanned arms and vacation photographs poked out of his black short-sleeved shirt, the surgical scar on his shaved head the only visible testament to what brain cancer put him through 10 years earlier. A moustache and goatee give Peter's face the touch of an outlaw, yet his demeanor would make him a great bedside doctor. His eyes have the twinkle of a child and the long stare of a thinker, his voice the cadence of a stream.

"There's nothing scary about radiation," he told Noreen. "It doesn't hurt at all. Little bit noisy, takes about 15 minutes, of which the radiation itself is less than two minutes. Most of it is lining up the beam of radiation."

Peter knew the ins and outs. He'd been there, lying on that table as the big machine hovered and whirred above him and the lasers threw crosshairs on his skull.

"About halfway through, regardless of how many weeks you go, you'll find yourself getting tired. With some people it's fatigue; other people don't feel it as much. When you're tired, take a nap. Conversely, when you're not tired, do something. You don't want muscles to atrophy. The good news is, once radiation is finished it dissipates and within a couple of months you'll feel like yourself.

"Noreen," he added. "Don't stop having fun. Just enjoy what you can. Why deprive yourself? You're deprived of enough things with this tumor."

All the support group members chimed in, and it made for a meeting more upbeat than usual. People like speaking from experience; people like to help and offer hope. It provides a sense of purpose. What better way to invigorate the spirit?

The mood spread around that big table made of smaller tables pushed together. Jane, one year removed from surgery, was looking good. She had an MRI scheduled for that day. Elias, treated for anaplastic astrocytoma in 1999, was doing well—on break from work and chowing down a hefty lunch.

There was Faye, and Faye wasn't so upbeat, at least at first.

Her glioblastoma had been removed in early March and she wore a kerchief to cover the residual bald spots from the radiation treatments that had followed. Quiet and withdrawn, she'd entered the room sullen and seemed determined to remain sullen, but the humor and camaraderie got to her, too. She brightened within the hour.

Common bonds: It was good to talk. David, an older, husky man who had been diagnosed with a glioblastoma two years earlier, recently suffered a grand mal seizure and was having a tough time with anti-seizure medication.

"This becomes like a family," David's strained, yet indomitably chipper wife Shoshe told Noreen. "You see people over and over, day in, day out."

There was little gloom and doom on this day. There was a lot of laughter, even from Tom, who was in a wheelchair. He tried updating the group on his condition, but his wife kept interrupting.

"Hey," he finally spouted. "What am I here for?"

Peter giggled. "He's getting better."

"Expect that every time, Tom," Rob chimed in.

Peter kept digging. "Tom, don't let her ever stop you. And when she's talking, interrupt her."

"You sound much better, Tom, than the last time you were with us," said Betsey D'Andrea, the neuro-oncology department's clinical coordinator who ran the support group sessions.

"Ah, thank you," Tom said. "I feel better mentally and in other areas."

The group moved on to other topics: medications and their side-effects, listening to music during MRIs, alternative medicine, religion. Noreen got her boost, and yet she didn't really need a big one. She'd been over medical hurdles before. Both of her sons had suffered from cystic fibrosis when they were younger.

"Some people say, 'Why is God doing this to you guys?' I don't believe God is doing this," Noreen told the group. "You're handed cards and these are the cards we're playing out and I think God's going to help. He's helped my boys. Now I'm hoping He continues his good work."

"Amen, Noreen," said Rob. "Stay in the positive; life is still good."

There was a blue note. Rob's friend Andrea Mann wasn't there. Rob was anxious to see her. A few days earlier he had called only to learn Andrea was back on chemo. Her cancer had grown more aggressive and she was participating in a new trial treatment offered out of Massachusetts General Hospital. Andrea was able to take it at home. A port had been implanted in her chest; an IV line hooked directly into it. The stuff was potent. When Rob called, Andrea came to the phone, but sounded utterly wiped. The conversation was brief, a damper on the day.

The same tumor, the same exact tumor.

"These tumors are very different, even if they look similar under the microscope," Dr. Baehring had assured Rob. "Do not be frightened by what you see because the tumors have behaved considerably different."

Rob had a follow-up exam with Dr. Baehring the same day as the support group meeting. I tagged along. Against a lighted screen, Baehring lined up the MRIs that had been taken Saturday at MidState. There was Rob's brain from about every possible angle—top, bottom, sideways. I could see where the tumor had been. There was a hole, a pretty big one.

"About two-thirds of the temporal lobe was removed," noted Dr. Baehring, so clinical, so matter of fact.

"Jesus, how can this guy even talk?"

"It shows the capacity and plasticity of the brain," Baehring said. "It can compensate for a lot."

There were a few small white spots around the excavation. Some of that was scar tissue from the surgery. Some were the tumor cells Dr. Piepmeier dared not touch. Baehring was looking for any visible changes from Rob's previous scans. Later, in his office, he'd make side-by-side comparisons with minute measurements. For now, he just had to eye them up for anything that might indicate new growth.

"It looks good," Baehring said. "One thing I can say for sure is there's no enhancement. It's the same size."

Baehring still had to put Rob through the paces. Was he having any symptoms, any headaches? He checked Rob's vision, his balance, his reflexes, the sensations in his extremities.

"Let's see you walk a few steps," Baehring said.

Rob took a step and pitched over into my lap. We all cracked up. It was a good check-up, but the MRIs would continue every three months.

"How do we get rid of those guys up there?" Rob asked Baehring. "I want to take a scan and have you say to me, 'They're freaking gone.' Any way they can miraculously disappear?"

"We don't know. There may be cases like that. There certainly are cases where the tumor does not grow again."

"This one's not going to grow again," Rob said.

"That's what we're trying to accomplish here."

Observation mode would continue, more wait and see. If the tumor started to grow again, chemotherapy would resume. Until then, there was no reason for treatment.

And with the clean check-up Rob boarded a plane. Diane had come up with a capital idea: a spur-of-the-moment getaway week to St. Martin.

* * *

This was a solo trip for Rob. He and Diane didn't have the

money for both of them to go, at least not for two last-minute airfares. Besides, Diane said, it would be good for Rob to remove himself entirely from the tension and turmoil generated by the Maloney coaching drama.

Rob felt at ease the minute he landed and plopped down on a lounge chair on the fine-grained sands of Orient Beach. He popped a Carib beer. The sun passed in and out of billowy white clouds and the water rolled in wave after wave after wave. Young ladies strolled by in their birthday suits.

"This is my home for the next seven days," Rob wrote in his journal. *"The hardest decisions I will have to make during that time will be where to eat and when do I shed it all and blend in with my new friends?"*

He lounged, he sipped, he wrote. He carried that journal everywhere. He thought about how one of the motivating forces throughout his illness was to return to coaching high school football. Now that dream was gone, at least as a head coach. Rob had spent 26 years completely steeped in motivating players and young coaches, and his chance to return was gone. Rob chided himself.

I shouldn't have picked a public fight with Kogut. I shouldn't have seemed so eager about coming back. I should have been low key, more diplomatic. Being excited may have played into the opposition hands—"See, he did have a motive in reporting that coach swearing at the kid."

But there had been no conspiracy, no undermining. It didn't matter. Rob felt like he'd taken a major public relations beating.

Later in the week Rob met a gentleman from New York who worked in education. He mentioned the Family Emergency Medical Leave Act. Under that act, Rob was supposed to have been told of his rights to a partial leave of absence. Essentially, you can step down while ill and, when healthy, return to your job. Rob was never informed of that. Should he take that avenue to get his coaching job back? Rob thought about it, but kept coming around to the havoc it would wreak on the program.

Besides, for most of the trip Rob didn't dwell on the rough road of the previous month. He thought about what he'd survived and how he was still striving to live to the fullest. He read Lance Armstrong's second book, *Every Second Counts*, and it reaffirmed his fighting spirit. He read about the ravages of drip chemo and felt humbled. He only had Temodar, a pill once a day for five days every 28 days. He was fortunate.

He also read about the nay-saying that had accompanied Lance's comeback, about how he could not possibly have won the Tour de France without taking performance-enhancing drugs. Rob could relate to those personal attacks.

The trip also got eerie, but in a good way. Rob began meeting people who had recently weathered trauma or tragedy. He met them at dinner; he met them walking down the beach. It started on the connecting flight from Florida to St. Martin. Rob sat next to a guy named Pete from Sarasota who'd just lost his wife. "The perfect wife," Pete said.

There was a Long Island family that had just lost a son in a car accident.

There was a family from Westport, Connecticut—Westport, the town to which Rob had been bound that fateful first day of September 2001. This family had a daughter-in-law who had died from cancer. Their son—the woman's husband—was with them. He was now raising a young son alone.

There was another couple whose daughter had died from cancer that began in her appendix. There was a gentleman on the beach battling back from melanoma.

One night, while waiting for dinner in a restaurant, a waitress saw Rob busy with his journal.

"What are you doing?"

"I'm writing a book about surviving a brain tumor."

The waitress grasped Rob's hand.

"Feel my arm!"

The hair was on end.

"My mother just died from a brain tumor."

It was all around Rob in St. Martin. He was on an island, and yet he wasn't. Everywhere he went someone had a story to tell about disease or disaster and how it had touched them. The coincidences were uncanny, and yet Rob didn't believe it was coincidental at all.

I am being constantly reinforced. All these people have suffered, but are forging on because that is what they believed their deceased loved ones wanted them to do.

Rob thought about Mike Falis and his wife Linda. They had lost Ryan. It had been very, very difficult, but they'd soldiered on. How they doted on those grandkids. They were living in the positive. Rob, too, had to keep living in the positive.

That wasn't difficult to do on St. Martin. The weather was so fine, the people so friendly. There was also a heavy Christian element on the island. Every evening you could find a church service in progress on just about every block and hear the sound of voices singing and praying spilling into the tropical twilight.

The woman who drove Rob back to the airport for his flight home readily confessed to a deep religious bent. She was a buxom, dark-skinned native and she wore a colorful, long-flowing dress. When she asked Rob what he was so busy writing about, Rob went into detail. There was plenty of time to talk.

"God bless you," the woman said when Rob was through. "The Lord has spared you for a reason. Your body is only the home for your spirit. You're alive for this purpose. Your mission on earth is to write this book to help other people."

The words echoed as Rob flew home.

I believe that. There is a reason why I've been spared. I don't think I've fulfilled everything the Master Coach in the sky has planned for me. It could be this book.

Journal pages filled.

* * *

Rob came back so tanned and unshaven that Diane didn't recognize him in the airport. He gave her a big hug. After meeting the young Westport man whose wife had died, Rob had a greater appreciation for Di and what she had done to help him through. He was recommitted to working out problems with her, many of which were brought on by the stress of not driving.

"I'm going to attack it like a football game, Diane. What are our problems? How do we fix them? Let's get a little bit better every day. By the end of the week we're going to be pretty good. By the end of the month we'll be very good. By the end of the year we're going to be back on track."

There was another call to make. Andrea was in the hospital and the prognosis was not good. Rob paid her a visit at Yale-New Haven.

Yale-New Haven: The same hospital where Andrea had worked in a lab in her healthier life, before the tumor, before the operations, before the rounds of radiation, before the chemo, before Grade 2 passed to Grade 3, before the trial treatment out of Boston that was so powerful and yet too late.

Andrea was up and out of bed when Rob ducked in. His eyes were immediately drawn to her bloated, swollen face. It was unrecognizable from the face he'd looked at so many times over lunchtime tables after good checkups and support group meetings, the clear-sailing days that were supposed to have bought more time.

Andrea mustered a smile.

"Oh, Rob. How nice of you to come up here."

"How are you feeling, Andrea?"

He was trying hard to hide his shock.

"I'm much better today than I was yesterday."

So swollen, so bloated. *What is in that chemo?*

"Andrea, you look much better than I anticipated."

He hoped she didn't pick up on the white lie.

"You should have seen me yesterday or the day before."

Peter DeBona had seen her a few weeks back. Andrea was not herself, he'd told Rob. Still, there was no preparation for this; no getting used to it no matter how long he stayed. Outside, a lovely July afternoon whiled away. Blue sky, full sun.

Rob left feeling low and sick. So when the call came the night of July 28 from Betsey D'Andrea, he expected it.

"Rob, I've got some bad news."

Betsey, who had brought Rob and Andrea together. She knew every patient that came through Yale-New Haven's neuro-oncology unit, their triumphs and their setbacks, their families and their friends. She had made calls like this before.

"Your friendship was always very good for her, Rob."

"Likewise."

Rob could hardly whisper. So expected, yet so devastating. It was something all brain tumor patients thought about: the call in the night, the news being spread about someone who had just been sitting around that support group table, just the other day, just last month.

And Rob and Andrea, well, they had gone down such a long path together. All those lunches, all those parallels. The same family background, the same age, the same tumor. Oligodendroglioma, right temporal lobe. An operation, chemotherapy: Andrea going first, Rob following like a kid brother. Except for the radiation.

"Is it painful? How many days do you have to go? Will you lose your hair? What about that mask they put over your face?"

"You're not following me, Rob, understand? You're not following me anymore."

Brown curly hair and brown eyes across the table, merry even when exasperated with his endless optimism, gentle even when bringing him down to earth.

"OK, Rob, if that's what you want to believe."

Rob welled up. What that woman suffered. He thought of Andrea's husband—another Rob. Andrea would talk about her Rob, about how supportive he was. Rob would say the same about Diane. Who really suffers the most, they'd ask each other. Who really carries the load? They knew.

Rob called Andrea's husband and extended his condolences. There would be a small memorial service. Yes, Rob would be there.

The phone went back on the receiver. Again the house was quiet. Diane was not home. Mr. Diffley slept on his sofa. A Wednesday night in late July: twilight still long but imperceptibly growing shorter. Amid the silence, the old conversations echoed.

The reality is we have an affliction we're living with and may have to live with the rest of our lives.

The reality was they had the exact same tumor in the exact same place. Rob was doing great. Piepmeier and Baehring said he was doing great. But what does it take for a little deviation of DNA to set off a chain reaction? What all of a sudden had made Andrea's tumor start to grow again? What pushed it from Grade 2 over that crucial dividing line to Grade 3? What made it keep growing to the point where the doctors looked at her MRI and said, "She isn't going to make it?"

What was it?

The same tumor. It's up there. I've got a tumor.

Would it grow at an unreasonable rate for some reason? Reasons? There were no reasons. What had triggered it in the first place? What could trigger it again? Who knew? No one knew. If we did, we'd all be home free. No worries. Rob had kept his positive attitude, but he'd also watched Andrea go through radiation, new rounds of chemo and second and third operations knowing he could be in her shoes at any time, any moment.

Andrea: His reality check.

Now she was gone and, yes, death felt like it was at the doorstep, had descended over the eastern ridges and found its way all the way to the top of the hill at the end of Oak Ridge Drive.

"Rob, I've got some bad news."

News spread in the night: When comes the night the news is spread about you?

Rob went upstairs to pray.

"I believe. I hit my knees," Rob once told Andrea. "I don't pray for myself to get healthy. I don't."

"What do you pray for?"

"That I can just live the life He put me on this earth for, to help other people, to fulfill the mission He put me here for. I've been told by people who are far more religious than I'll ever be that I haven't fulfilled His mission. Otherwise I'd be gone. That may be true."

What if it wasn't? Sometimes the game ended too soon. Sometimes the Spartans would be driving, in sight of the go-ahead score, and time just ran out. And once it ran out . . . *the reality is . . .*

Tears were falling as Rob fell to his knees in the quiet house.

Tears fell onto clasped hands, clenching, and he waited for the words to come and flow into the hum above the silence.

And that's when he heard her voice.

Oh, it was her voice. Just as Father David had heard Millie's voice the day of the blood clots, Rob heard Andrea's voice on his knees in his bedroom on the night she died.

"You're not following me, Rob."

He heard it in the darkness.

"You're not following me anymore."

Rob raised his head, listening in the darkness.

"You're not following me, do you understand?"

He began to laugh. He laughed through the tears. Both poured out of him.

"I understand, Andrea. I understand."

Downstairs, too, the silence was broken. Mr. Diffley barked and stirred from the sofa. A lock released. The door from the garage opened. A light came on.

Diane.

Rob rose from the floor, rushed to her, embraced her.

"What is it, Rob?"

"Every minute," he said, "is precious."

Rob and Kevin Savejs

CHAPTER 17

Green Bays in the Gloaming

THE GREEN SHIRTS, white pants and white helmets fade into the deepening darkness of early November and disappear . . . and then reappear amid hard breathing and the pounding of galloping cleats.

"Don't show weakness! Don't show weakness!"

Once the clocks fall back an hour in late October, football practice ends after dark. Collectively, the lights that ring the Maloney practice field are hardly stronger than the spotlight on somebody's back stoop, like that one over there in the neighborhood of small capes and ranches beyond the schoolyard fence. Here on the field, all you can really see is what's right in front of your face.

Unseen traffic hums on the north-south highways beyond the dark trees. On the field you hear the pounding feet and the heavy breathing of the players, the steady bark of the coaches and the shrill punctuation of their whistles.

"Toes on the line! TOES ON THE LINE! On three, on three."

Sh-weeeeeeeeeet!

"Go . . . go . . . GO!"

Off go the Spartans. They run the last of their ten 100-yard sprints, with the eight 80s, six 60s, four 40s and two 20s still to go. Green Bays in the gloaming: feet pound, fade, pound back out of the darkness.

Mike Falis, wearing his trademark shorts and scowl, is counting by one-one thousands—"13 one thousand, 14 one thousand!" Rob is pacing up and down the line as the boys come in.

"Nice job! NICE JOB!" he shouts. "Way to work! WAY TO WORK!"

When Bob Zito was hired he made a tactical move to bridge the divide in Maloney football. The new head coach extended an offer to the Old Guard: Join me on staff. Perhaps this was part of Shugrue's "resolution." Zito made overtures to Falis and Steve Hoag, the defensive coordinator. They said OK, but it was conditional. They wouldn't sign on without Smaz.

"Looks like you're the key guy," Zito said the night he spoke to Rob.

The pain of summer was still fresh, but the pull of football was too strong. Rob said yes, and that sealed it. The old Maloney coaching staff was back, signed on for the 2004 season. Also back was the weightlifting coach, Pablo Valentin, and the stat guys, Les Zimmerman and his son Brett. Back, too, were the traditions, such as the brutal Green Bays.

"Toes on the line! TOES ON THE LINE!"

The Spartans settle into the eight 80-yard sprints. Quarterbacks take turns calling the count. Players assume stances by position: linemen down, running backs upright, arms on thighs, receivers standing, arms pumped, fists chest high.

"On two."

Sh-weeeeeeeet! A long, drawn out whistle, then a sharp "Go!" Then a pause just long enough to allow one more crucial lungful of air, and then "GO!"

Feet pound, forms fade. The trampled, muddy ground where Mike Falis once burnt his son's jacket and Rob once burnt a Land's End shirt goes silent, then vibrates anew. A tread first heard, then seen. Back come the boys, out of the dark, running with the wind . . .

It was exhilarating for Rob to return to the sidelines. The Spartans won at Ceppa Field on opening night against Glastonbury. They won again on the same field a week later against Wethersfield. The wins weren't pretty and they didn't come against strong opponents, but they were a huge psychological boost for players who had endured one win and 21 losses over the previous two years.

They were a huge boost for Rob, as well. I covered the Wethersfield game. Brilliant late afternoon color streaked the warm September sky during warm-ups. We caught each other's eye and winked. After the game, Rob ran the team over to the bleachers, where the band was jumping up and down. He led them in the Maloney fight song, still the All-American boy, still the 1960s square peg, belting out corny old school songs in the era of hip hop, and yet there were the kids, merrily swept up in the joy.

There were also frustrations and mixed emotions. Rob wasn't head coach, he was an assistant. He had to adjust to playing second fiddle in a program he had orchestrated for 26 years. He found some of the new practice drills too violent. One of Rob's cardinal rules had been avoiding contact that could get players hurt in practice. Sure enough, one afternoon early in the season, a Spartan went down and had to be taken to the hospital for precautionary tests. The boy was OK, but he wound up quitting football.

Nor did Rob care for the new offensive scheme. Zito brought in the wing-T, a formation that relies on a lot of misdirection and lateral movement. Under Rob, Maloney had long been an I-formation team, running downhill. His frustration grew as the

Spartans struggled to score. The wing-T wasn't an easy offense to learn, and the Spartans hadn't taken it up until August. Too many plays were going for negative yards. Thank goodness for defense and special teams. The win over Glastonbury had largely been the product of two blocked punts returned for touchdowns.

After another game, Rob found himself tending to a backed-up toilet in the Ceppa Field locker room. It was certainly a moment ripe with symbolism.

Rob let a lot sit inside. He vented only to Diane. This was his program and he felt he'd been screwed out of it by the political maneuverings of a few. But he did like Zito, who was a good man worthy of loyalty.

"The welfare of the kids is always at his heart, no doubt about that," Rob told me. "You can coach for a guy like that and there's never a problem. But just to see things run differently than you did them . . ."

Rob and head coach Bob Zito outside the Ceppa Field locker room

Rob started as the quarterbacks coach. That was too limiting. He needed to do more. He wanted that old feel of getting up before the players in the hot, stuffy team room before practice, diagramming plays and showing film, seeing eyes widen at something that could work and feeling spirits feed off his excitement. One day, heading to a youth football game they'd been invited to, Rob said to Zito, "Coach, I can do more than just coach a position."

Zito was agreeable to that. Rob gradually realized that many frustrations were his own doing. Sometimes all he had to do was ask.

There were disagreements at times. As the Spartans continued to struggle with the wing-T, Steve Hoag calculated that when points produced by defense and special teams were discounted, Maloney had the least productive offense in its conference. Rob, itching to re-inject some of his old I-formation plays, passed that information along to Zito in a note. Zito wrote back angrily. "We do not have the least productive offense. Get your facts straight."

That was as tense as it ever got that season. In time, Zito gave Rob leave to add some I-formation plays—"toss" one week, "belly" the next. Rob admired Zito for giving him such latitude. He wondered how he would have handled being in Zito's shoes: Hired amid controversy, hired over the native son, the guy who was synonymous with the program, and then coaching with him and the Old Guard. Rob wondered. *Would my ego have allowed me to do the same?*

. . . the boys run back with the wind, then turn their faces back toward the north end zone, back into the brisk, biting November wind, breathing hard.

"Good work! Way to go! DOWN TO THE 60s!"

Darkness deepens. The field lights throw what little light they do. Brighter lights flare up in the kitchens of homes beyond the south end zone. It's dinner time, but the Spartans are not done.

"Don't show weakness! Don't show weakness! We win the fourth quarter! WE WIN THE FOURTH QUARTER!"

Rob used to run Green Bays with the guys, back in his younger days. If he tried now, he says, his back would lock right up. He mentions nothing about how the residual effects of a brain tumor might hinder the performance. He has that way of making you forget all about it, as if it were some once-jarring detail in a lush landscape—say, a lightning-scarred tree that in time healed up enough to blend in with the rest of the forest, so much so that when you see it you must jog your memory: *Remember that storm?*

The cause of brain tumors still remained unknown, though there were plenty of studies aiming for an understanding. In Connecticut, a cluster of Pratt & Whitney workers had developed brain tumors and the state's Department of Health launched an investigation in 2004 to see if environmental exposure was the cause. Other studies were focusing on stem cells in the brain, the immature cells from pre-natal gestation and development that maintain the ability to proliferate and migrate. Were those "resident" cells the source of tumors? Researchers were pursuing multiple paths.

"I would anticipate during our careers we're going to have a handle on it," Dr. Piepmeier had said that summer. "It's not tomorrow, but there are a lot of people, many laboratories, investigating this."

. . . the Spartans move closer to the end zone, breathing hard, spitting. The 60-yarders are complete. Just the four 40s and two 20s remain. For the first 40, the count is "on three," but half the team jumps on two. Rob's whistle shrilly goes *Sh-weeeeeeeet!*

"Get back on the line. GET FOCUSED! That's what this

drill's all about. When you get tired, you lose discipline. Don't lose it! DON'T LOSE IT! Toes on the line. On three: Go . . . Go . . . GO!"

The National Cancer Institute, under the ambitious new leadership of Dr. Andrew von Eschenbach, was hoping that by 2015 cancer would be known only as a chronic condition, not a fatal one. In the meantime, the American Cancer Society was estimating 12,690 people would die from the disease in 2004.

Rob would not be one of that number. Surgery, chemotherapy and a fighting spirit had bought him time. It had been three years. How much time lay ahead?

"Even now, just not knowing where it's going, that's the scary part," Diane had said back in the summer on a gorgeous afternoon. "I'm not sure this is all over with. You never know that. Every time he goes for an MRI, I hold my breath. For me, it's not the kind of thing that's just going to go away. At some point, 10 years down the road or whenever, if something else doesn't get him first, this will eventually get him. Because we don't know when it started, how long it sat there and grew. It could have been 20 years. They took the bulk of it out, but that little bit that's there could just hang around for another 20 years and start growing again. You just don't know. It's not like life is over. You don't know what to expect. We still don't know what to expect. But life goes on and it can be good again."

That was Rob's mantra. Life was still good in 2004 as he returned to the Maloney sidelines. Life would still be good in 2007 when he walked out of Maloney and sailed into retirement. "And I look forward to long, healthy retirement," he said. "Maybe a month and a half in St. Martin rather than just one magical week."

Sure, six weeks to kick back on the beach and watch those Caribbean waves roll in . . .

. . . back go the boys, fading, disappearing. "Good job!" call the coaches as the Spartans reappear like waves on a night beach. Isn't that the essence of high school coaching? Years pass, one class follows the next. In its turn, each wave rolls in, small and dormant, power and potential unformed, just waiting to be gathered and harnessed into a force of nature that builds, crests . . . only to break, recede and be replaced, its spent energy feeding the wave that follows.

"Good job! GOOD JOB! Down to the 20s!"

The Spartans would wind up going 6-4 in 2004. They'd lose on Thanksgiving to a playoff-bound Platt team 55-20.

Of course, if Rob had helped turn the program completely around, even as an assistant coach, and the Spartans had won the city's first state championship in football, this book might have had its fairy tale ending after all. But fairy tales are hard to come by and most stories are slow to end—like Green Bays on a November night. The 40s are done, but there are still those 20s left to be run.

So toes on the line.

TOES ON THE LINE!

PART II

CHAPTER 18

Interlude: January 11, 2005

I WRITE THIS entry knowing it begins another chapter in Rob's book, with snow falling on a January night, coating the evergreens, suspending them in white.

I look out the study window of my new house, gazing at dark hills, finding myself foolish to think time and situations ever freeze.

This book began last summer with Rob and I recreating history even as new events played out and muscled themselves onto the pages.

Then it was finished to a certain point, tinkered and enhanced a bit, but with Rob busy with football, I found there was only so much I could do. Plus, I got busy with other tasks, including buying this hillside home in a small, quiet town on the east side of the Connecticut River. My wife and I moved in and put fresh coats of paint on all the walls. The book was left alone. Life was still good.

As if the story could just end that way, or remain fixed in one place until we got back to it and polished it up and got it published and displayed front and center in every bookstore in America in tall, towering displays . . .

. . . snow falls, accumulating . . .

Rob got word today his tumor is growing back.

The future course is not yet known. Maybe there will be more chemo, maybe another operation. That's to be decided in the days ahead. It was enough today to learn that the son of a bitch is growing again.

Rob told me on the phone. I'd called from my newspaper office to reschedule our next work session.

"Hey Diane," I said when she answered the phone. "You mind if I stop by an hour earlier tomorrow?"

"No, that's OK."

Pause.

"Here, you better talk to Rob."

The news was sad and infuriating and grim, yet not surprising. Rob's seizure activity had spiked recently. It had never really gone away—it had gotten pretty bad in the summer, in fact, when the bitter coaching controversy was running in the newspapers and burning even deeper behind the scenes and Rob was stressed out and distracted.

The seizures were nothing major. We'd be working and Rob would just zone out for maybe 10 or 20 seconds, lose his train of thought completely. At first he wouldn't tell me. He would try to cover it up by focusing on a page of manuscript or a photograph, but I quickly caught on. After a while, he'd tell me.

"OK," he'd suddenly announce. "I'm having a simple-partial right now. Pretty good one: On a scale of one to ten, about a seven and a half."

"Are you OK?" I'd try to keep my voice quiet and level.

"Yep," he'd say, though his eyes would seem to bulge and he'd swallow several times in rapid succession.

"Can I get you something? Water?"

"It'll pass."

Quieter, calmer: "What's it feel like, Rob?"

"Like a hundred heartbeats in my arms."

Dr. Baehring had said an increase in seizures would be the

clearest indicator of renewed tumor activity. Those words, delivered in Dr. Baehring's deep monotone with the German accents, never left me. Yet Rob's scans were clean in the summer, and these seizures could easily be chalked up to stress.

Now, in the first fresh days of 2005, Rob and I were finally getting back to work. I crossed the river and drove over to his hilltop house on Sunday, January 9. The pale purple light of winter slanted low off the ridges. And there was Rob, dressed not in the usual sweatshirt or coaching accoutrements, but in a flannel shirt and work boots, looking every bit the woodsman, complete with a fire going in the fireplace. He showed me the new snowblower he'd received for Christmas and I teased him because I take perverse pleasure in shoveling my new driveway, even the section by the garage bracketed by high brownstone retaining walls.

We laughed and jostled and wrestled a bit and I tensed up my skinny arms and shoulders, which I always do when Rob and I jostle or embrace because, you know, he's a football coach and I want to show I have secret strength in me, too.

"I was out there shoveling two days ago, Coach."

"Were ya?"

"Yeah, but my driveway is nowhere near as steep as yours."

We resumed our work at the kitchen table, exactly where we had worked all summer. The conversation darted and danced across topics and chapters, exactly like it had all summer. Rob mostly wanted to talk about the problematic Chapter 13, which he'd been working on. He wrestled with describing the events leading up to and following the firing of his hand-picked successor at Maloney. It was hard for Rob. The experience had hurt him. He'd been frequently attacked by the supporters of the other coach and he felt defenseless. My newspaper had run articles as the story played out, but Rob found himself double-damned.

Given the book project, which everyone knew about, the newspaper could never seem impartial in the eyes of some readers. In Rob's eyes, the newspaper overcompensated for our relationship by trying to avoid the appearance of defending him, and thus left him dangling even further in the wind.

The book offered Rob a chance to state his case, but he continually wavered on how heavy he wanted to come across. In angry moments the fiery competitor emerged and wanted to spell out the string of dirty details that eventually got his successor canned. Those moments never lasted. Inevitably, the smiling sensitive side of Rob resurfaced and he came around to saying, "The more I try to rework this, the more my inner gut tells me it's going to reawake a nasty situation. I just don't want to open up old wounds. I think about families and kids and someone having to hear from a classmate, 'Hey, I read Coach Szymaszek's book and I heard about what your dad said.' "

"You've got to go with what you're comfortable with, Rob," I'd say. "It's your book."

We went over that ground again on Sunday, as well as some of the revisions I'd been working on without him, when out of the blue he said, "Did I tell you my seizures have come back again?"

His eyes, so big and blue behind his glasses, locked on mine. Rob could sling the BS with the best of them, but this look always prefaced candor. I warmed to the confidence, but dreaded what I knew he was about to say.

"No, you didn't."

"Yeah, buddy, I'm up to about 24, 25 a week."

A week? I tried not to show alarm. While working with Rob, I always avoided playing any kind of worst-case scenario around a guy so unfailingly optimistic. I strove instead to play the upbeat realist. Sometimes when Rob had a plan or a theory, I actually believed in it—or wanted to believe in it—even when my "inner gut" said pie in the sky. Rob is so damn positive it's usually irresistible, and it sure as hell beats the negativity that infiltrates too much of our lives.

But my gut reaction to this news was tough to override. He talked about knocking out alcohol because, as he said, his fondness for good wine and holiday champagne had probably undermined his anti-seizure medication.

"They told me alcohol was OK in moderation, but you know me. I cook a good meal and I like to have a good time."

He smiled and I smiled, but Dr. Baehring's deep monotone resonated in my head. I said only, "Good idea. Bag alcohol altogether."

"And if that doesn't work," Rob said, "my epileptic doctor will tweak my seizure meds."

Later, when Rob went upstairs to retrieve some notes, Diane brought over bowls of soup and sat down next to me.

"Did he tell you about the seizures?"

"Yeah."

"I'm worried about these. He's foggy after he has them."

Diane was calm and matter of fact and, I thought, very brave.

Two days later, on the 11th, they got the latest MRI results down at Yale-New Haven and it had to suck the wind and guts out of even Rob, because that's how it felt when he told me, and I knew it was coming.

Still, the eternal optimist strove to put his best face forward, at least to me when we spoke on the phone that night.

"At one point I'm standing between Dr. Baehring and Dr. Piepmeier, and they're talking about what to do next, and I'm thinking, 'Why not do a PET scan like we did last time to see exactly how much it's grown?' and I was about to say, 'Here I am standing next to one guy who went to Yale and another guy who went to Harvard and here I am, a Southern Connecticut State guy. How come I know what to do?' But then I saw the look in Dr. Piepmeier's eyes, just a look of concern and compassion. So maybe we do chemo again, maybe another biopsy. But boy, Bry, I don't want to have to go through that again."

No, not again. That storm had been cleared away; those chapters written. We go forward. There were defeats, but the bigger game's been won. Life is still good, right?

No. Life is good, but never fixed.

As I spoke to Rob, the light in my newspaper office seemed to diminish as if I were looking through the wrong end of a telescope. It was dark outside, the forecasted snow coming down at a steady clip. The streets of downtown Meriden, always so poorly plowed, were already covered.

"I think about my friend Andrea, how she had the same tumor as me."

I perked up.

"Rob, chemo wouldn't be a bad option. It worked last time."

"It didn't shrink the tumor, but it did keep it from growing."

"That's right."

"Hey, whatever it takes. This is part of the game. Like Dr. Piepmeier said, I'll be seeing him three-four times a year, just like you go see your dentist. Sometimes they say we'll see you in sixth months; sometimes they say we'll see you in two weeks and we'll get that cavity. Instead of drilling my teeth, they'll be drilling my skull."

We giggled, and Rob said, "You take care of it, right? Huh, buddy? OK, so you're coming an hour earlier tomorrow?"

I left work and drove home slowly through the snow. It's a

longer drive now, almost twice as long, with the river to cross. It was slow going, especially over the bridge, but I got home all right. My wife looked out, smiled and waved through the lighted study window.

I shoveled the driveway before I went in, even though it was still snowing. It would mean less to do tomorrow, and I wanted to move my arms and shoulders and breathe cold air.

And it made me feel like I was staying ahead of the storm. With each pass of the shovel a little bit of order was restored.

When I finished, I went inside and my wife made me soup.

Now, as I write these words in the study we just repainted and carpeted, I glance at the snow still falling through the light of the street lamps and hear my wife flip through Welcome Wagon coupons in the kitchen. My gaze vacantly falls to the floor and I force my mind to drift to Rob's house and what it must be like to contemplate the sort of news he got today and know you're not dreaming or watching TV or reading about someone else's story.

Or writing it.

I raise my eyes and see the clock and hear my wife and notice the brightness of the kitchen and the straight lines of the table and consider the miracle of a day of good health and no ill tidings. A wave washes over me that leaves me smiling and weeping all at once.

CHAPTER 19

Back into the Breach

AS UPBEAT AS he'd been on the phone with me, the news of January 11 hit Rob hard. Part of him was down and depressed. He and Diane cried when they got home before he bucked up and gave me that call at work.

Just as he had that summer night in 2000 when he wrestled with giving up coaching football to become the head of the Maloney guidance department, Rob put thoughts on paper.

Am I prepared to go through this again?

Do I want to go through radiation?

I'm feeling very vulnerable right now.

These were followed by:

Comeback! Get things in order for the book.

Living in the positive: Rejuvenate.

"I think for the first time I'm having self doubts," Rob said to me the next night. "Going through it once: Can I muster up the endurance to do this again? Those were the thoughts. I know I will."

He thought about what lay ahead and memories of what came before flooded back.

The pain and the morphine drip.

The hours of lying in bed, listening to the sirens of incoming ambulances and wondering, as he had when he was a boy and his dad took him around the police station and he saw the guys in lockup: "What's wrong with that person? What affliction do they have?"

He remembered slowly regaining strength, getting out of the hospital bed and walking around the floor, looking into other rooms, seeing people wheeled in after their operations.

He remembered a lot of crying and very little laughter.

When Rob first got the news his tumor was growing back, the football coach in him came to the fore. "What are the options?" he asked Piepmeier and Baehring as if they were trusted coordinators. *Let's game plan, from the least invasive (chemo) to the most invasive (surgery).*

There was some talk of doing a biopsy to draw a tissue sample and see how it was behaving. Diane spoke up. "If you're going to do that, why not take out the rest? If you're going to do chemo or radiate, why even bother opening up his head again?"

"I thought it was very good you said that," Rob told Diane when I stopped by on the night of the 12th.

"You were telling me to shut up at that point," Diane reminded him.

"I thought you were stepping on Joe's toes a little bit. Joe is like a god to me."

"Somebody's got to ask questions."

There was an edge in Diane's voice that softened away. "You ask good questions, too, Rob."

Rob and Diane had gone down to Yale-New Haven expecting a turn for the worse. Diane had been worried since October. Even Rob had taken the December brain scan and held it up to the kitchen window. Against the gray backdrop of the early winter light, he thought he saw something.

Rob's sister Sharon had called the morning of the appointment and detected a strain in Diane's voice. She told Diane she was driving up from New Jersey to meet them at Yale-New Haven.

Even when anxious, Rob couldn't resist teasing his big sister. Sharon hadn't arrived by the time Rob and Diane got to the hospital, so as they checked in at the reception desk Rob said, "My ex-lover might be coming up to find me. She's a blonde and she may be ranting and raving, but please, let her know where the room is."

Rob and Diane were already meeting with the doctors as Sharon came down the hallway. She froze at the door as she heard Baehring say, "There's been a change."

"You look so good Rob," she later said. "How can anything be wrong with you?"

"Yeah, I feel good. I feel real good."

But Rob really hadn't felt good. There was no denying those seizures. They were coming in waves like the ones he experienced that first week in the hospital after the fateful car crash in September 2001. He tried to downplay them. He was familiar with them. He could feel them coming about half a minute in advance. He could better handle them, disguise them, but there was no denying them and what they signified.

After the meeting with Piepmeier and Baehring, Rob grew irritable on the ride home. The first flakes of the January 11th storm were starting to fly, and he hoped for a snow day on the 12th. He didn't want to go to school. He hoped it would snow through the night. But there was no closing, only a delayed opening. It proved to be for the best. Rob got to work, and helping kids got his mind off his health. A student who had just moved to Florida needed a transcript. He got a call from a girl whose alcoholic father had shown up drunk that morning, and he helped ease that crisis.

"Thank God I came to school today. It got me off my situation," Rob told me. "I've got to get back on the path and be the guy I know I am and not that mean son of a bitch."

This helped Rob put his game face back on. The night before, he'd asked Diane if the time had come for him to start putting some things in order. Now he was back in the huddle, game-planning for a showdown. "We'll call out the first team," he vowed. "We're not playing around. I want the same team. I want the same team that's good in the fourth quarter."

* * *

The initial game plan was the least invasive route. Rob would resume the Temador, the pill form of chemo he'd been on back in 2003. Five days every 28 days, with regular scans to monitor the progress. Temador had held the tumor in check the first time around; perhaps it would again be successful.

Winter pressed on and gave way to the long barren stretch of March. Hot stove football came to the fore. Rob was still involved in the Connecticut-Rhode Island All-Star game, and he spoke at a press conference called to hype the 2005 game. I was there in my journalistic capacity, and there was Rob, a tumor regenerating, more vibrant and more energetic than most of the guys who would be coaching in the game. When it was his turn to speak, Rob had his arms wrapped around both sides of the podium as if he were about to tackle it.

He spoke again in April at a Hall of Fame induction at Lyman Hall High School in neighboring Wallingford. The ceremony honored players who had beaten Rob's Maloney team on their state title march 20 years before. Again, there was the same vibrancy, the same energy, the same two hands firm on the podium like he was doing all he could to restrain himself from hauling that sucker up and drive-blocking it halfway across the auditorium. His voice boomed. There was no need for a microphone. Every word carried its own exclamation point.

"THE THEME OF GETTING BETTER SEEMS TO BE THE CENTRAL THING THAT MADE THIS TEAM SO SPECIAL!"

Getting better . . . who could read between the lines? Few in the crowd that night knew that just a couple days earlier the stoic Dr. Baehring had been on the verge of tears looking at Rob's latest MRI. What it revealed was clear. Small, no bigger than a shelled peanut, the cancer cells were still reforming. The Temador wasn't working.

The Yale-New Haven oncology team sized up the treatment options and laid them on the table for Rob mere hours before his scheduled Hall of Fame speech. There were three choices: stronger chemo, radiation or surgery. The doctors were recommending the first. It wouldn't be easy. No more pills: The new chemo would be of the IV drip variety, a pair of two-hour cycles starting in May. Compared to radiation or surgery, which were still in the cards if this new chemo treatment didn't work, it certainly was the least invasive option. Still, Rob wasn't sure. He held off making a decision and headed to Lyman Hall High School to make his speech.

"I could be standing here telling you I'm going under the knife again," Rob told me when we met in the lobby. "I guess we got good news."

Then he turned to his fellow Maloney assistant, Steve Hoag, who was originally a Lyman Hall guy and still a driving force in the school's Hall of Fame. Hoag had arranged for Rob's speech that night, and while Rob never had considered begging off, he had placed a call to Steve en route to Yale-New Haven.

"Where are you going to be today? I might need a pep talk."

Now Rob cracked a smile. "I know what you're thinking, Steve. I'm calling the Maloney Spartans offense this year and *nothing* is going to keep me from calling plays."

And later, to the assemblage: "THE LYMAN HALL FOOTBALL TEAM FROM GAME 1, WHEN WE PLAYED YOU—I WISH I COULD HAVE FOLLOWED YOU THROUGH THE SEASON—JUST GOT BETTER AND BETTER AND BETTER!"

I wrote about the Hall of Fame induction on deadline that night. Long before I filed the story I sent Rob an e-mail:

I'm sitting here on Friday night writing a story about you that you will read tomorrow morning, and while I write most stories with a certain emotional detachment in order to really wrap my mind around them, I find I cannot do it with this one.

Truth is, I've never been able to. Not from the beginning, not throughout the book, not tonight.

And I find each time the feeling gets stronger.

I'm not sitting here crying or despairing or cursing or anything like that. You wouldn't want that anyway. I'm just sitting here smiling and shaking my head, filled with f'ing admiration . . .

Too bad I can't use that last bit in the newspaper. Doesn't matter, though. Those who know you already know exactly what I mean.

After the buzz of that night faded, Rob still had a decision to make. Would he go on the stronger chemo? The more he thought about it, the more he leaned against it. Rob had always been leery of drip chemo. He hated seeing other patients so weak and decimated next to their IV poles with looks of horror in their eyes. *Is that going to be me some day? Will I become one of them? No! I will be spared this awful treatment.*

Why hadn't the Temador worked? As Piepmeier explained, chemotherapy latches onto DNA in a tumor and causes a strand break. If the DNA can't replicate itself, bingo: that tumor cell dies. But tumors do contain repair enzymes, and as soon as the chemo's alkalating agent latches on, the tumor makes an enzyme in an effort to shuck it off and repair the damage. Sometimes it's successful. Even if a tumor has this repair enzyme, it doesn't mean chemo can't be effective, Piepmeier added, but it explains why when it isn't.

Rob noted that his rounds of Temador had never devastated him physically.

"Why don't you just jack that crap up?" he asked Piepmeier.

The surgeon laughed. He really admired Rob's fighting spirit.

"And knock your bone marrow out, huh?"

Besides, Piepmeier said, increasing dosage wouldn't necessarily increase effect.

With Rob opposed to the stronger chemo, radiation moved to the fore. Baehring was recommending it. But Rob didn't want to go that route either. He had seen the havoc it, too, could wreak. He had seen what it had done to Andrea—the swelling, the bloating, the face that was hardly recognizable.

"Radiation scares me," Rob said.

For a while Rob had been growing dissatisfied with Dr. Baehring—largely, it seemed to me, because he didn't like what the oncologist had to tell him. To many of Baehring's suggestions Rob would reply, "How does Dr. P. feel about this?"

Rob began to wonder: *I don't mean to make it seem this way, but am I giving Dr. Baehring reason to think I have no faith in him?*

Finally, on one visit, Baehring brought it all to a head—and to a quick resolution. "If you want to change oncologists I wouldn't have a problem with that," Baehring told Rob.

"Dr. B.," he said, "I want to stay with the team."

Now the team had put the dreaded R word on the table. *"You're not following me Rob. You're not following me anymore. Do you understand?"* Andrea had said it and we all wanted to believe it. Now here we were: radiation.

When? Not just yet. When school let out in June, Rob and Diane took off and went to St. Martin. Cut and run for a while. Why the hell not? My wife teaches. I know how it is when the school year ends. You need to cut out, even if you don't have tough medical decisions to make on the other side of R&R.

Every morning on this trip Rob stopped in at Baywatch, a breakfast place on Orient Beach run by a guy named Andy, a Vietnam vet from New Jersey. It's the one place on the island where you can get an American breakfast. Everything else is French.

Andy had a big ol' belly and a big ol' attitude.

"Don't worry about nothin'; just fahgeddabout it. If you're lookin' at life, I'm lookin' at you, and I'm not goin' anywhere, so fahgeddabout it."

You can get eggs over easy and watch the topless girls stroll by.

"Who can have a better job than me?" Andy wanted to know.

Andy suggested Rob ditch everything and retire right then and there to St. Martin. Just fahgeddabout it.

But, no, not yet. Too much remained in Meriden. There was school. There was the team. There was a brainstorm: A line of clothes, "Life is Still Good," to go along with the book. The clothes would be tailor-made for cancer patients, Rob explained, with lots of flaps and lots of layers.

As for the book, it was in hiatus. The manuscript was sent out. Some took a pass; some didn't even respond. I steeped myself in newspaper work on a former pro football player going through divorce and alcohol rehab at age 70. Then I went on my own vacation.

"How's the book coming?" I'd be asked.

I'd say, "I'll be getting back to it soon" and left it at that, without saying how I knew that new chapters would soon need to be written.

So when I got back from vacation and the phone rang at work on the last Friday in August and Rob was on the other line, not with his usual rip-roaring "HEY BRY," but with a gosh-shucks, sorry-to-let-you-down "hey Bry," I knew the story was about to resume.

* * *

Rob's latest brain scan had been taken earlier in the week. On that Friday, he and Diane met with Dr. Baehring to get the results. The continued regeneration of the tumor was plain to see and it was growing faster than expected.

Baehring was again talking radiation. Then Piepmeier stopped in to say he could operate and would operate. A two-pronged plan emerged. Piepmeier would operate and, once Rob's brain had healed from the surgery, they'd go after what cells were left with radiation. It would be intensive therapy: five days a week for six weeks, but if all went well it could stem the tide for 7-10 years.

"This could be good," Rob said to Diane.

Diane looked up through her tears. "How could this be good?"

"They're talking about operating and radiating. Maybe we can kill those bastards for good. Seven to 10 years: I'm looking forward to frolicking in that warm Caribbean water till I'm 65, 67. You've got to look at it that way."

Rob's news was very grim, no doubt about it, and yet I wasn't floored by it. I guess part of it was because the news wasn't unexpected. But it was more: It was Rob's attitude. The man was just never beaten. A crap hand had been re-dealt. *Hey, we're going to cut your head open one more time and after that we're going to zap it with radiation.* But there was Rob, ready to play.

This wasn't denial. This wasn't pie in the sky. This was valid.

Besides, it beat the alternative. I got off the phone with Rob and left my newspaper office, leaving behind co-workers who were down in the mouth about—you know, I don't even know what about, other than it was always something and almost always penny ante. So I left to go enjoy the more upbeat company of a guy with a regenerating brain tumor.

The late afternoon of that last Friday in August was beautiful. It had been cool all week, which was nice for the football team. In recent years preseason had been marred by dreadful heat. As sticky and humid as the summer of 2005 had been, this week was a sweet reprieve. There was plenty of soft dry air and blue sky and lazy breezes. Wisps of white cloud were streaked, as if brushed, across the sky.

As I pulled into Maloney's back parking lot it occurred to me how this afternoon was probably much like that first day of September back in 2001, the day the ordeal started. Here it was, starting all over again, almost to the day.

The Spartans were down on the field. Kids in shorts and t-shirts, with white helmets emblazoned with that great big green block M. I could hear Rob's voice wafting up. I could hear it above the fast-flowing traffic on the north-south highways beyond the screen of trees. I glanced further eastward, to the ridge lines. They were marked with sun and shadow. Down on the field, shadows were starting to edge across the track, cast by trees on the hillside where the legend, Ed McGee, had stood that August in 1966 when Rob attended his first practice as a player.

I often wondered why Rob referred to McGee as "The Legend." Ed had coached only 12 years or so. Rob had coached more than twice as long. He had coached longer than anyone in school history. He had won the most games in the history of Meriden football. He was the legend.

And four decades later he was still down on that same old field where he'd been a wild-eyed boy, coaching with the same fervor and that same wide-eyed look, head cocked as if looking at angles others could not see. A head for the game. A head with a tumor growing back inside of it.

Rob had the quarterback and wide receivers running skeleton drills to work the defensive backs.

"Booba!" he called to sophomore Johrone Bunch, one of the best athletes on the team. "You're like a free safety right now. Front tilt. QB, front shoulder."

Hut, hut: The play ran. Patterns splayed out across the fresh green field and the ball went up against blue and cotton-swab sky. A deep route, a deflection.

"That's when to look! That's when to look!" Rob encouraged.

The next pass was incomplete, too, but there was contact.

"OK, hey, Orlando, the hand on the shoulder's gonna get the yellow flag. A hand on the hip, you got a chance. And you don't want to look until the receiver looks, alright? Not bad coverage, though. Not bad at all."

Rob had been given the reins to the offense, and he wasted little time re-installing his old Maloney I-formation. The Spartans were looking more like the Spartans of old. If only it could be so in all ways . . .

If anything could take Rob's mind off the news received earlier in the day it was this: To be here, at football practice, with the boys, going through the paces. Rob felt good. He looked good. That was the kicker. Here this tumor was growing again and Rob seemed fine. Even the seizures had subsided in number.

They'd come on, but they wouldn't blossom. It was like a budding sneeze that would dissipate rather than explode.

I joined Rob on the field as the Spartans regrouped and ran another play. "Nice, Orlando, nice! Jo-Jo, are you coming out of the backfield?"

Rob had seen the city school superintendent, Mary Cortright, earlier that day. Everything was arranged, ready to go. A guidance counselor had been lined up to come in while Rob recovered from surgery. Heck, Rob had accumulated nearly 400 sick days. He could retire now if he wanted. But he couldn't walk away from this team, and if he was to coach he'd have to keep working.

"Bob's got my offense all set to go," Rob said laughing. "I'd hate to give this up now. God dang it, I worked too hard to get back."

Rob was excited about the team. They'd lost seniors from the year before, but had a number of key returnees, including a kid eyed for quarterback and another who had already proven himself as a running back. Rob cooed over the team's speed. The Spartans had size, too. Mike Falis had moved some guys around on the offensive line and the right side was particularly strong.

"And the backs—God!"

More than that, this was a team Rob and the other coaches were connecting with, the threads of day-to-day contact and camaraderie quickly intertwining. The bad vibe of those long losing seasons was long gone. Bob Zito set a good tone.

"These kids are happy," Rob said. "Mike Falis is down there coaching his ass off. It's a good situation here again."

Hut, hut: Another play.

"Nice! Nice!" Rob called. "HEY! That's a great move to the ball, Booba. Jo-Jo, don't let him get an inside release on you. Don't let him get an inside release."

It went on like this for another hour, the practice playing out with an exhilarating exertion as the sun went down. The day was so fine. It wasn't until afterward, when we were in the parking lot and the players had dispersed homeward, that Rob let out a long exhale. One of those weight-of-the-world exhales.

"I'll have a lot more details next Wednesday."

A pre-op consult with Piepmeier was scheduled for that day. Rob spoke with his usual optimism. Yet in the spaces between the words, where thought moved silently ahead or where perhaps the echo of the said words slammed home, waves of doubt and even fear washed over Rob's face.

This wasn't weakness. This was knowing what lay ahead.

Rob studied the ground with wide, distant eyes—a look that, were he talking football, would indicate he was zipping through mental reels of game film, searching for a specific play of reference. But this wasn't about football, and this time he didn't give utterance to every thought he was poring over.

Nor did I even though it was floating right there between us, so big and obvious. But it served no purpose to be dire, so I found myself saying what I believed to be a stronger truth, because I saw it first hand when my sister was a little girl suffering from advanced-stage neuroblastoma and the doctors said her chances to live were 5 percent.

"Take the shit out, Rob. I know it's your head that's going to be cut open and not mine, but there it is. You know, when my sister was sick all my mom wanted was for that tumor to be taken out. 'Take it out. Take it out. Take it out.' Then one day a doctor in Boston said he could take it out, and that's why my sister made it."

"It probably sounds crazy," Rob replied, "but I like to think you always have to look at things optimistically. I look at this . . . this is a stroke of good fortune."

"But on the other side," he continued, "nobody likes to be cut open. Any time somebody's operating on your brain there are all these inherent dangers, and we've got to worry about the embolisms again. I just picture, with my eyes closed, the feeding tubes, the weekend nurses—all that crap. But, hey, it's a small price to pay to get this over with once and for all."

There were upsides to surgery. Technique had been improved since the first operation, and this time there would be no biopsy. There would be just one incision. And, again, it was Joe Piepmeier, Rob's go-to guy. Successful surgery and radiation would also buy more time.

"If I can go on living like I lived the last four years, that's pretty good. A lot of zuppa di pesce," Rob chuckled. "I guess I didn't kick its ass completely, but the game is far from finished."

We said our goodbyes for the day. Before driving off Rob stuck his head out the car window. "Keep the title of the book *Life is Still Good,* " he said. "Life *is* still good."

CHAPTER 20

Pray For You, Coach

IT WAS THE waiting that always got Rob. Waiting for surgery wasn't much different than the interminable wait before kickoff. Body and mind were committed to the task and risk at hand, geared up for it, and now the revving engine was left to idle.

"Schedule the damn thing; let's go," Rob said the day I visited him at practice. "I wish I could go in tomorrow. I really do, so I don't have to think about it any longer."

Waiting left too much space for thinking. *How long will I be out? When will radiation start? When can I coach again? When can I counsel again?*

When, how long: Let's have the game plan.

Dr. Piepmeier took care of that during the August 31 consultation at Yale-New Haven. I went down with Rob and Diane and heard Piepmeier confirm and detail his impressions from the week before. He could operate and operate successfully.

Even sitting down, Piepmeier was like a rock. Blue eyes, white hair fringing male-pattern baldness, well over six feet tall: a steady rock above the tide, looking down and regarding the ebb and flow without visible alarm even when dangers were so evident to his practiced eye.

"It's clear you need more treatment," he told Rob. "The decision to observe was OK. We've reached the end of that decision. So what do we do?"

Surgery was the route. With the help of new technology that would provide a 3-D scan of Rob's brain during the operation—technology not available during the first operation in 2001—Piepmeier could go after not only the new growth, but perhaps some of the embedded cancer cells he deemed to risky to touch the first time.

Interestingly, those cells had been quiet. The latest tumor activity was exactly where Piepmeier had operated the first time, and it appeared that a small portion of the growth had burrowed in deeper than before. But with the new technology Piepmeier could better pinpoint and be more aggressive without taking risks. He couldn't get all of it, but there would be a significant reduction.

"Even better than last time," he said. "This is a pretty good option for you."

Piepmeier did caution surgery wouldn't do it alone. Follow-up brain scans and post-op testing of the removed mass would dictate future treatment. It might just be some more wait-and-see, but radiation could be in the cards. Piepmeier seemed to tread carefully with that topic. He was well aware that, for Rob, the word 'radiation' was synonymous with the late Andrea Mann.

"I know you're reluctant to consider radiation," Piepmeier said. "I think that, in part, is based on the experiences of other people. I think at some point we're going to have to look at that. If everything goes well with the surgery, then I would feel better about continuing with observation rather than jumping right to radiation—unless we find something in surgery."

All surgeries come with risks. Rob's tumor was near an artery. Piepmeier would have to pay close attention to that. Then there were those blood clots, so common after brain surgery and such a frightening aftermath to Rob's first procedure. This time, Piepmeier said, treatment would be more proactive. They'd get

Rob started on blood thinners in advance and get him on his feet and moving around as soon as possible.

For Rob, it was a plan, and once a plan was in place no opponent was too big. "All right," he told Piepmeier. "There's nobody I trust more. How soon can you get me in? Let's get this done."

Diane asked a few questions and they were good ones. In a nutshell, she wanted to know where they were ultimately headed.

"My intent is curative. That's what we're after," Piepmeier answered. "We're not palliating; we're intending to cure. I think we stack the deck in our favor by doing this, by reducing the burden we're asking other treatment to take care of. Fortunately, this isn't in an area where I can't go. I can go here. I can fix this."

"You're saying curative," said Diane. "I've never heard that term from you guys before."

"That is my intent."

"Cure completely?"

"Cure completely. Gone."

The brain surgeon locked his blue eyes on Rob's and regarded his patient from the height of the rock. "I want you around for my retirement party, and that's not for another 10 years. You even get to sit at the big table."

We chuckled.

"Heart of hearts," said Piepmeier, "I'm out to cure this. I'm not pissing around. That means we've got to get aggressive; that means we've got to face some treatments. I'm happy we can do this; I'm happy we can go back. This gives us more options. Let's fix it."

We bounced out of there, weirdly happy for people who'd just been talking about brain surgery. "Hey, d'ya hear that? Dr. P. wants me at his retirement party."

"Yeah, Rob, and not at some table in the back. You're at the head table."

We formed a pool, speculating on the date of surgery. Di won the three dollars when Yale called later that afternoon to say it would be Sept. 15.

I spent most of the day with Rob and saw the full gamut of his personality: the trusting patient, the beloved coach, the zealous competitor, the sower of happiness, the family man at turns soft and scratchy.

On the way into the hospital we had passed a young mother and her young daughter in the parking garage.

"HELLO!" Rob boomed out to the little girl.

"Say 'hello,' " instructed the mom.

"Hello," said the little girl.

"HOW ARE YOU TODAY?"

"Say 'good.' "

"Good."

"THAT'S GREAT! YOU HAVE A NICE DAY! What a beautiful kid."

The first thing Rob did on the drive home was phone his daughter Jennifer in New York to fill her in.

"I think this is a call for a celebration tonight," he remarked to Diane as he clicked off the phone. "Where we gonna go for dinner? Let's go out to dinner tonight."

Then he started debating whether he should head into work. It was the first day of school. Rob had visions of kids lined up outside his guidance office. Maybe he could get in for the afternoon.

"Should I go in, Diane? I think so. I feel funny not going to work today."

The road slowly bent homeward. Rob got to talking about Diane's driving, how it reflected their different personalities, how Di was so non-aggressive. As if on cue, another driver cut in front of us as two lanes merged into one.

"Where the hell is that guy going?" Rob yelped. "Don't let that bastard go! Don't let him do that!"

He was half laughing, half raging. The dulcet tones of Diane's Enya tape provided a bizarre counterpoint.

"He's an old guy who probably doesn't know where he's going," Diane said. "Let him go."

"He's not an old guy. He's a young kid."

"Rob, stop."

"Ah, it pisses me off," Rob said, laughing. "He just took advantage of you."

"Am I really worse off, Rob? This is what we deal with all the time, Bryant."

The mood was light, and yet Rob's anger was pure.

"You just lost, Diane."

"Who the heck cares?"

"I care. He just beat us. I don't lose well."

Ah, there was the old football coach, and it just so happened the Spartans had a scrimmage that afternoon over in Cheshire. This was an annual meeting, and a good one. There was a lot of friendliness and mutual respect between Rob and the Cheshire staff, which was headed by 40-year-old Mark Ecke who, like Rob, was a native son coaching the program he once played for. Every preseason Rob's team and Ecke's team would meet in a controlled scrimmage—no kickoffs or punts, coaches on the field during plays—then chow down with a post-game cookout. All the hot dogs and soda a kid could want. It was like getting out of detention after all those three-a-day practices and conditioning drills.

What the Spartans didn't know as they boarded the bus on this warm, but rain-spattered day was that some hard news was waiting back at Maloney. Rob coached during the scrimmage, but opted to wait until the end of the day to let the team know about his upcoming surgery. He wanted to tell the players what was up before they started hearing rumors or reading things in the newspaper.

Down in the narrow hallway to the locker room, which was almost always clamoring with shouts and clattering cleats and clanging lockers, the team knelt in a silent ring as Rob gave the word he'd been keeping from them for over a week. He'd be gone for a while, he told the Spartans, but he'd be back.

The kids were stunned. With the way Coach was at practice, darting here, striding there, hardly ever shutting up, who could have guessed?

"He's such a big part of bringing our spirits up and keeping everyone going in practice, and then something like this happens and he's still going to come out and coach us? I don't know how he's dealt with it so good."

Rob and Jay Evans

That was Jay Evans, one of the senior captains. Another captain, the quiet and steady center Jon Kovach, said the news about Coach Smaz would hopefully take some selfishness out of the team. What really was so big about their problems?

"It's a great lesson," Bob Zito remarked to me. "We had triple sessions the other day and the kids were tired and Robby's running around and I was thinking, 'Here's this guy who's got this medical situation and would never complain about it.' You talk about someone to emulate, admire and model your life after."

The players filed out, each with a word for coach.

"Hey coach, I know you'll be fine," said the unheralded senior halfback Patrick Wrenn.

"Coach, expect flowers," said Shoquan Stevens, a young, lanky defensive end who played with an unbridled passion and joy that was a delight to watch. "I'll get you anything you want. I'll get you the playbook."

"You know what I want, Shoquan," Rob replied. "I want you to come out and work hard each day."

Rob hated to leave these kids. Every day the fabric tightened. Every night at dinner he'd tell Di about this player, that player. White kids, black kids, Latino kids: The bonds were forming quickly.

During the consultation, Piepmeier had asked how the team was looking and that reminded Rob to ask when he could get back to work and to coaching. Piepmeier, noting that he'd keep the stitches in a little longer because it was a second surgery, figured it would be at least a couple of weeks. On the drive home Rob pulled out his pocket calendar and started counting days—four or five in the hospital after surgery, maybe another week recuperating at home—and "at least" a couple of weeks became two weeks at the most. By the end of the day, with the kids filing out of the locker room, each with a word for coach, it was down to eight days.

"Friday night the 23rd? Maybe just sitting in the press box? Is that being overly optimistic?" Rob asked me.

It certainly wasn't being out of character, and I certainly wasn't going to try and talk him out of it. I wasn't going to remind him of what Piepmeier had said: "In terms of returning to coaching activities, you tell me. I think the only real issue is fatigue. You're going to come out of this and you're going to be whipped."

Whipped? That was a subjective thing. It all depended on who was in the arena and who they had in their corner.

One of the last players out was Tommy Flores. He played defensive back, just as Rob had as a boy. But Tommy didn't have that nurturing family structure Rob had enjoyed. Not even close. Both his parents had scrapes with the law and Tommy had transferred in from New Britain to live with an aunt in Meriden. Rob took him a little deeper under his wing. Tommy was the one Rob called out to after most plays, praising or correcting him on his positioning, his steps, his tackling. "OK, good drop, Tommy . . . OK, you've got to wrap him up first, Tommy."

Now it was Tommy, shuffling out, head lowered, heavy duffle bag over one shoulder, who called out to Rob, though it was really no more than a whisper in the depths of that locker room of big echoes.

"Pray for you, Coach."

CHAPTER 21

Game Day, Round 2

ROB'S SECOND SURGERY was on September 15, 2005, almost four years to the day from the first. And like the first, the medical crisis of Coach Ron Carbone's All-American boy played out against the broader canvas of national catastrophe. The terrorist attacks of 9/11 had been replaced by the destruction Hurricane Katrina had wreaked on New Orleans and the Gulf Coast.

The Northeast was bone dry. Overdue rain came the morning of surgery, though as I drove over to meet Rob and Diane for the ride down to Yale-New Haven, patches of sun and blue sky were breaking through in the west—the sort of rainy-day clearing that can somehow seem more uplifting than a full day of sun. Diane, coming in from walking Mr. Diffley as I drove up, noted that morning's saying in a little daily book of wisdom she was reading: "Rain is heaven's water."

I liked the symbolism of light returning after darkness. "I believe in signs," I said to Rob, then asked him if he was wearing clean underwear.

Rob smiled. His sense of humor was undimmed, but it rode on palpable nervousness. He was quieter than usual, subdued. Part of it was that old ballplayer edginess. Pre-game butterflies: Once you take your first hit or have that first pitch thrown, you can settle down. In the meantime, you just want to get on with it.

That morning's paper featured the high school football preview. The Maloney Spartans would be kicking off their season in two days in Glastonbury. Rob said he wanted to read the articles on the ride down to the hospital, but it was unlikely he'd be able to focus on them. Diane's anxiety showed too. She was constantly moving around. Even Mr. Diffley sensed something was up. He, too, couldn't sit still.

Rob's sister Sharon showed up. She'd driven up from New Jersey earlier in the week. Just the day before, she'd dropped by Maloney to see Rob with their nephew, Jan's son Michael John, who was leaving shortly to study in England. They found Rob in his guidance office, hunched over his desk, making a play sheet that Maloney's rookie quarterback would wear on his wrist in Saturday's season opener. Little coded notations, the whole galaxy of a system distilled onto a square of paper. Perhaps, even if just for a day, it would make a single young man, a single team, a star. Perhaps, when faced with enormity, there is comfort to be found in the simple routines and details of our lives.

Rob went into his second operation with optimism, belief and strength that countered moments of doubt. For one thing, there was the unwavering confidence in Piepmeier. "It's almost like I want to insulate him, to put five guys around him and drive him around to make sure nothing happens to him," Rob had joked after the consultation two weeks earlier.

Well-wishers had him on the phone for much of the day before the surgery. School folks, football folks, just plain folks: It was a force of energy. "With that kind of support," he said, "how can things not go well?" Rob learned he was on many prayer lists at churches and in prayer groups. He spoke with Phil Ottochian and John Skubel, former coaching colleagues who were wrestling with health issues of their own. He spoke with Mother Shaun Vergauwen, who ran the Franciscan Life Center, a Catholic retreat tucked off a rolling back road on the Cheshire-Meriden line. Rob loved bringing his team out to the Center to do community service work. He wasn't alone. UConn basketball coach Jim Calhoun was so close to the sisters that they were often seen sitting behind his bench at games, including Final Fours.

Rob loved Mother Shaun and the sisters. "There's a radiance that comes out of their eyes," Rob said, and he was right. There was a vibe of goodness about the place, a sense of sanctuary from the world's hard ways.

"Rob, I'm putting you back on the top of our prayer list," Mother Shaun told Rob as his surgery approached.

"Well, I don't think I need to get the top, Mother Shaun. How about somewhere in the Top 10?"

People would stop Diane in the grocery store. "I pray for Rob; I pray for Rob." Rob believed in the power of those prayers. Though his practice waxed and waned, he strove to live a Christian life and the Catholic beliefs in which he was raised never wavered. He believed in the hereafter, in heaven, hell, and purgatory. He believed and accepted that the tumor was his cross to bear.

He did have doubts. These he confessed the afternoon after the consult with Dr. Piepmeier. When the tumor started growing again, Rob started thinking about who he wanted for his pallbearers. One of his former assistant coaches, the rambunctious Aldo Scoffone, used to joke, "Screw 'em all but six." Was it time to pick the six?

"I don't think pessimistically, but at the same time we all want things done. It's not doom and gloom, but sometimes you . . . as much as you think positively and optimistically, I don't know why this time I'm thinking in terms of the possibility . . . death never even entered my mind last time. It crept into my mind this time."

"I think that's only natural to think that," I said.

"Yeah, but I didn't last time."

Earlier in the year, when the tumor seemed inoperable and wasn't responding to chemo, Rob had asked Baehring, "Doc, should I start getting my things in order?"

At the time, radiation seemed the likely option. The anniversary of Andrea's death was approaching.

"No," Baehring said. "You're far from that."

* * *

Sharon's perky, playful sense of humor helped chase the gloom on the day of surgery. She drove Rob and Diane to the hospital, and as they checked in, Sharon comforted her brother in her own unique way.

"It's not like they can mess it up. It's not like they can take the wrong one, like a kidney. You only have one brain."

"Well, I've got some news for you, Sharon," Rob replied. "We need to take out a piece of your brain to give to me."

"Oh, that's OK. I hope you get the sensitive part."

"I hope it's not the feminine part."

While Rob was in a bathroom trading his dress shirt and khakis for surgery pajamas, a nurse we'd never seen before came into our private waiting room.

"Who's getting operated on today?"

Sharon pushed me forward. "He is."

Rob reappeared in the hospital-issue pajamas and that drew laughs and photographs.

"Now I know what it's like to have a dress on," Rob remarked as Diane and Sharon snapped away. "This will be one for the book, huh Bry?"

"Maybe the centerfold."

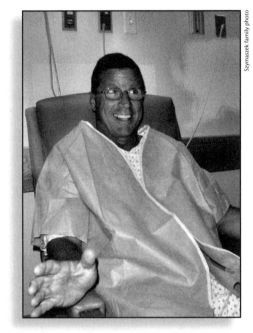

"This will be one for the book."
Rob just before his second surgery.

Jennifer arrived from New York City. She was just back from an expedition to Colombia that had Rob and Diane worried sick. She and another young woman from New York were putting together a documentary. With the help of a Colombian nun, they visited families displaced by that country's drug trade and attendant violence. Some had parents and siblings simply vanish.

When it came to courage, Jen was her father's daughter, and then some. The fields she'd traversed weren't defined by yard lines or accepted rules. There was no safety to be had on the sidelines. There were no sidelines. Now Jen was back in New York, doing freelance photography for the Associated Press and for diplomats.

She'd gone from Third World dirt floors to a party at the United Nations thrown by the Prince of Monaco, but she would be going back to Colombia to do more work on the documentary.

Arriving with Jen was a parcel of Mrs. Fields cookies sent by Rob's friend Jimmy Staszewski. Jimmy had been a teammate; he'd been best man at Rob's wedding. Now he was a cognitive psychologist living in Pittsburgh. Jim knew his stuff. The cookies, he indicated, were for the nurses on the recovery floor. He knew how to ensure steady attention for his buddy after surgery.

The operation was still some time off. Rob sat in a recliner and you could easily kid yourself into thinking he was settling in at home to watch a movie—maybe *Rudy* for the 10 gazillionth time. A nurse came in to take Rob's vitals and they talked about cruises and dogs. Rob said he was going into surgery thinking about St. Martin. He'd close his eyes and see the clear blue water and sunsets at Orient Beach and the eggs over easy at Andy's place and (wink, wink) the skin tones of the locals. Everything wrapped in an easy breeze: *Just fahgeddabout it.*

All the humor, however, could not chase the growing anxiety as the minutes ticked away. "Wow," Sharon whispered to Diane, "this is really happening."

Betsey D'Andrea stopped by. Betsey: a warm, familiar face, shouldering the emotional load of the neuro-oncology department, still running the support group meetings. Her husband had died without warning only a few months before.

"How are we this morning?"

Rob asked if there were any last-minute changes in his brain scans. "Being the eternal optimist I am, I thought maybe it shrank."

Betsey managed a smile. "We're sitting here, so I have a feeling that's not the case."

"Oh," Rob chuckled, but it had a rueful edge.

"I'd like to say, 'Go home; there's been a mistake,' but I don't think that's going to happen."

"OK, Betsey, OK."

"You all right?"

"I'm fine. Let's get this over with, right?"

"Absolutely."

"This is good."

"This is the right thing to do. After you recover from this, we'll talk about what the next step is."

It would be a numbers game. If the pathology report indicated the tumor was still a Grade 2, it would be wait-and-see; but if it had elevated to Grade 3 then there would likely be radiation.

"We like the number two," said Betsey.

"What if it's two and a half?" Diane asked.

"We like the number two. Go to sleep thinking two."

"Is there such a thing as a one?" Rob asked.

Betsey managed another smile. "I'm surprised you're not out in the hallway pacing," she said.

"We're blocking the door," said Sharon.

Betsey gave Rob a long look, smiled. "You're ready."

"Let's kick the ball off and get this thing rolling."

Outside in hallway, Sharon talked with Betsey. "People are always asking me 'How's your brother?' and I always say 'He's doing great' because that's how he's handled it. The bottom line is he's got a cancerous tumor in his brain, yet the way he's handled it is like he's got a cold."

Sharon paused. "He's always so optimistic on the outside, but I know on the inside he's worried."

"That's to be expected," Betsey said. "It would be abnormal if he weren't."

Dr. Piepmeier and Dr. Baehring stopped in.

"Hey, Dr. Piepmeier," Rob called out. "I was almost going to call you last weekend and tell you not to do any yard work involving sharp tools."

Piepmeier smiled, but like Betsey's, it was a mustered smile. He was all business, wearing plum-colored scrubs and green rubber clogs. Rob would be his second patient of the morning. The first surgery ran a little longer than expected, he explained, and the operating room was just now getting cleared and cleaned.

Orderlies wearing similar scrubs of plum or powder blue passed in a steady stream up and down the hallway, which frequently jigged and jagged like a house out of Dr. Seuss. The intercom emitted a thin tinny voice at regular intervals. *Attention please. Will the surgical clinical advisor please dial extension eight-nine-three-oh-two.*

Rob reminded Diane about his last-minute advice for Coach Zito. "Tell Bob to make sure all the assistant coaches remain real positive around the kids for the next few days. Everybody's upbeat, OK?"

Finally, the orderlies came for Rob. It was go time. They had Rob lie down on the stretcher and they took off his glasses. A wave of anxiety washed across his face. We started to wheel him down the hallway, but there was only so far we could go. The name of one of the orderlies was Reggie, and Sharon tried to bribe him with the Mrs. Fields cookies to let us proceed further.

"Reggie," Rob called up from the stretcher, "don't listen to her. Whatever she tells you, do the opposite."

We laughed one last time, but there, at the door of the OR waiting room, we had to stop. This wasn't like last time, when Jen could stand right outside the door to the operating room itself and give her dad one last vision of love to take into that room with the brightest lights he'd ever seen. Husband and wife embraced. Diane was wearing Rob's wedding ring on a chain around her neck. Father and daughter embraced. Brother and sister kissed. Two friends shook hands. Tears and smiles. Then just tears as the stretcher was wheeled down the hall.

Sharon and Di embraced.

"It's in God's hands," Sharon said.

"He's going to be OK," said Diane.

The stretcher went away. Rob had closed his eyes as he left us, but as he got to the final turn, passing under a clock, I saw him look up.

* * *

The OR waiting room was full at noon. People awaited word on their loved ones. People with messy hair and craggy faces. People who hadn't been getting enough sleep. People lulled by the tedium and slow time of waiting. The tinny voice maintained its monotone on the intercom. *O-R-two-A-seven for a neuro pickup please, O-R-two-A-seven for a neuro pickup. Thank you . . .*

There was a monitor on the wall, much like the ones at airports. It listed each patient's name, the time they went into surgery and the time they were due out. The names were in alphabetical order and they rotated. I monitored the scroll as if waiting to pick Rob up from a return flight from St. Martin.

Diane and Sharon did a lot of handholding. Sharon commiserated with her sister-in-law. She knew the strain and stress the ordeal had put on her, not to mention the times when Rob was cranky or in pain, or just a pain in the ass—the details of which Diane would never tell me. That's Diane. As much as Rob was boisterous and comfortable living in public—it comes with the territory of coaching, and after 20-some-odd years it's no big deal—Diane was quiet and preferred keeping to herself, certainly on deeply personal matters. She was never really enamored with the idea of the book mostly because she knew the unpleasant, uninspiring side of it—again, the details of which she'd never tell me. Or she'd say "way off the book," sometimes even when giving the most innocuous detail.

Sharon and Diane did a lot of talking. It occurred to me Sharon was much like her brother. Quick to smile, quick to laugh. She didn't want to be vulnerable or show it. It also occurred to me she was probably a lot like Millie. She wasn't just a big sister; she was a second mother and had always been so. She, too, doted on Rob and could make him the absolute center of the universe. For a moment, I had a glimpse into Rob's boyhood and one of the major forces that had shaped him. No wonder Rob had sometimes found Diane's attentions to be lacking—and unfairly so. Sharon and Diane spoke of this after Rob went into surgery. There was an easy and warm openness between them and it was comforting to hear them confide.

We didn't hang around the waiting room for the duration of the surgery. Rob had given Diane some cash earlier in the day. *Go out to lunch while I'm in. Don't just sit there worrying.* So instead of keeping vigil, letting anxiety eat at us, we ate at a nearby restaurant where Rob and Andrea had often had lunch. I could hear Rob's voice in my head. *"You know me. I like to cook a good meal and I like to have a good time."*

On the way back to the hospital, we ran into Mark Padilla and his mother Madeline. Mark should have been in his junior year at Maloney, getting ready for the start of the season with the rest of the Spartans. Instead, he was not in school thanks to a 180-day expulsion, a penalty that resulted, as best as I could tell, from the maneuverings of a few determined school board members.

"180 days?" I'd asked Rob when the expulsion was announced. "Why don't they just take him out back and cut his arm off or burn him as a witch?"

Rob agreed. He'd always found his school to be far too eager to dole out suspensions and expulsions as if they were a point of pride, as if some sort of quota had to be met. Mark's expulsion stemmed from a shouting match at a spring track practice with an assistant coach. From what I heard, the coach had been as responsible for the incident's escalation as much as the kid, if not more so.

We all have our angels and our devils. The day Coach Smaz underwent brain surgery for a second time, Mark was there.

He and his mother had bought a Box o' Joe from Dunkin' Donuts. We crowded onto the elevator and headed back upstairs to wait out the remaining hour. But coming down the hall, we could see Dr. Piepmeier at the waiting room door. This was much earlier than expected. And as much as that flicker of fear—*what's gone wrong?*—flared through our hearts, it quickly dimmed. You could just tell by the way Piepmeier was standing there. The high shoulders, the easy confidence. Maybe he even smiled, but he didn't have to.

He led us through the waiting room to a more private room behind it and closed the door. There were couches around a small table, bare save for a box of tissues. This was where every family received its news.

"We got everything done that we wanted to do," Dr. Piepmeier began. "It worked, in terms of the surgery. We didn't have any problems."

There was the slightest pause, but no change in Piepmeier's tone.

"The tumor looked a little different. It looked a little more vascular."

"Meaning?" Diane asked.

Dr. Piepmeier didn't beat around. "Meaning more blood supply to the tumor. More than he had previously."

Jennifer seized on the implication. "Meaning it could be a higher grade."

"I can't tell yet," Piepmeier answered. "That in itself doesn't answer the question. His is behaving like it."

Only the pathology tests would tell. In the meantime, Piepmeier didn't want to dampen the day's success. Cancer battles are best fought that way.

"I'm glad we did this. I feel much better about it now. Everything we thought we'd get out, we got out."

"What's left?" Diane asked.

"He's got some infiltration that we knew we weren't going to go after. It's far less–"

"Than last time?"

"Than what we had three hours ago, in terms of what the burden now is to treat with radiation. It's much less."

"So you're thinking probably radiation?"

"Let's wait and see what pathology says. I'm probably going to push for that, too. Let's wait and see what pathology says. I don't want to presuppose that. But it went well. I'm pleased."

"Dr. P.," said Sharon, "You amaze us."

Piepmeier left to attend to his next surgery. Diane, while relieved, mulled the likelihood of radiation, the road Rob didn't want to take. The enhanced blood supply would indicate a more severe grade, we agreed, but the operation left a smaller area to radiate. Plus, the operation had bought more time. More time for enhanced technology, more time for improved treatment.

Diane let go a long exhale and stood up.

"OK," she said. "He's alive."

* * *

We were able to see Rob in about half an hour. Diane went in and Sharon, Jennifer and I waited our turn in the ICU waiting

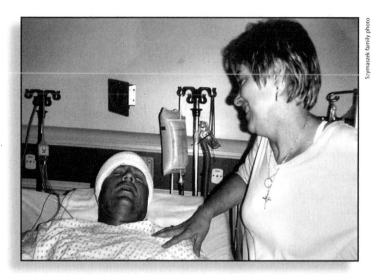

Szymaszek family photo

Diane looks over Rob after the second operation at Yale-New Haven.

room. Betsey D'Andrea stopped by on her way home. Jen asked her about the significance of the enhanced blood supply.

"Hey," Betsey said. "We can take care of this."

Jen went in to see her dad. In a while, Sharon and I were ushered in.

In the darkened recovery room, Rob was looking about as good as you could look, I imagined, after having your brain operated on. His head was wrapped in a turban of white gauze. His face looked normal. There seemed to be no swelling. There was an IV bag and all sorts of machines that beeped and monitored pulse and heartbeat with silent green numbers.

Rob was lucid, though the pain medication was starting to kick in. He was able to speak—slowly, but with certainty. I asked a question I knew he'd want to field.

"Hey, Coach, any message for the team?"

"What's today? Thursday? Forty-eight hours there should be

a happy bus ride home. Stay focused. Don't let me distract you from the mission. Beat Glastonbury."

It had been an off-and-on day of showers and sun. The Gulf Coast continued its long recovery from Katrina. Rob slept in ICU.

Mist was clinging to the cliff faces as I got back to Meriden. And then, I kid you not, the clouds cleared a bit and a rainbow arched across the sky. The sun glowed off the ridges as the mist cleared away. I tried not to pay attention to the dark clouds looming behind them.

CHAPTER 22

Escape from Oak Ridge Drive

IT WAS WEEK 2 of the 2005 football season, another Saturday morning in September, and this time it was Mike Falis pulling into an empty parking lot at Maloney High School.

Mike: The nice guy who can be a hard ass, the guy who got mad at Coach Ed McGee all those years ago when he was a senior captain because McGee wouldn't let him play just because he was pissing blood before the game. Well, on this Saturday, Mike pulled into the Maloney High School parking lot at nine o'clock in the morning and didn't see the Szymaszek white Acura and got all sentimental. He punched a speed dial number on his cell phone. "Hey, I miss you."

If Mike was like a schoolgirl that morning, then Rob was the schoolboy. He'd been pacing, pacing, thoughts racing, antsy since he woke up. Diane had already left for a conference at nearby Wesleyan University. As she was heading out the door Rob told her that, no, he supposed he wouldn't be going to Maloney's game at Wethersfield that afternoon but, hey, just in case he changed his mind, maybe she should leave her cell phone on. Diane stopped and made her preference for Rob's activities that day perfectly clear.

With the house empty save for Mr. Diffley, the scales of Rob's inner debate kept swinging one way, driven by silence and unanswered phone calls and isolation. Then Mike's call came in. Rob started babbling like a grounded kid who's about to be let out to play in the sand pits but can't stand the last five minutes of his three-day sentence.

"I've been calling down to the locker room! Where is everybody?"

Rob paced the kitchen, pulling the long phone cord across the kitchen table.

"Diane's mad at me. *I wanna go!*"

He came back across the kitchen. Back went the long phone cord across the table.

"We got in an argument. *I wanna go!*"

Mike took a politician's tack. He talked good sense and took a position, then hedged on both in the very next sentence.

"I think maybe it's better to stay home and give it another week, but you call me if you want me to pick you up. The bus leaves for Wethersfield at 10:30."

So that's where it was left for the next 90 minutes, but was there really any doubt? The prior Saturday, two days after his operation, still hospitalized at Yale-New Haven, Rob placed a call to Mike's wife Linda, who works for an ambulance company. The Spartans were opening the season that afternoon about 40 minutes away in Glastonbury, a Hartford suburb that managed to be upscale and colonial-quaint at the same time.

"Hey Linda, how much would it cost to have an ambulance pick me up at Yale-New Haven, drive me to Glastonbury and then bring me back after the game?"

Perhaps her answer, along with further consideration of how to get past nurses and security with an IV in tow—again, all of 48 hours after brain surgery—convinced Rob to forego Maloney's season opener.

It was just as well. The Spartans made some early mistakes—an interception, a blocked punt, another interception—and a more experienced Glastonbury team capitalized on each one for an almost immediate 19-0 lead. It was 26-0 by halftime.

The young Maloney team did not know how to respond. Deflation was palpable along the sidelines, which were virtually silent. No chant of "DEE-FENSE! DEE-FENSE!" No howls of "PASS!" or "RUN!" to help alert the defense. No rallying cry of any kind.

Kids were getting banged up, too. Maloney's trainer, Jessie Wylie, was ubiquitous, carrying ice bags and diagnosing knee sprains. Key players hobbled out, and as the afternoon wore on and the cloud cover broke, the heat rose. It was a tough game to play in. Plenty of players on both teams cramped up before the contest came to a merciful 33-6 close. The Spartans had played their opponent evenly after halftime, one score apiece, but that was lost amid an almost spiritual malaise that hovered over the team.

That lack of emotion bothered Rob when he heard about it. So did the struggles off the new offense he had installed. Bob Zito was unfamiliar with the I-formation, but he'd let Rob shape the playbook. Rob felt a deep responsibility to Zito. "What if it were the other way around?" Rob thought lying in his hospital bed. "What if I was the new guy and he put in his wing-T, then got sick and I was left with an offense I didn't really know?"

Moreover, tradition and reputation were on the line. This was Rob Szymaszek's offense. For all the spread and option wrinkles that had been added, this at its core was the tried-and-true Spartan offense, the toss-and-belly staple that had once made Maloney known as "Tailback High." Mustering just 55 yards on 51 plays—Maloney's output against Glastonbury—was embarrassing and unacceptable.

So a week later, nine days after his operation, five days out of the hospital, back home in Meriden and in closer touch with the team, there was really no debate about where Coach Smaz would be for Maloney's second game of the season.

Mike called back promptly at 10:30.

"What do you want to do?"

"PICK ME UP!"

What was it that he had told Diane? Well, it was unfortunate, but it seemed her cell phone wasn't on after all.

"Hey Mike, remember that drill we used to run: Escape from Saigon?" Rob asked once the two were northbound on I-91 to Wethersfield. "Well, this was Escape from Oak Ridge Drive."

* * *

The effect of Rob's appearance was obvious and immediate. The players perked up as they saw Rob come onto the field as they were warming up. He hadn't been on the bus, of course, and

Rob at the Wethersfield game after getting bandaged by Jessie Wylie

they had no idea he'd be coming. Yet there he was, the right side of his head bare and slightly swollen and seemingly misshapen as if it had been kicked at. The black stitches were plainly visible. There was a salve on the incision and it glistened in the noon sun until Jessie Wylie rigged a gauze covering.

Nine days after brain surgery, up and walking and on the sidelines. Did anyone really need a pep talk?

"This game was for him," Johran McCaw announced after galloping for 157 yards and two touchdowns in a 16-0 Spartans victory.

A few more kids got hurt or aggravated injuries, but there was no letdown. And there was no silence along the sidelines this time. Every defensive down drew a prompt and prolonged cry of "PASS" or "RUN."

"Just seeing him walk down to the field brought everybody's emotions up," said Jay Evans, one of the senior captains, a two-way guy at fullback and linebacker. He was a cut from the Maloney mold: not very big, not very fast, just very hard-nosed and committed.

McCaw was another cut from the Maloney mold: athletic, speedy kid who ran with the ball. "We wanted to win that much more," McCaw said. "It's not the same without him on the sidelines."

Rob was on those sidelines, out in the full sun for the whole game, and he wasn't merely a bystander. "I didn't come here to stand on the sidelines," Rob had said as he strode up and shook Bob Zito's hand. "I came to call some plays."

One bit of information Rob didn't make widely known was that pathology reports confirmed what the operation had made suspect: The tumor cells had elevated from Grade 2 to Grade 3.

Nor did Rob tell anyone he'd stopped taking his pain medication at 2 a.m. the night before. He had a hunch he'd be at this game. The last thing he wanted was to feel drugged up and spacey. He wanted to be clear-headed. That meant pain. Adrenaline and joy carried him early on—seeing the kids, seeing the coaches. I was covering the game, and when I heard he was there, I bolted out of the press box and sprinted down to the end of the field where the team was just breaking its final pre-game huddle. I was laughing wildly as I grabbed his shoulders.

"You are a goddamn nut!"

I wasn't alone in the sentiment. The other coaches, myself, Diane—she eventually got Rob's message and showed up to watch the game with Mr. Diffley, noting with a resigned chuckle, "when I left this morning, he wasn't going"—we absolutely admired Rob for his guts, his passion. We questioned his sanity, but not his fortitude.

Coaches from other teams marveled about it when they heard. "He is one tough son of a bitch," said Cheshire assistant Greg Ferry, and he meant not a drop of disrespect to Millie Szymaszek.

Rob was ferried to and from the locker room at halftime on a golf cart. The same cart took him out to the parking lot when the game was over. He was a hurting unit by then. He denied it, of course, but it was plain to see in his eyes, even behind his sunglasses. His usual sparkling, wide blue eyes were dull and in a perpetual squint. It was also plain to see in his posture. As the game went on, Rob had become something of a Leaning Tower of Szymaszek.

"That day in Wethersfield, Rob," I asked weeks later. "How much pain were you in?"

"On a scale of one to ten? Probably at an eight."

The sheer happiness of not just being at the game, but contributing to victory, helped overcome the pain, or at least make

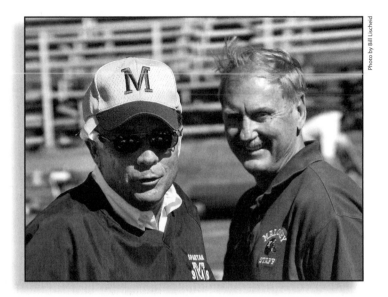

Photo by Bill Lischeid

Rob and Mike Falis after Maloney beat Wethersfield

it bearable. Certainly his mental clarity never wavered. Rob had to have done something right. A week after gaining 55 yards on offense, the Spartans racked up 321 against Wethersfield and maintained possession of the ball for about three-quarters of the game.

That ball wound up at Rob's house by the end of the night, up on the football shelf next to the game ball from that first game against Guilford way back in 1976 and next to the post-game photograph from career win No. 100. All the kids on the team signed this latest piece of the collection and the senior captains brought it up. Johrone Bunch's comical nickname, "Boobutt," was printed in particularly large letters and seemed to radiate off the ball as if etched in neon.

It was on that day in Wethersfield, Rob would later say, that his comeback from his second surgery commenced. The pain reached its pinnacle, but his fighting spirit was back on its feet. He vowed it was true, even months later, when the comeback was under attack and the battle was being waged on the front he'd always wanted to avoid.

CHAPTER 23

Piece by Piece

THE JIGSAW PUZZLES in the waiting room of Yale-New Haven's Hunter Radiation Therapy Center were always in a state of progress. Spread out on small tables, with some effort made to contain the sprawl, they never seemed to get finished. The frames were done and, within the frame, pieces forming a scenic feature—a Vermont barn, say, or a Maine lighthouse—had been lumped together, but awaited the pivotal piece that would link them to the big picture.

Radiation patients would come in each day and slot together a few pieces while awaiting treatment. They'd come back the next day, find a few more, undergo treatment until, after a month of days—for that's how long most treatment cycles lasted—they'd come in and announce with proud finality and relief, "Today is my last day."

Maybe the radiation would work. Maybe it would prove the pivotal piece in a cancer patient's treatment.

For Rob, this was the part of the puzzle he never wanted to dabble with. This was the building he never wanted to enter. Yale's Hunter Radiation Therapy Center sits across York Avenue from Yale-New Haven's main building. Whenever he'd go into the hospital for consults or to review scans, Rob would cast a rueful glance across the street and think, "Boy, I hope I don't have to go there." Yet here he was, coming down daily for a treatment

293

cycle that would run from early November into mid-December 2005.

Radiation seemed likely after the second surgery and became inevitable once the pathology report confirmed the cancer had elevated from Grade 2 to Grade 3. Now was the time to radiate. That was the point of surgery. As Dr. Piepmeier had said, it set up radiation by reducing the area necessary to treat.

Yale radiologist Dr. Jonathan Knisely designed the protocol. Knisely had earned his undergrad degrees at Yale in the early 1980s and, after acquiring his doctorate at Penn and putting in residencies in Chicago and Toronto, was back in New Haven as an associate professor at the Yale School of Medicine's Department of Therapeutic Radiology. Researching and using radiation to treat brain tumors was his field of expertise.

Knisely's track record helped put Rob at ease. While Rob said he didn't fear the radiation itself—Andrea had told him it was painless—he was worried about the side effects, namely the effect on healthy brain tissue and his health in general. Rob read a lot, including an account from a woman who said radiation turned her husband into the shell of the man he was.

"He couldn't do this; he couldn't do that because they didn't really pinpoint the radiation. That scared the shit out of me," Rob said. "He couldn't get dressed himself. Jesus Christ, the thought of not being able to dress myself in the morning."

Dr. Knisely reminded Rob that after two brain operations he was still able to do what he always could do. As for radiation, he added, the tumor was in a good position to be treated. Above all, the improvements in radiation therapy had been tremendous, even from the time Rob's support group buddy, Peter DeBona, had gone through it in 1994. Using state of the art machines called "linear accelerators," Yale technicians could pinpoint the radiation beams on diseased cells with far less collateral damage to the surrounding healthy cells. Also, Knisely had been using image fusion between MRIs and CT scans to plan radiation treatments since 1996.

These points were underscored in e-mails sent to Rob by Peter DeBona, who was still in remission and now living in Arizona.

"They just bombarded that poor guy's head and look at him," Rob said. "He's unbelievable."

So Rob sized it up: *OK, there are cells that Dr. Piepmeier couldn't remove in surgery and we couldn't eradicate with chemotherapy. As good a neurosurgeon as he is, Joe couldn't go there. So what options are left? Let's have Dr. Knisely design the program and let's do it. Let's finally eradicate this disease once and for all.*

"We're not dealing with a Grade 2 cell anymore," Rob said to me one morning as I drove him to New Haven for a radiation treatment. "I'm dealing with a Grade 3 aggressive tumor cell up there. I don't want to think, in all honesty, what could happen if I don't do this. My options—let's face it, there aren't a lot of options left. So across the street, into the radiation center I go."

First, however, other health complications arose. Rob said the second surgery was not as painful as the first, but there was more swelling and the swelling lasted longer. It was so persistent there was talk of using a needle to drain the fluid, but Dr. Piepmeier said that procedure was too intrusive. Let it happen naturally, he advised.

Then there were the blood clots. They were an all-too-common side effect of brain surgery and the horrific experience after the first operation had taught Rob to be on the lookout for symptoms. So two days after the Wethersfield game, when he noticed some swelling in his leg and Diane suggested they take a run down to Yale-New Haven, there was no resistance.

Precaution prevailed. An ultrasound revealed a clot in his leg. Rob was admitted and filters were put implanted through a vein in his neck. It was a painful process. Rob felt every little movement.

"Does it hurt?" asked the attending physician.

"Yeah it fucking hurts."

Rob was already irritable from a nearly six-hour wait in the emergency room. Even on a Monday night Yale-New Haven was packed and chaotic. There were swarms of sirens. Patients were rushed in from motor vehicle accidents, even a shooting.

Maybe the ER is where Rob picked up the infection that really leveled him later that week. Or maybe it was the strain of going to the Wethersfield game, though Rob didn't think so and neither did Diane. I thought with dread about two water bottles I'd given Rob at halftime. I'd bought one for each of us, but he looked so drained from the sun I handed off both as he was driven to the locker room on a golf cart. I had taken a few sips from mine. I was healthy, but had I passed on some dormant germ?

As Maloney's home opener rolled around the following Friday night there was no question Coach Smaz would not be on the sidelines or in the press box or anywhere close to Ceppa Field. He was still in the hospital, suffering headaches so acute the pain made him vomit. He hurt so badly he turned off the ringer to the telephone in his room and begged off on visitors. I didn't get through until Saturday afternoon.

"I'm heading down to Long Wharf Theater to see a play tonight. Why don't I leave a few hours early and pay a visit?"

"I'm afraid I won't be much company," Rob said before handing the phone over to Diane.

"Through this whole ordeal—everything—this is the sickest I've seen him," she said.

Rob got home Sunday night, but was feeling very weak. He

readily capitulated to rest and recuperation. "For the first time I don't have the stamina," he told me the following Friday as Maloney played its fourth game of the season.

Plus, Rob hadn't been at practice all week. Just showing up on the night of a game flew in the face of his long-standing team rule. And if Rob needed any further words of wisdom, he got them from Dr. Piepmeier: You'll get better; don't push it; it will take time; this was your second operation.

"I'm listening to the big guy," Rob said.

So that night, instead of watching the Spartans, Rob tuned in to the new ESPN movie *Four Minute Mile* about Roger Bannister, and it fired him right back up.

"You know, for the longest time people believed the human body was not capable of running a four-minute mile and that anyone who did it would die from the stress," Rob remarked. "Along comes Roger Bannister, who was studying to be a doctor and knew otherwise. It's just more proof that what the mind can believe, the body can achieve."

Up on the shelf sat the ball from the Wethersfield game. I'd often noted how Rob's football memorabilia contrasted to the other end of the shelf, upon which sat Diane's pottery and primitive art. And on the shelf holding their DVD and video collection, *Rudy* stood side by side with The *Power of Myth*. I would come to see them as pieces of a kindred puzzle.

* * *

By early November, Rob had recuperated enough to start radiation. He had already put in 10 days by the time I took him on November 16.

The accumulated traumas of the past two months had affected his appearance. There was a slight diminishment, but only by

Rob's standard. He's usually so robust he seems to give off waves of energy. On that day, it was more like a deflation, like a body just out of bed that hadn't turned itself on yet.

I noticed his memory was a little sketchy and that the hair shaven away for the operation had grown back, but looked dry. On top of it, Rob informed me, he was on antibiotics for bronchitis. Radiation does inhibit the immune system—not a whole lot, but enough so that it's wise to get treated right away for any illness. Rob was also on the blood thinner Lovanox, which he injected each night, and on the steroid Decatron, which had been prescribed to reduce swelling in the brain after the operation and through radiation.

Despite all this, Rob had hoped to return to work during the treatments. He wanted to schedule the appointments early so he could get to school by 10 a.m. It remained a point of pride to punch the clock. He even asked Dr. Knisely for a letter saying it was OK for him to return to work part time. Rob got the letter, but it wound up having an unforeseen effect.

To Whom It May Concern . . . Mr. Szymaszek is a patient in my care in the Department of Radiology at the Yale School of Medicine for his treatment of cancer.

Rob read it, re-read it.

Treatment of cancer.

Rob said it was the first time he'd seen the words in writing and they just floored him. "Wow, I guess I really have this."

Rob was also exchanging e-mails with Mary Cortright, Meriden's superintendent of schools. She didn't expect Rob back until after the Christmas break at the earliest. She all but ordered him to stay home until then.

My advice to you is to take the time you need to really feel good and not rush back to work! This is really a time when you need to concentrate on yourself. Of course, the choice is yours, Rob, but it really is OK to think about yourself and your wellness.

Rob e-mailed back:

Thank you for your sincere and genuine concern and advice. The more radiation patients and professional people I have talked to in the past few days reconfirm memory issues and fatigue.

So, OK, he'd target an early January return.

However, my own personal philosophy is diabolically opposed to taking lengthy periods of time off.

I was about to tease Rob about using the wrong word, then it occurred to me that "diabolically" was the absolute right word. He's such a battler he sometimes doesn't know when to back off even when it's in his best interest. Radiation, though, was denting the armor. "You see my dilemma," Rob said. "I need to stay active, but I am truthfully concerned about whether I can pull this one off."

Rob pulled out two light blue baseball caps emblazoned with the Life is Good logo and handed one to me. He'd read about how the hair loss that accompanies radiation kicks in around the 15th day of treatment and was wondering if he should get a toupee.

"Uh-oh, Bry, as we speak," Rob said, pulling a single strand from the band of his cap.

"I can match that."

I held out my cap, tousled my hair and extracted a single strand.

"Here ya, go. Matched it."

Rob grinned, donned his cap.

"OK, Day 11, 19 more to go."

* * *

There was a low groaning as the big machine moved into place. It stirred like some giant sci-fi microscope come to life, large and looming and slowly probing this creature lying on its plate. Rob certainly seemed like some kind of specimen immobilized there. He was wearing a mesh mask—it looked like the mask fencers wear—affixed with a couple squares of medical tape marked with crosses. Lasers were lined up on both sides of his head.

Radiation looks imposing, and there's no denying it's a heavy treatment. At Yale, it's administered underground in the Hunter Building. You take an elevator down one flight to get to the waiting room. As for the treatment itself, think of a red-hot poker. That's how the radiation beam is applied: a daily guided missile strike to kill cancer cells and keep killing them while the surrounding healthy cells continue their normal division cycle.

It's in the precision that radiation treatment has made the greatest gains. Patricia Roy and Helene Civatello, the technicians who worked with Rob at Yale, talked about this as they prepped him for dose No. 11. Pat and Helene had a great touch. They were efficient yet friendly, happily explaining as they went about their work. They'd done the same when Jen had brought Rob in for an appointment before heading to back to New York. She left feeling a lot more comfortable about her dad's latest course of treatment.

It started with the brain scans, which pinpointed the areas to be treated. Then came the mask. It was form-fitted to Rob's face and the mesh front allowed the radiation beams to pass through while protecting the rest of his face, especially his eyes. In earlier days of radiation, before the masks, patients would have the targeted areas X'd off on their skin with marker or medical tape.

Once Rob was situated, Pat and Helene retreated into a control room. We could see Rob on two TV monitors, lying stock still under that giant microscope, mummy-like in the mask, left hand by his side, right hand on his hip, the state coaches Hall of Fame ring twinkling.

The technicians called up Rob's profile on the computer. There was no guesswork here. It told them precisely how to set the beam—the size, the distance, the dosage. It told them precisely where Rob was to be treated and where he was not. On a grid defined by coordinates, Rob was literally lined up in the crosshairs.

He had six areas of treatment. They were delineated by little green holes on the computer screen, little scattered pieces within a tidy frame. I was dismayed. I had been under the impression that, after the second surgery, there was only a small area left to radiate. I now saw that it was the size of a fist.

A red box appeared on screen: BEAM ON. When it clicked off, Pat and Helene went back into the treatment room and repositioned the machine. This allowed the radiation to blast the cancer cells from multiple angles.

Radiation works much like a flashlight. The full beam hits the target area and diminishes in strength as it radiates away from the focal point. The periphery gets some of the dose, but not full bore, which is key. It's critical to protect healthy tissue because it's often more sensitive to radiation than the diseased areas—the sort of collateral damage that so concerned Rob.

I mentioned to Pat and Helene how leery Rob had been about radiation. Pat pretended to be taken aback. "He didn't want to come here?"

"Well, as much as he likes you guys, he probably would have preferred to meet you in a different context."

"Everyone who's had chemo and radiation has told us this is much easier to go through," Pat said.

"Just the connotation of radiation is scary," Helene

acknowledged. "Especially for older ones who saw Hiroshima: They just heard horror stories back in the day."

Actually, the stories aren't even that old. I told Pat and Helene how my sister had gone through radiation for treatment of her neuroblastoma in the late 70s. Just recently, 25 years after the fact, residual complications required one of her kidneys to be removed.

Helene wasn't surprised. She'd been a radiation tech since age 18. Back then, she said, they had to assume what they were doing was working. There were no computers, no MRIs. Helene didn't even use a calculator. Now she worked with precise lines, defining grids and 3-D imaging. Compared to what my sister had gone through, to what Peter DeBona had gone through, radiation had come out of the Dark Ages.

When the day's treatment was over and we rode the elevator back up to daylight, I asked Rob how it felt being under the beam. Like being under a sun lamp, he said, or being on the beach all day.

"I can smell the same burning of the skin."

"Can you feel it or is it just a smell?"

"No pain, no discomfort."

"They really have that thing defined."

"Compared to what Peter DeBona had. They just bombarded his whole freaking brain."

"He turned out OK."

"He sure did."

We passed a shirt in a gift store reading "It's All Good."

"I like that one," Rob said.

Mostly, though, we were subdued. Normally on the ride home from New Haven Rob and I joked around quite a bit. Not that day. My mind kept circling back to the green dots on the computer screen, the treatment area that was the size of a fist.

But I wasn't going to tell him anything that wasn't encouraging. I wondered if perhaps that made me some sort of an accomplice.

So I talked about football, a trump card I sometimes played to chase lurking gloom. Rob brought up the story about how he ran into Bill Parcells a few years earlier on a horse trip to Saratoga, N.Y. This was back when Rob was retired from coaching, and when he told Parcells how he used to coach high school football, Parcells looked at a guy who still appeared to be in his prime and asked, "Coach, how come you're not coaching anymore?"

So Rob told him about the tumor.

Parcells was transfixed. His younger brother, he told Rob, had just been diagnosed with a brain tumor.

Rob had been reminded of that meeting earlier in the week. At the head of the Monday Night Football telecast of the Dallas-Philadelphia game, Al Michaels said if Coach Parcells seemed distracted, it was because his brother Don had just passed away from brain cancer at age 62. Mere hours before the game, Parcells had been at the funeral.

Now Rob had that note from Dr. Knisely spelling it out in black and white. *Mr. Szymaszek is a patient in my care in the Department of Radiology at Yale School of Medicine for his treatment of cancer.*

It was a warm day for November, but gray and very windy. The wind played through bare trees that had only recently given up their last leaves, seeming bleakest as they do in November, when we have yet to adapt to the new season.

Rob continued gazing out the window.

"But I'm going to get through this," he said. "This is the start of it."

He glanced over.

"You know, I have to stay optimistic. I have to think I'm the lucky one."

* * *

I took Rob for another radiation appointment on December 1. He was more energetic, more like his old self. He wasn't congested as he had been three weeks earlier while suffering from bronchitis, though he did say he had a cold he couldn't shake. I wondered if he still wasn't mentally sharp. He seemed to struggle for the right word—or maybe just being around me brought that out.

"How's my co-author?" as he had taken to calling me.

We donned our light blue Life is Good hats and hit the road.

Rob wasn't searching the cap for fallen strands anymore. During a timeout in the Thanksgiving Stoddard Bowl he'd tromped onto muddy Ceppa Field and, as he gathered the Spartans, pulled off his green knit hat and laid bare a scalp reddened and hair thinned by radiation. A small gesture, yet a revelation. I wondered how many other people crowded around that muddy patch of earth in the middle of Meriden, sinking in ooze up to their shoe tops standing along the sidelines or huddled in blankets sitting in the bleachers, took its full measure.

Earlier in November, I had covered a game up in Glastonbury and overheard two men working the chains on the sidelines.

"Hear about Szymaszek?"

"Yeah, I hear he's in rough shape."

Infuriated, I stomped away cursing under my breath, "What the fuck do you know about it?"

I had been at Rob's house just a few days previous. He was getting ready to return to the team at a time when the Spartans, beset by injuries, were unraveling. Rob talked about team chemistry, about how a coach needs to approach it just like a cook preparing zuppa di pesce, a dish Rob had once prepared for my wife and me. It was easily one of the top three meals either one of us ever ate.

"You need to balance the ingredients just right," Rob explained.

Inspired by the thought, he cooked up some linguine and marinara sauce that night. When Diane got home, candles were lit on the table.

Yeah, I hear he's in rough shape.

Rob had settled into a routine with radiation. On the morning of December 1 we drove down to New Haven, walked into the Hunter Radiation Therapy Center, took the elevator down one flight and entered the waiting room, passing by the jigsaw puzzles. The same frames, it seemed to me, with the same clumps of Vermont barn or Maine lighthouse unattached.

Rob said hello to Mary Ganter, the receptionist, and we made selections from the handsome tea box on the refreshment table. There was a woman there from Meriden and she recognized Rob. Her daughter had gone to Maloney at the time Rob decided to stay with coaching rather than become head of the Guidance Department.

"That's where you belong," the woman said.

"Yeah, thank you," Rob replied.

"Really," she said. "You've done so much for these kids."

Rob later struck up a conversation with a Yale intern whose father coached a junior college football team. Rob wrote down his name and number.

"I've got some kids who are Division One Double-A," Rob told the intern. "I've heard a lot about that school. It's good at getting kids to the next level."

Maybe for some kids on this year's team. The Spartans had finished a disappointing 3-6-1, but had played well in a 24-21 Stoddard Bowl loss to favored Platt. What a great game. Mark

Padilla had been cleared to play and he took over at quarterback, engineering a dramatic late-game comeback bid. He scored a touchdown, somehow keeping his balance in the mud, to pull the Spartans to within one score. The defense held and the Spartans had one last chance. They got inside the 10. The game ended with a pass falling incomplete in the end zone.

Both of Rob's sisters were at the game. We briefly congregated on that field where there was absolutely no firm ground to be found. Wasn't Ceppa Field always like that by the end of the season? The Szymaszeks had been gathering there every Thanksgiving for 40 years and, while Rob's medical issues now gave the day a different perspective, the stakes of Thanksgiving hadn't changed. Maloney had lost to Platt and Rob was not happy and it had nothing to do with radiation treatments.

I noticed there were red lines across his forehead, and as we sat in the waiting room on December 1, sipping our tea, Rob mentioned he was using cream to help alleviate the burning sensation on his skin. He was particularly sensitive behind his ears, where the radiation beam exited his head. But mostly Rob felt blessed. He saw other patients who had blisters and looked badly sunburned.

That day's session with Pat and Helene brought the number of remaining treatments down to single digits. Rob was looking forward to December 15, the morning when it would be his turn to stride into the waiting room and, amid the puzzles and the patients, announce, "Today is my last day."

Rob was feeling good and our ride home was far more upbeat than the one on November 16. Rob talked about how he was using imagery with radiation just as he had when he was on Temador, though now, instead of dropping bombs with each pill, the radiation was napalm.

"They're moving faster because they're grade threes, but we're getting them, we're getting them. Every day they try to move a little bit faster, but I just feel like we're killing them."

Since the operation, Rob had not experienced any seizures. That certainly was a good sign. The seizures, he now confessed, could be harrowing, especially when they happened around other people.

"I couldn't tell my wife—she'd worry too much—but every day was an adventure. Now it's nice, so nice, not to have to worry about those. It's so nice not to have to apologize to someone because I look like I'm zoned out. No more, 'Excuse me, I'm having a simple-partial seizure right now. I'm going to get up and walk outside my office door. I should be out of this state in a few seconds.'"

Rob would see looks of unease, of fear. I imagined him making that announcement to a student in his guidance office.

"That's nonexistent in my life now, so I really feel we're into this brand new chapter. It's like closing a book on this saga, this

Szymaszek family photo

Rob hugs Mary Ganter on the last day of his radiation treatment at Yale-New Haven.

horrible saga I've been through. I think it's all over. I really do. And I want to continue to believe like that till it's over."

An MRI scheduled for January 25, 2006 and reviewed by Dr. Baehring on the 27th would tell the story. By then, radiation would be over for a month and the scan would measure the effectiveness of the treatment. The scan would probably show a white mass. The question was, was that mass white scar tissue from the cells fried by radiation—'necrosis' it was called—or was it new cancer forming?

Rob remembered Andrea having that post-radiation scan.

"Can you believe it, Rob? There's another white mass. They don't know if it's necrosis or another tumor."

It was another tumor. Not long after, Andrea underwent her third operation.

"The poor kid," Rob said as we pulled back into Oak Ridge Drive. "I don't know how I'd deal with that, Bry, between you and I. Being the optimistic son of a gun I am, I don't even want to entertain that idea. But I'll tell you what, when they're looking at the scan outside that door on the 27th, that's as nervous as I'll be out of all the scans I've had.

"But if my system tells me no seizures, my energy level is good, my mental thought process—everything seems to be functioning at the highest possible level. There's nothing that tells me something is up there. And I know myself pretty well because I've been through this for four years and five months."

Diane went with Rob on December 15, the last day. They bought muffins—blueberry and cranberry, good and warm—for Helene, Pat, Mary and all the girls at the Radiation Therapy Center. They gave him a diploma. Radiation was complete.

On the Saturday before Christmas, Rob and Di threw a party to celebrate. The house was filled with teaching colleagues, football colleagues and friends. Jen was home for the holidays. Food and drink were in ample supply, Millie-style, and the house was decorated in red and green. Upon one window sill sat two teddy bears. One held a red heart reading "Live Well, Laugh Often, Love Much." The other bear was wearing a white shirt bearing a green 'M' and holding a football and a helmet, also emblazoned with the Maloney logo.

Rob was decked in a red sweater and was in great spirits. It wasn't until mid-January that the post-radiation effects became manifest. Rob was fatigued. He'd put on a little weight from the ravenous appetite brought on by the Decatron. His memory still seemed a little sketchy, though he certainly hadn't forgotten about his sister Jan's fast-approaching 50th birthday party.

By then Coach Ron Carbone's All-American boy had shaved his head into a Mohawk. Little white burn spots had surfaced on his head. What did it look like on the inside? What had become of those areas that had been treated by radiation, the spots that collectively seemed the size of a fist as the big radiation machine hummed and Rob laid still and the monitor screen read BEAM ON?

As we headed to Yale-New Haven on January 27, 2006 to meet with Dr. Baehring to go over the critical MRI taken two days before, it finally occurred to me why those jigsaw puzzles in the radiation waiting room were best left unfinished. The little pieces weren't supposed to come together. Radiation was supposed to blow them apart.

Had it worked for Rob?

The 27th was very cold and very clear. Frost had formed on the windows, but the sunshine was brilliant. Rob did the driving this time, with Diane riding shotgun and me in the back. The sun was creeping over the east-side ridges as we headed out. James Taylor drifted from the speakers.

In my mind I'm going to Carolina. I'm going to Carolina in my mind.

That reminded Rob of the time his former player Rahshon Spikes played at North Carolina State and he'd gone down to Raleigh and given a speech to Rahshon's new teammates.

Rob zipped along in the left lane, doing 75. Cars ran southward.

Mexico, I ain't never been, but I'd like to go.

Rob played over the scenarios. If the tumor was growing again: then what? More chemo? Other treatments?

"I don't think that's going to happen," Diane said.

Rob still wasn't having seizures, but did say, "Should I mention the other day that I was lightheaded?"

"I would," Diane replied, "and how you were tired the last few days."

Rob was still injecting the blood thinner Lovanox daily and he was still on the Decatron, not to mention the anti-seizure medication Keppra. Rob reminded me to ask Dr. Baehring when the dosages could be reduced, if not eliminated entirely.

We got off the exit for downtown New Haven.

"I got to hate this ride after 30 days," Rob said. "It made me appreciate the short ride to Maloney High School."

We passed the New Haven Coliseum, which was being dismantled. New Haven's old downtown arena had hosted so many hockey games and rock concerts. Now it was being reduced to rubble, taken apart from the outside in. Passing by, we could see the seats. How many shows had I seen there? It seemed so small from this vantage.

In the hospital, up on the oncology floor, sun poured through the windows. Only the spaces up by the cathedral ceilings were unlit. It was morning-quiet, the day just getting started. Only two other people were in the waiting room. Another patient was wheeled in on a stretcher. In the distance came the sound of crying. What would our news be?

In the all-too-familiar examining room an unfamiliar nurse came in to take Rob's blood pressure. She commented on the Mohawk and told us about a friend of hers who had breast cancer. She'd lost her hair in treatment, but it actually grew back better than before.

"She just got back to work and, let me tell you, she's got the most beautiful hair I've ever seen," the nurse said. "She used to be a platinum blond, very thin. Now it's thick and curly and it's so beautiful. She looks so European."

"That's the look you strive for, right Rob?" I said. "That European look."

I kept it up.

"Hey Rob, I was just telling Di how much you want her to take you to see *Brokeback Mountain*."

The "gay cowboy" movie had been out for a couple of months. Rob had an unconscious habit of calling it *Backbreak Mountain*.

"It ain't gonna happen, Bry. It ain't gonna happen. John Wayne is one of my all-time favorite guys."

"Oh, he's not in it."

And then Dr. Baehring walked in without any fanfare, like a main act taking the stage without introduction, without any hype. He wished us Happy New Year, asked Rob about his hair and then, without prelude, said, "The scan looks excellent."

"Hmmm?" said Rob.

"The scan," Baehring repeated, "looks excellent."

Three pronounced exhales filled the room.

"All right," said Diane. "Tell us more."

"It couldn't look better," Baehring said. "There's nothing there."

But that was actually a qualified statement. It really meant there was no new growth, no necrosis. The scan did show an area that contained either dormant cancer cells or maybe just scar tissue from the operations. Those were deep-rooted and unlikely ever to be eradicated.

"I don't want to hear that," Rob said with heat in his voice. "I want to get those son-of-a-bitches."

Dr. Baehring steered the focus to the positives. There was no new growth. The cancer was in check. Rob would continue having scans taken every three months. In the meantime, the seizure medication and the Decatron could be reduced and eventually phased out.

When you sized it up that way, it had been a very good day. Rob recognized that.

"We're on our way back," he said as we walked out of the hospital and into the cold, but sunny January morning. "Hey Bry, know of any head coaching positions that are open?"

He wasn't waiting for an answer. He had his arm around Diane.

"What would I do without you?" he wanted to know.

And then they kissed.

CHAPTER 24

Testimony

TWO PHOTOGRAPHS RAN on the front page of the Meriden
Record-Journal the next morning. The one of Diane and Jennifer
with Rob was striking and would wind up matted and framed in
their house. But it was the other one that told the story: a long
line, three and four bodies wide, stretching out the door, waiting
to get in.

Above: Rob, Diane and Jennifer
at the testimonial. Right:
The line to get into the Aqua
Turf for the testimonial.

Photos by Christopher Zajac, courtesy of the Meriden Record-Journal

313

The Aqua Turf Club in Southington is the premier banquet facility in central Connecticut. There's rarely a day it's not booked. It's a hot spot for weddings, the place to be on New Year's Eve. Virtually every major awards banquet in Connecticut high school sports is held there. Prime rib is the specialty of the house. How many had Rob enjoyed through the years? How many glasses of wine?

On March 1, 2007, Aqua Turf glasses were raised to him in "A Tribute to Rob Szymaszek." Dan Hatch and Mike Falis and Rob's colleagues from Maloney put it together. Howie Hewitt, the school's basketball coach, was a key player even with his hoop team in the midst of an undefeated run to the state championship game.

The testimonial was an overdue event, hastily put together, but still drew more than 500 people on few weeks notice. The ballroom chandeliers were muted to a low gold. A slide show compiled by Bill Lischeid played on a large screen, flashing the whole gamut of Rob's coaching career, from the wild-eyed buck hardly older than his players to the seasoned, bespectacled mentor whose passion hardly dimmed with age. And the most recent: The brain cancer patient, haggard and under a winter cap, who somehow found the wherewithal to get back on the sidelines.

So much flashed before your eyes, and you didn't have to look hard to see how Rob, in his fashion, had transcended reality. Rob Szymaszek, the boy with no brothers, was an esteemed member of a coaching fraternity. There was Mike Falis, Steve Filippone of Madison and Rob Cersosimo of West Hartford, men who Rob truly considered brothers. There was Marce Petroccio, all the way up from Westport, where Rob had been bound that fateful first day of September 2001. And there was Tom Ryan, who only a few months before had retired from coaching. He'd been head man at Platt for 27 years, one more than Rob's 26 at Maloney. Like Rob, his final game ended with defeat in the Stoddard Bowl. Neither loss diminished what they had done in their time. Rob and Tom gone from the sidelines: Truly the end of an era in Meriden.

Plenty of teaching colleagues showed up for the testimonial. Football referees, too. A year before a state referee's association had given Rob its "Golden Whistle Award."

Mostly, though, the testimonial was a reunion of players and coach, and here, too, was transcendence. Rob Szymaszek, father of one daughter, who had always wanted a son, a little man he could dress up, actually had hundreds of sons, and they had always dressed the part—once in shoulder pads and helmets, now in sport coats, suits and ties.

Jennifer attested to it. She grew up watching Rob treat players to steaks on Friday nights and even to Thanksgiving dinners, players who didn't have a family or were in difficult filial situations. She grew up watching Rob stay behind in the locker room to listen to a player or stick up for kids in school when it was the least popular thing to do. Jennifer, the face at the operating room door, the furthest you could possibly stand; Jennifer, Rob's one and only, with all these brothers.

There was Patrick Hatch, team captain that fateful season of 2001. He had gone on to a college career after Maloney and was now coaching at the collegiate level, an assistant hardly older than his charges, one in the next generation of coaches. He was among the testimonial's scheduled speakers, and when he got to the podium he grabbed it two-handed like I'd seen Rob do so many times.

"Coach Smaz," Pat said, "your impact as a football coach should never be measured by just your accomplishments on the football field. Your influence on my life and the lives of so many others has had a greater meaning than any play you've ever called.

You always made it clear the great game of football was truly a metaphor for life, and you were always a shining example of that. You instilled in us how to be men."

Speeches were slow in coming this night. A long meet-and-greet sweep swirled around Rob for more than an hour. People hugged him, shook his hand, chatted, laughed and posed for pictures. "Coach should run for mayor. He knows everybody," said Tommy Flores, who'd just finished up his senior season under Rob's protective wing. On Senior Night, when parents accompany their sons out to midfield, Rob walked out with Tommy.

It took me a while to sidle up to Rob, and when he saw my wife he was even happier because he knows she appreciates good food and likes to cook a good meal as much as he does. They hugged, and then Rob pulled a thick wad of cash out of his pocket, peeled off a $50 and put it in my hand.

"What the hell are you doing?"

"The wife of my co-author is not gonna pay to go to my testimonial."

"Get out of here, Rob," I said, giving it back.

He stuffed the $50 back in my hand, smiling, laughing, but looking like he was about to drive block me into the head table all the same. "The wife of my co-author is not gonna pay to go to my testimonial!"

There were appetizers and pasta stations, an open bar. It was the kind of night Millie Szymaszek would have liked. Rob, in fact, said he had heard his mother's voice while deliberating over a free ride to the testimonial offered by Danny Hunter's Meriden limo company. Diane was balking; it was awfully ostentatious. Millie overruled.

Take the limo; ride the limo. Rob, enjoy the time of your life right now.

For who knows how long the time will last?

2006 had opened well for Rob. It had not ended that way. Radiation held the line against cancer, but by summer a new problem emerged: a bone infection in the skull, right where Rob had undergone the two operations. So on August 29, for the third time in five years, Dr. Joe Piepmeier performed surgery on Rob at Yale-New Haven Hospital.

Unlike the first two procedures, Dr. Piepmeier was not pleased with the results. While relieved the infection hadn't passed into the brain, Dr. P. wound up removing a bigger piece of bone than he expected. There was a pipe-sized dent on the right side of Rob's head—a hole, really—and it would require follow-up plastic surgery to fix.

See, it was never just the cancer. All along it had been the collateral damage—the blood clots, the infections—that made the ordeal twice as hard, and it was taking its toll. We were all a little less filtered. As he retreated with Diane, Sharon, and me into the same private meeting room where we sat a year earlier after the second surgery, Dr. Piepmeier shucked off his latex gloves and fired them across the room into a garbage can. He tried to buck up, but there was weary frustration in his voice.

"He's an amazing, amazing guy. He just keeps getting kicked down, kicked down and he keeps bouncing back."

"But that's just on the surface," Diane said. "He's not like that at home."

"You might want to talk to him about getting some professional help," Dr. Piepmeier said.

"Forget it," Diane answered. "He won't listen to me about that. You better talk to him."

"Oh I will, because he's not going to like hearing about this. He's a good-looking guy. I mean, he really is a good-looking guy, and this will have an effect on his vanity."

The news discouraged me. Seeing Dr. Piepmeier rattled

discouraged me. That's why I don't believe I ever admired Rob more than when I saw him in ICU after this third surgery. Diane was sitting by his side, holding his hand. Sharon stood at the foot of his bed, rubbing his feet through the blankets. He was groggy, but battling to maintain clarity. He looked worse than he had after the second tumor operation, and this was discouraging, too. There were traces of blood on his pillow, most of it dried, some of it fresh. An oxygen mask covered his nose and mouth. He was clearly in severe pain. Yet when he called out in the darkened room it was to say, "How's my brother Bry doing over there?"

I moved out of the corner and sidled up alongside the bed. We squeezed hands. Our grip tightened, lingered, drifted into tenderness. I found, for the moment, I wasn't so dispirited. Then, through the oxygen mask, eyes closing, the pain medication starting to kick in, Rob muttered, "Couldn't move the ball yesterday against Weaver. Most talented group of kids we've ever had. Friggin' wing-T."

I half chuckled, half wept and told Rob we'd talk about it more when he got home. Because there would be more football, right? There had to be more football. Brain cancer was far, far away when we talked football.

Rob intended to return to the Spartans, but it would be different. The one-year resurrection of Rob's trademark I-formation was over. Bob Zito, now in his third year as Maloney head coach, returned to the wing-T offense he knew so well. One bad scrimmage against Hartford's Weaver High School aside, it complemented the Spartans well. Zito was also running a two-platoon system—separate units on offense and defense. The Spartans were no longer looking for their best 11; they were looking for their most strategic 22. And it worked. Maloney got off to a 5-0 start.

Rob, meanwhile, went through a month-long regimen of

antibiotics to make sure the infection was totally gone. It was heavy stuff. A PICC line was put into his upper chest and, for the first time, Rob had an IV pole to tote around. Diane learned how to change the bags and re-set the machine. One night in early October she and Rob hauled the contraption down to Gaylord Hospital, the famed rehabilitation hospital in Wallingford, to speak at a cancer survivors' meeting. They brought Mr. Diffley, too, and he curled up at Diane's feet as Rob and the IV pole stood at the podium. When the machine beeped, Diane knelt down and pulled out a new bag, connected it to the drip line and placed it atop of the pole.

Rob also had that hole in his head. Until a prosthetic piece of bone could be surgically inserted—and that wasn't likely until February—a mere flap of skin covered it up. When Rob returned home from the hospital in early September he was given a hockey helmet for protection. It was cumbersome and, frankly, the sort of thing that eats at pride. He wore it on only a few occasions. At the time, there was a student at Maloney by the name of Chris Giacco who was recovering from a traumatic head injury suffered in a car accident. He was wearing an almost identical helmet to school every day. Rob's respect and admiration for Chris were boundless. All the same, his helmet stayed home.

* * *

The antibiotics did their work; the infection cleared. Rob was able to return to work for the homestretch. This would be it, the 35th and final turn around the track. He was due to retire at the end of the 2006-07 school year at age 57.

Rob also returned to the sidelines, rejoining a Spartans team that, three years removed from 1-21, was bound for its second trip to a state championship game. Rob's role was limited and he accepted that. He was not involved in any of the play-calling.

Steve Hoag, Bible in back pocket, tie knotted and black high-tops laced on game day, was in charge of the defense with the help of Tyrone Abrams, a coach in his second year with the Spartans. Bob Zito ran the wing-T offense. Mike Falis handled the O-line. Rob worked with the defensive backs. Limited role or not, Rob was protective of his guys, like the week the staff wanted to pull Tommy Flores out of a game.

"You take him out, you better tell me to go home, because that kid is doing exactly what I told him to do and he's having a great game," Rob barked into his headset. "You're going to break his spirit and his heart if you take him out of the game."

Rob won a reprieve. Then he called Tommy over.

"Tom, you're that close to being taken out of the game, but I'll tell you what, I'm not letting them take you out of the game." He leaned closer, whispered, "So don't screw up."

"Coach, I love you."

"I love you too, Tommy."

Rob and Tommy Flores

Rob was a living, breathing morale boost for the Spartans. In turn, the Spartans looked out for him. Rob wore nothing to protect his head, and whenever a play or errant pass careened toward the sidelines the kids would yell "Coach, watch out!" and scramble to shield him.

The great season rolled on. Heading into Thanksgiving, the Spartans were 8-1 and already assured of a postseason berth. And Rob was feeling well. He had completely recovered from the bone infection. The PICC line was out, the IV pole long gone. He was suffering few seizures and feeling few ill effects from the cancer.

Which is why he and Diane were so stunned that mid-November afternoon down at Yale-New Haven. It was just a routine visit, a routine follow-up to a routine scan. But what is ever routine about illness? As Rob and Diane sat, Dr. Joachim Baehring stood silently, sizing up the latest scan, poring, pausing, until finally he said, "I don't like the look of this scan."

Against a backlit panel, the new scan next to the previous, it was unmistakable. There were more white spots. White spots in new places. They looked, Rob said, like spray off waves at the beach. The cancer was spreading.

The Yale-New Haven neuro-oncology team laid out the cards. Rob bought a new journal and wrote on paper with numbered lines.

O.K. Another bad scan. This time the options are not good.

The tumor is in an inoperable area. No radiation either, leaving one option only: the dreaded chemotherapy.

Here I am in my 35th yr. of education, my retirement year, having just a great time with my counselees and my football players.

Rob didn't breathe a word about it as the Spartans prepared for Thanksgiving and the postseason. There was such a good vibe around the team and Rob didn't want to deflect any attention.

The Spartans capped a 9-1 regular season with a 26-20 Stoddard Bowl win over Platt on a frigid, rainy Thanksgiving, then played their first-ever playoff game at Ceppa Field and romped past Berlin, their old rival to the north, 40-14, to reach the Class MM state championship.

Would we get our fairy tale finish after all? No. At Central Connecticut State University, where Rob had stolen the homecoming show from Sharon nearly 40 years before, the New Canaan Rams routed the Spartans 53-21 in a game that was never close.

And on the other side of this difficult loss lay a difficult decision. Rob's cancer had not only recurred, it had spread to new areas. The doctors were saying there was only one way to treat it. But this chemo wouldn't be Temador; it wouldn't be a pill. It was a potent intravenous treatment, a combination of Avastin and CPT-11, two drugs traditionally used to treat colorectal cancer and just starting to be used on brain cancer patients.

Rob resisted. In his mind, cancer patients often died from the treatment and not the disease. Hadn't that happened to Pete Sini? During the 2004 season Rob would pick up Papa Pete before games and the old guy would just be wiped out from a treatment. Then there would be a month-long interval between doses and, in the interim, Pete would get his color back, get his appetite back, get back to being the old Papa Pete. Then he'd undergo another treatment and get knocked back down. When Pete eventually passed away in 2005 Rob thought, *It's the chemo that killed this guy. This can happen to me.*

If his days were numbered, Rob didn't want to compromise their quality. But what was the alternative? After one of the playoff games, Rob spoke with Ted Moynihan, the retired senior sportswriter from the Meriden *Record-Journal*. Ted and Rob went way back. Plus, Ted's wife Fran was just starting follow-up radiation and chemotherapy after surgery for breast cancer.

Photo by Bill Lischeid

Rob and retired Meriden Record-Journal sportswriter Ted Moynihan

"If Rob's got to make a choice, he's a fighter," Ted told Fran when he got home. "He's going to do the chemo. I can't see him not doing the chemo."

Dr. Baehring was recommending chemo. A member of the Yale-New Haven brain tumor support group was on the Avastin/CPT-II combination and having good results. Rob asked for and received the Joe Piepmeier seal of approval. The gravity of the situation was clear. Chemo was the way to go. Still, Rob played for time. He pled with his doctors: *Please let me first spend some quality time with my loved ones.* He wanted one last fling, one last stroll in the sun. He set up a "bonding" calendar with the women in his life: Jennifer home for Christmas, Jan down from Northampton, a trip to Florida with Sharon, a trip to St. Martin with Diane. Rob felt he couldn't enjoy those moments if he was fitting them in between treatments. He didn't want to be walking down the beach with Sharon with a port in his chest. He wanted to enjoy good food and wine without worrying about counteracting chemotherapy.

The neuro-oncology team heard him out and said OK. Chemo could wait.

That still left Rob with another major decision: What to do about work. The treatment cycle would be grueling. No popping a pill in the morning at 76 Oak Ridge Drive and getting dressed looking at a poster of a stick figure saying "Staying home is not an option." He'd be down at Yale-New Haven once every two weeks, a full day given over to Avastin and CPT-11 dripping into veins, and then God only knew what sort of side effects. Rob's instinct was to see the year out, play all four quarters and finish the game. But how effective would he be on the job?

He had enough sick days to take a medical leave that would carry him to the end of school in June. After consulting with Mary Cortright, the superintendent, and Bob Angeli, who had replaced Shugrue as Maloney principal, that's the option he took. December 22, the day before the 2006 Christmas break, would be his last day.

Rob made the announcement in an e-mail sent to the entire Maloney staff. He thanked them for their support and friendship over the years and reminded them that they had a unique opportunity that many other professionals did not: making a difference in a young person's life each and every day. He mended fences with any colleagues he'd banged heads with. That part was easy.

Saying goodbye to the students who filtered into his guidance office was much harder. As he had in the troubled summer of 2004 when he withdrew as candidate for head coach, Rob gave himself pep talks to counter his second-guessing.

The reality began hitting home. What am I doing? However, family had to come first this time!

On Rob's last day, the Friday morning quiet of the guidance department was broken by a humming. *Ba-ba-bum, ba-ba-bum.* It gathered and grew. *Ba-ba-bum.* Heads popped out of office doors, curious and expectant. *Ba-ba-bum.* One by one they trickled in, music teacher Lynn Scarchuk, portable keyboard in hand, and the "Allegrettos" student choir. Christmas was three days away. It was the season of carolers. These were bound for one door. Once Rob emerged from his office *ba-ba-bum* they broke into "Stand by Me."

There, in the narrow confines of the Maloney guidance department, with counselors at their office doors and secretaries in their seats and Rob with an arm around Diane (who had come down from her art room because she knew what was up), the choir sang. Don Panciera, the assistant principal who once coached for Rob, came in and leaned against the back wall next to Ray Mainville, the retired athletic director. They were as silent and still and overcome as everyone else. There wasn't a dry eye as "Stand by Me" gave way to "I Have Been Changed" from *Wicked the Musical.* The singers were wiping their eyes, too, and even so, their voices were so clear.

"It may be that we'll never meet again in this lifetime."

Rob stood in his doorway, his doorway since 1976, the door that was always open. On the wall outside, where it always hung, was a clipboard holding a yellow signup sheet for the day's appointments.

"You taught me well; you gave me strength. You showed the way; I'll not forget you," the choir sang, and that was from Carl Strommen's "Like an Eagle."

The Allegrettos had chosen well. They segued into Josh Groban's "You Raise Me Up" and finished with "Seasons of Love" from *Rent*.

"How do you measure a year in the life? . . . How do you measure the life of a woman or man?"

There were a ton of cards, a ton of e-mails from staff and students. Before school let out, there was a ceremony—not in the gym, but in the band room, of all places. Football players and musicians are typically light years apart in the high school universe, but Rob had found a kindred spirit in Brian Cyr, the band's new director. He was as young and energetic as Rob had been when he took over the football program at age 26. Together they established a new tradition. After victories, the football team and band would gather, helmets and instruments raised, to sing the Maloney fight song, the same song Rob had sung when he hit the halls of Maloney High in the autumn of 1965.

And now 42 years gone: 42 waves of students and football teams, school days and game days, one wave after another washing through, each in its appointed time. Here, now, the last. Rob and Diane walked through the school foyer where they'd said their first awkward hellos and drove home.

Rob was torn as he recounted the day's events in his journal.

If their goal was to make this counselor feel loved, they accomplished their goal well. But I also felt like I was walking out on some of the kids who really depended on me for daily support and motivation. Who would provide that?

"Mrs. Smaz is only down the hall and I'm only five minutes from school," Rob had said, but as he said goodbye he saw some

Rob and Jennifer, Christmas 2006

hurt looks that said, "So many adults have walked out on my life and here goes the guy I've trusted for years."

It was a look that haunted Rob. It was the look Jennifer used to have when Rob dropped her off at nursery school. The one that said, "Dad, are you ever coming back?"

* * *

Jennifer flew home for Christmas 2006 after a trip to London and Poland. She was living in Mexico City, shooting for Reuters and other news outlets, with her boyfriend Greg, who wrote for Reuters. Soon they would shift careers and embark on doing documentary films. ("Why shouldn't we be able to do them?" she asked Greg; she was truly her father's daughter.)

After a rocky first six months in Mexico's capital city, Jen grew accustomed to the smog, the cement and the traffic. She had grown to like the chaos and the smell of tortillas mixed with the smell of gasoline. She knew the neighborhoods, knew where to go dancing. She wanted Rob to come visit, wanted to show him the Riviera Maya and all the places she had come to know. Rob was gung-ho until an infectious diseases doctor at Yale advised him not to go.

Coming home, Jennifer knew the change in Rob's condition. She e-mailed or spoke on the phone with her parents on a daily basis, and while she always knew there was a strong possibility this particular day would come, hearing the word "inoperable" was a blow. Being so distant helped her cope. It was a defense mechanism, she realized. Being home obliterated that. Now Jen could see the change, could see the mental and physical side effects of the spreading cancer.

All the same, Rob had his "bonding schedule" and he was sticking to the game plan. Jen was No. 1 on the list. She always liked Max's Oyster Bar up in West Hartford, so Rob made reservations and the two of them, along with Diane, went up for a meal two days before Christmas. It was a Saturday, warm for late December, but overcast and drizzly. The Szymaszeks had oysters, clams and shrimp for appetizers. They shared a bottle of red wine, though Rob was careful to have only one glass. Rob was subdued and Jen found herself constantly on the verge of tears, wondering how many more dinners she would share with her dad. Rob, picking up on this, laid it all out.

"Jennifer, are you concerned about Dad's mortality?"

Jen saw the look in Rob's eyes. It told her that, for the first time in a while, he was worried, too.

Those tears at the ready began to flow.

"Yes, Dad, of course."

"Well, now that that's out of the way, I want you to know that I'm going to continue to fight this thing to the end. I also want you to know, God forbid this thing does get the better of me, I have made sure you and Mom are going to be well taken care of."

Insurance, retirement plans, assets: The financial threads had been tied.

"It is a peace of mind for me to know this," Rob told his daughter.

Mostly, though, Rob was ready to renew the battle. They discussed treatments, how chemo was the recommendation. Jennifer had been doing more research on natural alternatives. She didn't want Rob to go through another toxic treatment that she believed wouldn't completely cure him. Why not try a natural therapy—say, a well-crafted diet that would be gentle on the system and could prolong life, if not cure him? Rob was receptive and promised he'd again look into alternative medicine before agreeing to go on chemo.

And yet, as Rob broke into a loaf of freshly baked bread, Jen wondered: Should I warn my dad about processed food like bread, which eventually turns into sugar, which feeds a tumor, or do I just let him enjoy life fully because who knows how long he has left?

Rob dug into the bread. It was delicious. Jennifer remained quiet.

* * *

After the holidays, Rob packed his shorts and polo shirts and journal and went to Sharon's condominium in Naples, Florida. Sharon told him to go and get settled in and she'd join him in a few days. It was a posh place, but like any condo complex, the buildings were exactly the same. So were some of the locks. One afternoon, Rob inadvertently walked into the wrong unit after unlocking the front door with Sharon's key. Another morning, descending in the elevator, Rob heard a beeping that reminded him of the sound an IV machine makes when the bag empties. It carried him back to the ICU at Yale-New Haven. But when the elevator reached ground level and the doors slid open, Rob saw palm trees, lounge chairs, an in-ground swimming pool and a sparkling Gulf of Mexico.

Third glass of Pinot as I write at lunch. What a setting, sitting over the bay, sun beginning to set. Boy, is life still good!

Sharon joined Rob and Rob made it a point to eat at the best restaurants, drink the best wine. He went to upscale H.T. Chittum & Co. and splurged on Tommy Bahama shirts and shorts.

The price tag would have staggered Diane, but the message that I was sending was I plan on living in these damn pairs of shorts and shirts for a long time.

Hadn't Rob done that in 2001, during the first Christmas of his illness? He bought himself the best tie he could find and put it away for Christmas 2002 because he was determined to be around to wear it. And hadn't he? Yes, that Christmas and the next four Christmases after that.

Sometimes when people get sick they stop buying clothes because they think pessimistically, "I'll never get a chance to wear them." Screw that thought process. I love what I just bought and plan on wearing it on my next bonding stop."

That was with Diane. After a few weeks in Florida, Rob and his wife hopped another plane to St. Martin. They hit up all the old haunts; they never grew tired of their favorite island. But at night Rob was having difficulty seeing. Maybe it was nothing, but the vision problems persisted when they got home. Rob was also getting headaches. Headaches, seizures, difficulty walking: These were some of the symptoms he was told might develop from the spreading cancer. There had been a few seizures on

Szymaszek family photo

Rob and Diane in St. Martin, January 2007

vacation, including a pretty severe one in Florida. Now there were headaches.

Another brain scan was taken in mid-January, and there were no surprises this time when Rob and Diane met with Dr. Baehring. The scan showed even more white spots, more spray off the waves, and it was no Caribbean beach.

"It was scary," Rob said. "We had to do something."

Chemo had to start and start right away.

* * *

On February 1, a port was put in Rob's chest. On February 9, chemotherapy began. Rob was slated for 12 treatments: a day-long dosage every two weeks. Both drugs were given intravenously: the CPT-11 for 60-90 minutes, the Avastin in diminishing doses: 90 minutes for the first, 60 minutes for the second and then down to 30—sort of like Green Bays, the ten 100-yard dashes winnowing down to the two 20-yarders. Ron Carbone told Rob to look at the treatment like two-a-day conditioning practices. Dive in fearlessly. Toes on the line! The results would be closely monitored. If effective, the cycle could be shortened. If not, it could be extended.

The CPT-II, introduced in Japan in 1994 and also known as irinotecan, was supposed to stop DNA replication. The Avastin, FDA approved in 2004, would target the protein that stimulates the creation of new blood vessels. Its mission was to cut off the blood supply to the cancer cells without harming healthy cells. Both drugs had a laundry list of side effects. Diarrhea and immunity suppression were the chief drawbacks of CPT-II. Avastin's were high blood pressure, blood clots, low white cell counts and weakness. Among Avastin's less common side effects were nosebleeds. They proved to be Rob's biggest repercussion after the first few treatments. He'd awake in the night with his white t-shirt drenched red, his nose a bloody faucet.

Actually, Rob was in rough shape even before the treatment began. His vision had deteriorated because tumor cells were pressing against his optical nerve. As Rob described it, the effect was much like the white spots you see after having your picture taken by a flash camera. Rob also had a blind "alley" on his left side. He stopped typing e-mails because he kept screwing up the a's and s's.

He was also mentally fuzzy, stumbling over words, struggling for words. His long-term memory was fine, his short-term memory shaky. Trains of thought shot suddenly onto sidetracks. He was scheduled to give a speech at the All-State football banquet at the Aqua Turf Club in late January and Diane was worried.

"I was afraid to let him go," she said.

Rob did go, though. The trophy that went to the MVP of the state Class MM champions had for several years been given in Rob's honor. For the 2006 season, that trophy went to a player from the team that had beaten the Maloney Spartans in the finals. Consider what that says about Rob's legacy to Connecticut football.

And consider, too, that Rob gave his speech.

"I think Diane was concerned I was going to embarrass myself based on what she was seeing around the house," Rob remarked to me a few nights later when I stopped by.

Diane was out and Rob was curious: "What exactly was Diane seeing that made her so worried? What isn't she telling me?"

He posed those questions to me rhetorically, but he was angling for answers. He was in the mood for a good heart to heart. He didn't say it; I could just tell. And I was up for it, I truly was. But I was sports editor at the *Record-Journal* now and I had to get back to work. I was tied to the clock and the rush of phone calls that would soon be flooding the office from basketball games that were just winding down. I had to leave and it killed me.

"Hey," Rob said. "Let me show you what I wrote the other day."

"OK."

Rob opened up a ring-bound binder to the pages with the numbered lines, where he'd confided the day of the bad scan and the day he left Maloney High School for the last time and the day he took Jennifer to dinner at Max's Oyster Bar and all the sun-filled days in Florida and St. Martin with Sharon and Diane. More material for a story that never stopped growing. Rob spread it out on that same old kitchen table beneath the same old clock. Beyond the windows, the lights of Meriden were tranquil in the night.

We leaned over under the kitchen light and I put an arm around Rob's shoulders as he began turning pages. He knew what he was looking for, but couldn't find it. He kept turning pages, moving front to back, back to front. When he got back to the first page the fingers of his left hand scrabbled against the inside cover, scrabbling for a page that wasn't there.

* * *

The head table was up on risers, running nearly full length across the head of the Aqua Turf ballroom. But no one sat at it save for Steve Hoag, the emcee. There was just Hoag, the podium and the microphone. There, the testimonial speakers held forth. Rob sat with Diane and Jennifer, and his sister Jan's family, at a table down in front.

The Rev. Donn Bradley offered a prayer. He had been a running back at Maloney in the late 60s, had once followed Rob's blocks on end-around plays. Now he was a minister with a church in western Massachusetts. He spoke with the cadences of the pulpit and closed his eyes tight.

"Lord, you created him and we thank you for that, for his life is a blessing to this community and to young people that he coached, to students that he worked with. And gracious God, I also, as I think about Rob, Lord, I ask for your healing hand to be upon him, and to anoint him with your presence, and to bless him in a powerful way, Lord God, and that he and his wonderful family will always know that you, in fact, are with him."

Most of the speakers were used to being in front of crowds and they, too, had known Rob for a long time. Many of the old stories came out—Scott Sundberg and Tom Gaffey on those first seasons Rob took over at Maloney. Gaffey was now a state senator and he presented Rob with a citation. Rob went up and held the plaque as his former player read the words printed there. Could Rob even see them? Rob stood quiet, dignified, touched and humbled. Then he flashed the impish little boy's face I had often seen bubble up behind his bravado, a touch of innocent mischief when the mood was light or he pulled off a joke or teased his older sister.

Or picked a fight: John Fontana, the head of the Connecticut High School Coaches Association, presented Rob with an engraved clock and mentioned the early years of the Connecticut-Rhode Island All-Star football game, when Connecticut had hosted Rhode Island to an Aqua Turf dinner only to be treated to a hot dog and hamburger affair the next summer in Rhode Island. Rob was so miffed he nearly came to blows with one of the Rhode Island organizers.

That was the Millie in Rob—the Bob Szymaszek, too. You host well. Your door is always open. You take care of friends and family. You let them know they are loved. Steve Addazio, a Connecticut native who went from winning state championships at Cheshire High to working as an assistant coach at Notre Dame and then the University of Florida, wrote a letter for the testimonial and said he always strove to emulate Rob—not for the X's and O's, but for his family-like pride in his program and for the fullness of his life beyond football.

Most importantly, Rob, I wanted you to know how much I admired you as a husband and a father. I would always listen carefully when you'd tell me about your relationship with Jen as she grew up and how much you enjoyed spending time with her. I loved to hear about you and Diane's Caribbean trips, drinking wine and watching the sunset. You could make having dinner at home with Diane and a dog and a dish of zuppa di pesce sound like heaven.

Ron Carbone referenced John F. Kennedy's *Profiles in Courage* and said Rob belonged in those pages. Like most of the night's speakers, Carbone's simplest words ran deepest. "I bless the day that he came into my life and I cherish his invaluable friendship.

If he were my own son, I could not love him any more. And judging by the size of this crowd, it's quite obvious that everybody loves Robbie."

The crowd stretched wall to wall in the big ballroom. As each speaker spoke, the room was silent save for the speaker and the high hum of the ceiling vents. Dan and Patrick Hatch both spoke—the father who had grown up with Rob and had played with him, starting on a junior high team with no names and no numbers on its uniforms; the son who played for Coach Smaz when he was a household name and on his way to the state coaching Hall of Fame. Patrick had been there when Rob burned the Land's End shirt on the practice field the night before Thanksgiving 2001 and spoke of the final destination that awaits all men. *"If you could be invisible at your funeral, what would you hear people saying?"*

More than five years later, Patrick Hatch had an answer, and no one was waiting around for a funeral. "Coach Smaz, the one thing I can assure you of is that every single day someone in this room thinks about you and it brings a smile to their face. Every single day someone in this room thinks back to the days they played football for you and they know they are a better person for it. And every single day someone in this room will make a positive difference in their life or in the life of somebody else because of something they learned from you. Long after this night is over, our part of the world will continue to be a better place because you have had such a lasting influence upon all of us."

The evening was ringed with applause. The first standing ovation, though, went to Diane. It was classic Di at the mic: short, sweet and quickly out of the spotlight. She wasn't there to give a speech, just to point out the people behind the scenes who had made the testimonial happen.

"Everybody said all these great things about Rob. Everyone knows how I feel about him. I don't need to say it. So, thank you. We love everybody here. We appreciate you all being here to share this wonderful night with our family."

Diane looked so lovely, her face and trademark blond bob so vibrant. In my mind's eye I saw her at Gaylord that night back in October, stooping and changing the bag on Rob's IV when the machine beeped. She had seen so much. She had seen everything. How many days had she spent at Rob's side down at Yale-New Haven? "Oh God, I hate that place, especially that floor," she once told me. She'd walk past the family center, see the families in there, see the strain and worry and stress so plainly etched on their faces. Did her face show the same?

"What can you do? You just go about it one day at a time," Diane confided. "I've had times when my stomach is just in knots. It's been five and a half years. I think the first one in 2001 was the toughest. That was the shock. Then you learn—never how to really deal with it, but how to go on with everything. But I'm tired. I'm tired of doing this. I don't want him to die, but I don't want to do this a lot longer. I don't know if I can.

"Fight it, definitely fight it, but how much can you fight this thing?"

It was March 1, 2007. Rob had been fighting brain cancer since September 1, 2001—five and a half years to the day. Some may have supposed he was losing. Others knew better. Others knew that for Rob Szymaszek, winning and losing was a case of how you defined the terms. Giving up always meant losing; battling to the end was a form of victory.

"The Maloney Spartans never lost a game," said Larry McHugh, a close friend of Rob's and the former coach of powerhouse Xavier High. "They just ran out of time."

Rob was last at the podium. A red rose pinned to the left

lapel of his dark blue suit, he slowly approached the head table, but once he got there he brought energy to bear. The dent on his head from where Dr. Piepmeier had removed the infected bone was plainly visible. So were the Hall of Fame ring on one hand and the wedding band on the other. These totems defined him: Family man, coach, cancer patient.

Rob didn't try to hide his vision or spatial problems. He told the crowd right off how he really couldn't read, how he'd be flying without a script.

"Everything I'm going to talk about is going to be from my heart, from my memory."

His voice toggled between soft and hard, interspersed with the occasional long pause.

"OK, bear with me."

He seemed to tilt as if losing balance on a tightrope, but calmly collected himself and moved on. It wasn't just the effects of brain cancer assailing him, but profound emotion.

"I . . . can't . . . tell you how . . . thankful, humbled I am . . . by the showing of people that are here today, from where you've come from, the sacrifices you've made to be here with me and my family."

How do you thank everybody? Rob didn't want to miss anyone. John Fontana had told him not to even try. He'd miss somebody and then beat himself up about it later.

The first thing Rob did was call out Steve Bedard. A one-time football official, Steve was also suffering from brain cancer. It had eaten away most of his nose.

"There is a gentleman out here right now who is fighting the same disease that I'm fighting. Is Stevie Bedard out here right now? Stevie? Did Stevie have to go?"

A hand went up from the middle of the room. Steve's head was bowed.

"Stevie," Rob gently pleaded, "please stand up."

Steve stood. The crowd applauded.

Only that morning Bedard had undergone a procedure with a gamma knife, a technology honed by the Swedish neurosurgeon Lars Leskell in which a narrow beam of radiation is used to perform brain surgeries without need of an incision. Yale-New Haven radiologist Dr. Jonathan Knisely was a big proponent. Yale-New Haven, in fact, is the only hospital in Connecticut that uses the gamma knife. Rob had asked Dr. Piepmeier numerous times if it could be used on him, but Joe explained it worked most effectively on tumors that were spherical in shape. Rob's wasn't like that. Rob's was shaped like a football.

But Rob didn't mention that last part to the crowd. He was cracking a joke instead.

"I'm really happy this dinner came upon us as quickly as it did because the advertisements that started on the sports page were getting closer and closer and closer—and the last time I looked—the advertisement was opposite the obituary page."

As exalted as the evening's testimony had been, if this night was to celebrate Rob Szymaszek, it had to be a celebration of other people. Rob told the crowd too much of the credit for Maloney football had been given to him. "There have been pillars in this program," he said, and then called out Dan Hatch and Mike Falis. Either one could be a head coach, Rob said. Either one could be in the state coaching Hall of Fame.

He turned to his health. If Rob Szymaszek was still in the game it was because of the people on his team. He cited Dr. Piepmeier and the neuro-oncology staff at Yale-New Haven. He cited his primary care doctor in Meriden, Jay Kaplan, the guy who never got the credit he deserved. Kaplan was there and Rob had him stand up.

Applause flowed, died away under the chandeliers, each with

its score of lights muted to a golden glow. There was a lengthy pause from the podium.

"OK, bear with me here."

He shuffled at pages. I knew the gesture and wondered where his energy came from and how he could regain focus when he really couldn't see. But I never thought for a second he'd fall apart, that Diane would have to go retrieve him and gently lead him away.

In another heartbeat, Rob was back, striding down the tight-rope, talking about his colleagues and the students at Maloney, how therapeutic it had been to walk into the building every day and hear kids say, "Hello, Coach; hello Mr. Szymaszek," and how hard it was to walk out for the last time.

"I really didn't want to. I had fought this disease. I thought that maybe, just maybe, I could still go through this last round of chemotherapy and still be able to counsel my kids like I did through the first round of chemotherapy. For the first time, my physical well-being started to deteriorate—a little bit; not physically, but my eyes did. Of course, being a guidance counselor, your eyes have to be sharp. You're looking at records daily. It became evident that I had to leave. It was a competitive thing for me; I didn't want to give into it, but I had to give in to it."

He told the crowd about how the choir sang.

"It was a day I'll never forget, like tonight. It was a very special last day. But I hated the thought that it was my last day as a guidance counselor and maybe as an assistant football coach at Maloney High School. But we're going to keep fighting and, as you know, we're only in the early rounds of this thing."

Rob was two cycles into the Avastin and CPT-II. The first had been no sweat. The second took a little more out of him. The terrible nosebleeds would start after the third. At the moment, he was riding the tremendous energy of the crowd. Love, support: It was always the best medicine.

"Seeing all you people here tonight, I'm going to be well for a long, long time."

Rob mentioned how Jacksonville Jaguars assistant coach Dave Campo, a Connecticut native, had called two hours before his team's December 10th game with the Indianapolis Colts.

"Davey, what are you doing. Shouldn't you be getting ready for kickoff?"

"Coach, we're just calling to wish you good luck."

"These are the types of things I'm talking about," Rob told the crowd. "These are the types of little things that have happened in my life. You talk about 'Life is Still Good' and what a wonderful life I'm living right now. Yes, I'm facing some critical health issues, but where would I be without you people out here? Where would I be without those phone calls, those notes, those letters, those cards? We live in a great town. Don't ever let anybody say anything about Meriden, Connecticut because we live in a great, great town."

From ridge to ridge, the sun rising over one and setting over the other in its daily round: 76 Oak Ridge Drive got the morning light out front and the sunset out back. Rob looked down at the table where Diane and Jennifer sat side by side, heads tilted, nearly touching; their hair so similar in color, Diane's short, Jennifer's hanging halfway down her back.

"My wife usually will say to me before these affairs, 'please don't speak about me; please don't say a word about me.'"

Yet there had been a ceremony in May 2006, in that very same Aqua Turf ballroom, a state coaches affair in which Rob received a prestigious award, and he hadn't said a word about Diane.

"Oh, boy, did I hear about it. *All* the way home. So tonight, I will speak about my wife—my lovely, wonderful wife; my high school sweetheart who has been my caregiver, caretaker. She has been just wonderful. The cards, the letters, the plants, the flowers should go to her. I got it easy. I've got a wonderful wife. She keeps this family going. The phone calls to my daughter, who lives in Mexico, the nightly calls—I can't even see the phone to make the calls. She makes those calls on that phone card, Jennifer."

Rob turned to his daughter, her head tilted toward her mother's.

"They're like two peas in a pod, the two liberals in the house. Oh, we have some interesting conversations at our dinner table, but it keeps things interesting in the Szymaszek household. And I love you, hon. Thank you for being here, for flying all the way from Mexico."

A long pause, the room silent save for the high hum of the ceiling vents.

"I want to relate one story to everybody out there."

This was the story Rob had told at the All-State football banquet in late January, the day Diane was so worried she didn't want him to go. But Rob had this story down. He got it from Lou Holtz, knew it through and through like the old Bill Curly-Columbia story. His voice flared back to full vigor.

"This gentleman, he's rather old, OK, and he's down in New York City, and he's got a seeing-eye dog. All of a sudden, the light turns green and the dog takes him across the street and he's dodging all these cars. They're beeping the horn at him; he barely gets across the street.

"Being alive, he reaches down in his pocket and takes a biscuit out and all of a sudden a guy comes running up to him.

'Hey, man, what's wrong with you? What are you rewarding that dog for? He almost got you killed.'

"He said, 'I'm not rewarding that dog. I'm just trying to find his mouth so I can kick him in the ass!'"

An explosion of laughter, applause. The impish little boy's face bubbled up. Millie Szymaszek's son had said a swear word right out loud, and he was staying out in those sand pits for as long as he damn well pleased. Bob Szymaszek would know where to find him. Jesus Cah-rist! We would all know where to find him. Coach Smaz would be there, spurring us on, with a shrill whistle, an encouraging word and a comforting pat on the back.

His eyes went round the room. There was vision in them still. People were already rising. "So," he said, "I'd like to ask all of you, if you're ever in my situation, when adversity comes your way, *kick it in the ass.*"

Post Game

MID-MARCH MOONLIGHT SPILLS through the living room skylights at Rob's house. High up there in a clear sky, the moon, just past full, is starting to wane.

Rob and I put some final touches on the book. He's got the clock from John Fontana and the state citation from Tom Gaffey added to his mantle and he's got a tube temporarily attached to his nose, which has been cauterized to stop the nosebleeds caused by the chemo.

He's home a lot now and the phone rings quite a bit. If you don't get him, leave a message after you hear "Life is still good," followed by the beep.

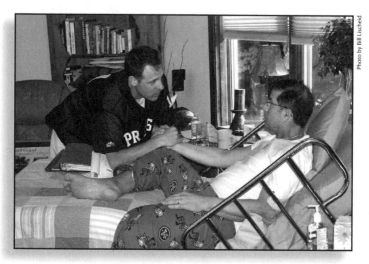

Bryant Carpenter and Rob Szymaszek, May 2007

Earlier in the day I had been on the phone with my sister Laura. She'd just celebrated her 37th birthday and I could hear her little boys in the background, my sweet rambunctious nephews Brady and Jake. My brother-in-law Lou and I often remark how we'll be watching Jake play linebacker in about 12 years, giving some coach that "wide-eyed, fanatical effort," as Rob would say.

Laura, who mercifully can't remember many of the harrowing details of her ordeal with childhood cancer, asked about the book and how Rob was doing and I told her.

"So this guy isn't sitting around feeling sorry for himself," she said.

And it sounded so strange to hear that—jarring, actually, as if I had missed a basic point of the story all along, because it's so obvious an issue for someone so ill.

But Rob was always so many miles beyond that. Being around him, you forget his baseline courage.

Don't. Then contemplate the rest.

Rob and I put in a couple hours of work. He's wearing powder blue pajamas emblazoned with flying footballs. Diane comes home from a yoga class and makes us tea and helps Rob recall some details. We are in the fourth quarter of his ambition. The book Rob first pitched to me in January 2004, on a day so cold it never got above single digits, has found a publisher.

Moonlight spills through the skylights. High up there in a clear sky, the moon, just past full, is starting to wane.

Some would say Rob Szymaszek is in a weakened state, but they are wrong. I know better and I don't stand alone. I'm in a long line, three and four bodies wide. It stretches well ahead of me and it stretches well behind.

I like to tell my sister she's my favorite miracle. I also like to believe—and I do believe, *will believe*—that when it comes to my good friend Rob Szymaszek, there is room for one more.

* * *

A cold March passes into a colder April. Just as the weather is improving Rob suffers another bout with blood clots. His legs and feet swell so badly he can't walk. He winds up in Yale-New Haven, then in a rehab center. He needs help getting in and out of the bathroom. He does exercises that involve moving his feet up and down in an effort to release the fluid that's trapped there. His old college teammate and long-time friend Rob Cersosimo spends a whole day driving around, looking for sneakers that will fit him.

When the therapists get him up walking, Rob pushes it, always wanting to do more. "Let's walk 300 feet—a football field."

Kentucky Derby day comes and Rob, who always counted horse gambling as his No. 1 vice, tries to place a bet over the phone, but his pain medication has him foggy, so he never confirms his wager. Naturally, his numbers come in and 15 grand falls through his fingers.

He tells me the story when I visit a few days later. I wheel him into the bathroom. He's just finished a rehab session and wants to wash up. In the mirror I watch him. Eyes closed, he splashes water on his face, over and over. The minutes pass. If only all of this could be washed away if we stuck to it long enough.

I help get him into bed, situate the pillows and blankets, pull down the Johnny coat that keeps riding up and nearly exposing him.

"Can I get you anything else?" I ask.

"Yeah," he says. "A .45."

Rob makes a gun with his finger and pulls the trigger like DeNiro near the end of *Taxi Driver*.

"No," I say quietly, "never."

We lock eyes. He nods, purses his lips. It is a bittersweet smile.

"OK," he says.

Just a few days before he's due to come home, Rob goes back down to Yale-New Haven for an MRI. The results are immediate: There is no shrinkage in the tumor. In fact, the cancer is still spreading.

"It's been up and down, up and down, up and down. So here we go again," Rob says when he calls me, his voice thin and tired on the other end of the line. "I'm always an optimistic guy. You know me. But I've had it with all of this—the situation here, the whole thing, everything. I just want to go home."

He tells me to call Diane. He's thinking of her, of Jennifer, of his sisters.

"I can handle the disappointment," he says. "I worry about them."

Then Rob tells me of a dream. During the MRI that morning he'd fallen asleep and in his dream he saw altar boys ringing a bell outside a church.

"And I saw a long black car—a limousine. It was a wake. And you know whose wake it was?"

"Oh, Rob."

Rob's dream actually is a harbinger. The very next day, May 16, Rob learns his father has died. Robert Szymaszek Sr., who at age 20 took one of the first tanks over the Remagan, who spent the last 17 years of his life unable to speak or write, who raised a devoted family in the years in between, is gone at age 84.

"It's like someone ripped my guts out and they haven't put them back in," Rob tells me at the wake.

"Big Bob's talking again," I say. "He's talking Millie's ear off."

We lock eyes. Rob nods, purses his lips. Comfort, acceptance, but still so painful.

Rob is sitting in a wheelchair. The swelling has gone down in his legs and feet, but he still can't walk and he still can't put on shoes. The next day, when he eulogizes his father, Rob is wheeled to the base of the pulpit at St. Stanislaus Church in Meriden and is helped out of the chair and up the stairs by his brothers-in-law. His back is to the church. His arms are extended outward and his broad shoulders sag inward. A collective moan issues from the sisters of the Franciscan Life Center seated in the pew before me. Tears spring to my eyes.

Rob still has vision problems and his short-term memory has deteriorated even further, so he instructs Diane to stand behind him and his sisters to stand on each side. They give cues to keep him on track.

Rob stands there, leaning against the lectern for support, and I find myself thinking about old pictures of FDR. Rob's slow to start, but as he goes along he gains steam. His energy builds and his voice booms and, aside from the occasional lapse in concentration, he shows more than just a glimmer of his former self. There he is, tapped back into that deep inner well of strength, coaching one last game, giving one last halftime speech, rallying the troops for the man he admired most.

And as I watch, tears verge into chuckling, head-shaking admiration, and I finally realize there's no need to sit around waiting for miracles; that when it comes to Rob Szymaszek, the miracle has been present all along. It's right there in the title: *Life*

Is Still Good. Not *Life Will Be Good* or *Life Will Always Be Good*, but *Life Is Still Good.* As in *right now.* The smallest word is the biggest.

Later, when the funeral party retires to Jacoby's over on the East Side of Meriden, the restaurant where Rob would often bring his players, Millie Syzmaszek's youngest brother, Bob Kosienski, gets up with his family and his sister Irene and they sing some of the Polish songs they used to sing at family get-togethers with Millie and Big Bob.

"Sto lat, Sto lat, nie-chaj zy-je, zy-je nam."

Good health, good cheer, may you live a hundred years.

Bob Kosienski, trim and silver haired at age 72, is one of the last of his generation. All but two of his 12 siblings are gone. Only he and Irene and another sister living in Florida remain. Bob and Irene stand behind their afflicted 57-year-old nephew. Rob reaches back. He and Bob hold hands. Rob has his glasses off and his eyes gather an unfocused, far away look. Irene reaches over and strokes his face. I see the face of a teenage football star, the golden boy.

They sing.

"Za rok, za dzien, za chwile, Razem nie bedzie nas."

A year, a day, a moment spent, and we may not be here.

Rob Szymaszek is now dying of brain cancer. But here, too, is truth: Rob Szymaszek is still living with brain cancer. He returns home and sets up shop with a hospital bed in the living room. The sisters from the Franciscan Life Center come by daily to provide medical assistance. Sharon is up from New Jersey to help, too.

On the opening day of spring football practice, Rob asks Sharon to locate a specific green Maloney football cap and a specific white Maloney football shirt he's got stashed somewhere in the house. Then he asks Diane to drive him down to Maloney so he can see the kids. His feet and lower legs are still swollen, but he's able to maneuver pretty well with the help of a walker. It's a humid afternoon in late May, and before leaving home he learns the golf cart that had been promised him to get around practice won't be available. Two reasons not to go. He doesn't say it, but I know that makes him determined more than ever to get down to the practice field behind Maloney High School and there's no way he'll be told otherwise.

Off he goes.

"Sto lat, Sto lat, nie-chaj zy-je, zy-je nam."

Good health, good cheer, may you live a hundred years.

That's my wish for Rob, for all those I love. But the truth is there will no such miracle. Not for Rob, not for any of us. After all, we too are dying. We're just not reminded of it every day and we do not yet know what card death will play.

Rob knows.

Rob knows, and life is still good.

It has been good. For the past three years I have seen it first hand, at first admiring Rob's unfailing optimism even when I questioned it, then coming to admire his greater strength: not merely the courage to battle illness, but to steadfastly believe he would win, and then the fortitude to go on and still play to win even when he knew he probably wouldn't.

But Rob is not losing. He's just running out of time.

The key lies in the definition, and the definition is ours to make. Are we losing the game or are we just running out of time?

Life is still good.

I hereby attest to the miracle.

Acknowledgements

THIS BOOK WAS three years in the making, and there are many people Rob and I would like to thank, both individually and as a team.

First as a team: George Geers and Plaidswede Publishing for recognizing the power of this story and the need for it to be shared; James H. Smith for opening big doors at the start and finish of the project as well as for his editing; Eliot C. White, publisher of the Meriden *Record-Journal*, for giving me the summer of 2004 off from work to get the book rolling.

We are also indebted to the photography of Bill Lischeid, which in more instances than one laid the groundwork for episodes in the book. We are indebted to the reporting of the Meriden *Record-Journal* sports staff, in particular Ted Moynihan, John Pettit, and Dan Champagne. We thank and respect William Dowling for his deep personal interest in this project.

Rob's acknowledgements could probably fill another book. He has been blessed to be surrounded by so many good and supportive people. His family is his anchor, starting with Diane—his high school sweetheart, his wife, his best friend and his caretaker—and his one and only, his daughter Jennifer. His love extends to his sisters Sharon and Jan and their families, and to his late parents Bob and Millie. (And, yes, to Mr. Diffley too.)

Rob would like to thank the faculty and students of Maloney throughout the years. "I realize how much I miss them," he said after retiring. "I tell that to Diane every day she comes home from work."

There are friends—"friends galore," and Rob thanks them, those in the city of Meriden, the state of Connecticut, in the football world and on the island of St. Martin. He thanks the Maloney football community—Dan Hatch and all the assistant coaches, players and parents who helped make Coach Smaz the winningest football coach in Meriden history. He'd also like to thank Larry McHugh and all the coaches he coached against. "Playing the best brought out the best in me and my program."

Rob thanks his mentors, Ron Carbone, George DeLeone, Paul Pasqualoni and the late Ed McGee. He thanks John Fontana and the Connecticut High School Coaches Association for its inspirational support. He thanks his brothers in the coaching fraternity, especially those who have truly been like brothers—Mike Falis, Rob Cersosimo, Marce Petroccio and Steve Filippone.

He thanks Mother Shawn Vergauwen and the sisters of the Franciscan Life Center for their spiritual support. He thanks the friend who truly was his best man, Jim Staszewski.

And Rob also thanks his medical team at Yale-New Haven Hospital, his neuro-surgeon Joe Piepmeier, his neuro-oncologist Joachim Baehring and all those who worked on his case.

I, too, thank Dr. Piepmeier, Dr. Baehring and all the Yale staff members who at first afforded me time as a writer and eventually accepted me as a de facto member of the Syzmaszek family.

That's not a stretch. Rob and I started as collaborators. We end up as much more than that.

I thank Diane, Jen, Sharon, Jan and the extended Szymaszek family for allowing me to get so close. And so we will remain.

I thank my wife, Colleen McClain, for her unwavering love, support and advice. As good an editor as Smith was, she was tougher. And, like Rob, I have been blessed with a family that has been the absolute and unshakable foundation in my life. This is for all of you.

Acknowledgements

And lastly, Rob, I look at you and you look at me and we wind it up as we so often do.

"Alright, I'll catch you later."

"Alright, buddy."

"Alright, my man, take care."

"You take care."

"Yeah, you too."

Love ya, brother.

TOWARD THE END, when he'd awake, Rob would look up beyond the skylights in his living room, see the bright blue sky beyond them, the passing white clouds, and sometimes he'd ask Diane or his sister Sharon, "Is that heaven?"

On Thursday, September 20, 2007, at 6:22 p.m., it was.

About the Author

BRYANT CARPENTER IS the Sports Editor of the Meriden Record-Journal, where he started his career before embarking on stops in Maine and the East End of Long Island.

He lives in Portland, Connecticut with his wife, Colleen McClain. *The Classic Experience* (1995) was his first published book.